Rethinking Attachment for Early Childhood Practice

Rethinking Attachment for Early Childhood Practice

Promoting security, autonomy and resilience in young children

SHARNE A. ROLFE

Department of Learning and Educational Development
The University of Melbourne

ALLEN&UNWIN

First published in 2004

Copyright © Sharne Rolfe 2004

Allen & Unwin
83 Alexander Street
Crows Nest NSW 2065
Australia
Phone: (61 2) 8425 0100
Fax: (61 2) 9906 2218
Email: info@allenandunwin.com
Web: www.allenandunwin.com

National Library of Australia
Cataloguing-in-Publication entry:

Rolfe, Sharne A.
    Rethinking attachment for early childhood practice:
    promoting security, autonomy and resilience in young children.

    Bibliography.
    Includes index.
    ISBN 978 1 86508 518 0

    1. Child care – Psychological aspects. 2. Attachment
    behaviour in children. 3. Child development. I. Title

155.44

Set in 11/13 pt Bembo by Bookhouse, Sydney
Printed by SRM Production Services, Malaysia

10 9 8 7 6 5 4 3 2

For my children, Jess and Sam, with love

Contents

Part IV

Part V

Part I

Introduction

1

Introduction

One-year-old Eli is happily exploring toys on the floor around her. She glances from time to time at other infants in her child-care room, and at adults as they come and go, but most often she looks at Zamia, her caregiver, as she moves around the room. Zamia smiles and talks to Eli often, and is the main person who attends to Eli's needs. Zamia frequently sits on the floor, and when she does, Eli crawls over and climbs onto her lap. Zamia gently strokes Eli's back as they play and chat together. Eli is settled and relaxed, attentive to her environment and confident to explore it. Over the past eight months in child care, Eli has formed a special relationship with Zamia. She has learnt she can rely on her for comfort, reassurance, encouragement and happy interactions. Zamia is Eli's special person at child care. She is Eli's secure base.

Two-and-a-half-year-old Ryan is in his father's arms at the start of his child-care day. His carer, Jung, walks over and stands chatting briefly with Ryan and his dad, then puts her arms out to Ryan. At first, Ryan leans away and cuddles into his dad, who speaks gently to him, rubbing his back. Ryan then looks at Jung, smiles and goes into her arms. He turns with Jung to survey the room, glancing back briefly to his dad, who waves as he leaves. After a minute or so, Ryan gestures to get down, and in moments is happily moving towards a group of other children playing on the floor. This morning ritual shows the security that exists in Ryan's relationship with Jung. This has developed from repeated experiences of having his needs responded to in predictable, caring and consistent ways.

Four-year-old Helina is playing happily with three of her friends in the outside play area of her preschool. They are laughing and making zooming noises as they ride their bikes around and around on the path. Unexpectedly, Helina and one of her friends collide. Helina bumps her knee and gets a fright. She starts to cry and, looking around, sees her teacher Malcolm standing nearby. She calls out to Malcolm, then runs to his side. Malcolm talks calmly to Helina and gently rubs her knee. Within a few moments, Helina wipes away her tears and begins to smile. Malcolm helps her back on her bike, and she is off again, calling out to her friends. Helina has learnt over time that she can trust Malcolm to be reassuring and encouraging when she is upset or frightened.

Each of these simple, everyday events tells us something important about attachment, security and child development. Eli happily explores her child-care world because she knows Zamia is sensitive and responsive to her needs. Ryan copes well with parental separation because he has built up an expectation of respectful, predictable transitions, secure in Jung's care. Helina settles quickly because she has learnt she can rely on Malcolm to be calm, caring and encouraging if she is afraid or upset.

This book is your guide to attachment theory and research. It explains how attachment relationships form and how they impact on a child's development. It explores the complex interpersonal dynamics of the early childhood setting, including relationships between adults and children, and between parents and early childhood professionals. It focuses on applying attachment theory to early childhood practices—how to promote security, autonomy and resilience in early childhood settings.

Attachment theory has a great deal to say about how we can make early childhood settings more caring, emotionally nurturing and developmentally supportive places for children and adults to be. It is therefore highly relevant to the practice of early childhood education and hence to caregivers and teachers of infants and young children. This relevance is evident in many aspects of the theory. These include viewing the infant and child in the context of significant relationships; the importance of sensitive and predictable caregiving; debates about the impact of non-parental care on the development of very young children; the relevance of adult attachment representations for patterns of caregiving; cultural differences in caregiving and attachment; and security of attachment as a protective factor in the development of at-risk children.

Why 'rethink' attachment theory?

This book invites you, the early childhood professional or student, to 'rethink' attachment. By this I mean to think again, and in new ways, about how attachment theory and research can help you to promote children's psychological health. This is a good time to do so. Interest in and enthusiasm for early childhood programs founded on attachment principles is growing (e.g. Harrison, 2003; Raikes, 1996). But perhaps it is some time since you studied the theory and your memory of it is hazy. You may wonder which of the ideas you once learnt about are still valid and which are out of date. Maybe you studied the theory only briefly and the implications for your practice are vague or not delineated at all. Or perhaps you are a new student of attachment theory, and need help to make sense of it and what it means for the early childhood setting in which you work, or plan to work. Attachment theory has been evolving for over 30 years or more, and much rethinking has been part of this process. Research continues to take it into exciting new territory. It is essential to keep abreast of these developments.

In Bowlby's earliest writings about attachment (e.g. Bowlby, 1958), for example, he assumed that attachment behaviour was focused selectively on one person. This is called the concept of monotropy and later became associated with predictions that non-parental care inevitably risks harm to a child's emotional wellbeing. But this assumption was dropped from his later writings (e.g. Bowlby, 1988) when historical analyses and cross-cultural studies, including the early research of Mary Ainsworth in Uganda (Ainsworth, 1967), did not support such a view. Attachment writers and researchers now know that it is usual for infants and young children to have more than one selective attachment, sometimes several, and they have similar purposes (Rutter and O'Connor, 1999). Most children form a network of attachment relationships—with family and other people who care for them. Research has shown that the nature of all these attachment relationships—including between children and their caregivers and teachers in early childhood settings (e.g. Howes, 1997; Howes and Smith, 1995)—have important impacts on cognitive and social functioning and development. The potential of attachment theory to inspire early childhood practices is only just beginning to be explored.

Themes for reflection

There are two main themes for reflection throughout this book: How can attachment theory inform better policies for early childhood services? How can attachment theory guide better early childhood practices? Material presented will encourage self-reflection on the following questions:

- How does attachment theory translate into ways of interacting with children that nurture emotional security, autonomy, feelings of competence and resilience?
- What implications does attachment theory have for the way we set up early childhood environments, especially the interpersonal dimensions of the setting?
- How can I use attachment theory and research to understand better the behaviours of those in the early childhood community in which I work—the children, the parents, other professionals and myself?

- In what ways might I modify and develop my interactions with children, parents and colleagues to best nurture their wellbeing?

What is attachment?

As we begin, it is important to define what is meant by attachment. Put simply, attachment is an emotional bond between two people in which there is an expectation of care and protection (see Goldberg, 2000). Usually we talk of the child 'becoming attached' to the caregiver, whereas the caregiver forms a 'bond' or 'becomes bonded' to the child. A recent child development text defines attachment as 'the strong, affectional tie we feel for special people in our lives that leads us to feel pleasure and joy when we interact with them and to be comforted by their nearness in times of stress' (Berk, 2000, p. 421). Most attachment relationships are like this. But as discussed in later chapters, not all attachments are so positive, joyful and comforting. Attachments can develop that are insecure in nature. If an attachment figure is insensitive, unresponsive or inconsistent, the child may become avoidant or resistant in response. In attachment relationships where the adult is abusive or neglectful, the child may show extreme behavioural disorganisation, dissociation and/or role reversal.

Attachment theory is a theory about close interpersonal relationships of all these kinds. It is a theory that helps us understand the nature of relationships between children and those who have the responsibility of caring for them. It informs our understanding of how these early relationships influence later psychological development. And most importantly for early childhood practitioners, it is a theory that provides many practical guidelines for caregiving interactions and relationships that nurture children's optimal psychological growth and wellbeing.

Attachment theory is relevant to all significant caregiving relationships in a child's life, not just those between parent and child. It has implications for the many different carers that young children may encounter in their lives, including extended family, foster and adoptive parents and certainly early childhood educators. In other words, attachment theory alerts us to the very important role that all caregivers—parents and others—have in contributing to a child's emotional health.

The importance of attachment relationships

Why are attachment relationships so important for emotional wellbeing? As discussed in detail in this book, the answer lies in the way these relationships bridge the personal and social worlds of the child. Attachment theorists use the term 'inner working model' to describe this. In simple terms, children learn about themselves, and how they can expect the world of people to be, through early relationships. As they experience interactions on a minute-by-minute, hour-by-hour, day-by-day basis, they build up a view of themselves and expectancies about how others will respond. If their experiences are of being responded to in caring, sensitive, consistent and reliable ways, then they develop a view of the world as generally a safe place to be, and people as generally to be trusted to have their best interests at heart. They also develop a view of themselves as loved and lovable, a critical foundation of healthy self-acceptance and self-esteem.

In contrast, children cannot develop the same sense of trust if their attachment figures are insensitive, harsh or unpredictable, or are psychologically unavailable or erratic all or much of the time. Instead, these children must develop strategies to cope. These strategies are psychological defences—which include avoidance or ambivalence—against rejection or uncertainty. Children with these sorts of experiences may become vulnerable to feelings of inadequacy and of being unloved.

At the extreme, children who experience abusive, neglectful attachment figures and/or who have attachment relationships severely disrupted by separations (as occurs in multiple foster-care placements) may develop a view of themselves as unlovable, with significant negative implications for future close relationships. These children may become 'parentified' in their behaviour, subsuming their own emotional needs in order to attempt to meet the needs of the adult attachment figure.

According to this model of development, the way a person

perceives their world and the people within it is profoundly influenced by the nature of early attachment relationships. In other words, how we are cared for sets up expectancies, and these are, in time, applied to the new relationships that we form. The child with a trusting view of the world would perceive (and probably respond to) the same interpersonal event quite differently to the child who has a view of the world as a place that is generally hostile. For example, imagine that while standing in the playground waiting for the swing, a child is accidentally knocked into by another child who is running past and not looking where he or she is going. The child with a secure inner working model is likely to perceive the event as just that, that is, as an accident with no deliberately hostile intent on the part of the other child. The event passes and nothing occurs to jeopardise future positive interactions between the two children. In contrast, children with a less trusting view of the world may inaccurately assume a hostile intent on the part of the other child and respond accordingly, perhaps with an expression of hostility of their own. Such retaliations may precipitate a truly hostile exchange, or other forms of rejection by the other child, thereby creating a self-fulfilling prophesy.

Children also develop skills of emotional self-regulation through their earliest attachment relationships. Sensitive, responsive care enables the young child to experience repeated cycles of emotional escalation and de-escalation, with arousal generally kept within comfortable bounds with the help of the caregiver. Children with insensitive, unresponsive carers do not have these emotionally supportive experiences. They may repeatedly become overwhelmed by their emotions, since at early ages self-regulatory abilities are limited. Difficulties with emotional self-control may contribute to the non-compliant, impulsive, aggressive and/or regressive behaviours we see in some children in early childhood settings.

Attachment theory and early childhood programs

The notion that the heart of an early childhood program resides in its interpersonal relationships is not new. What attachment theory allows us to do is pinpoint qualities in the caregiver–child relationship that are associated with the development of emotional health, empathy and optimism. In the early childhood community there are also other important interpersonal relationships, those between professionals and parents, and between the professionals themselves. Attachment theory is also relevant here. The work of attachment researchers in recent years has identified different ways in which adults represent the importance of attachment relationships and their own early attachment history. These representations impact on how we interact with others. Understanding this has potential to impact in positive ways on interpersonal dynamics between all adults in the early childhood setting.

Does attachment theory espouse a deterministic model of development?

Does attachment theory imply that certain experiences can leave a child damaged for life? Do early attachment relationships dictate later development? Case histories of children with traumatic, deprived early lives who have nonetheless developed into successful, happy and psychologically stable adults suggest this cannot be so. Bowlby's writings reject a deterministic model and instead emphasise risk, resilience and probable pathways of development (Greenberg, 1999; Rutter and O'Connor, 1999). From such a perspective, there is always potential for change. The direction of change—towards greater security, or towards insecurity—is determined by the quality of relationships experienced at the time.

The theory stresses, however, that children's ongoing psychological health will be put at risk by early insecure attachment relationships; that is, the emotional and social sensitivities that emerge from these experiences may remain. Careful study of the lives of resilient individuals often indicate the availability of at least one sensitive, responsive and consistently available attachment figure. This person (not necessarily a family member) was committed to their welfare, helped them feel valued and worthwhile and encouraged in them a sense of self-competence and self-worth (Werner and Smith, 1992). Sometimes it is not until adult life that a person finds their first secure attachment relationship with a partner whom they come to trust. However, the longer we are without a secure attachment, the harder it is for trust to develop and consolidate. This points to the critical importance of secure attachments and the experience of sensitive, responsive caregiving early in life.

The plan of this book

Following this general introductory chapter, Part II begins with an introduction to attachment theory itself, looking first to the founder of attachment theory, John Bowlby. Bowlby presented his theory in three main volumes, known as the attachment trilogy, first published in 1969 (Volume 1), 1973 (Volume 2) and 1980 (Volume 3). The first volume, entitled *Attachment*, outlines Bowlby's views about attachment behaviour as an instinctive response to the need for protection (in the child) and to protect (in the adult) and the place of attachment in the survival of the species. The second volume, entitled *Separation, anxiety and anger*, explores the links between separation, fear and security and how individual differences in anxiety may arise from particular attachment and separation experiences. In the third volume, *Loss, sadness and depression*, he examines how loss of the attachment figure and depression are linked.

Over the years Bowlby developed his ideas further and many of these formulations can be found in Bowlby (1988). The theory continues to be expanded and clarified by the ongoing efforts of many researchers around the world. In discussing these new developments, the work of attachment researchers in the United States, Canada, the United Kingdom, Europe, Africa and the Asia–Pacific, including Australia, will be presented. These efforts are adding to attachment theory by underlining the complexity of the attachment process as well as providing important new perspectives on cultural contexts and their impact on attachment behaviour. Why interactions matter and how they influence the development of the self and social understanding are also discussed in Part II. Quality of attachment, the features of secure and insecure attachment relationships, and the precursors of these various attachment types are described in detail. Their role in the development of resilience is explored.

In Part III, attachment and development at different stages of infancy and early childhood are considered in detail. In Part IV, a series of attachment topics and issues, including separation anxiety and cultural perspectives, are presented. In Part V, the implications of attachment theory for early childhood policies and practices presented in each chapter are integrated and summarised.

Each chapter concludes with a section exploring the implications of the material presented for early childhood practices. There is a case scenario for consideration, along with questions for reflection, discussion points and suggested further readings. All scenarios are hypothetical. They are based on compilations of real-life case histories and observations drawn from the author's professional experiences in early childhood settings and within the child protection field over many years. All names are made up. An annotated list of relevant websites is provided in the Appendix.

Terminology, language and some caveats

It is important to add a few words at the outset regarding terminology and language. Firstly, early attachment theorists, including Bowlby and Ainsworth, used the terms 'he' and 'his' to denote all children, of both genders. This terminology is no longer acceptable, but you will find all direct quotations from the writings of Bowlby, Ainsworth and others presented as per the original.

Secondly, Bowlby used the term 'mother' throughout his major writings as shorthand for 'mother figure'. A footnote in chapter 2 of Volume 1 (1969/1982) of the attachment trilogy makes this clear: 'Although throughout this book the text refers usually to "mother" and not to "mother-figure", it is to be understood that in every case reference is to the person who mothers a child and to whom he becomes attached. For most children, of course, that person is also his natural mother' (p. 29). These words are essentially repeated at the beginning of the other two volumes (Vol. 2, p. 3; Vol. 3, p. 9). Throughout this book, the terms 'attachment figure' or 'caregiver' are used to refer to the adult member of an attachment dyad, unless the comments being made relate specifically to the mother, father or a specified alternative caregiver (for example, an early childhood professional).

Thirdly, while focusing on attachment, this book acknowledges that caregiver–child relationships contain many elements that are quite distinct from 'security-promoting attachment features' (Rutter and O'Connor, 1999, p. 836). Rutter and O'Connor describe how there are attachment and non-attachment components of relationships. It also must be stressed that relationships of many different kinds influence development, and only some of these are attachment relationships (Dunn, 1993).

Further readings

This book aims to provide a scholarly overview of attachment theory and its implications for early childhood practice. In so doing, it draws on the work of others who have set out to evaluate systematically the multitude of research studies inspired by attachment theory in recent years. In particular, attention is drawn to three major current publications—an edited handbook of attachment theory, research and clinical application (Cassiby and Shaver, 1999), a single-authored attachment text (Goldberg, 2000) and an edited volume exploring attachment, culture and context (Crittenden and Claussen, 2000). The interested reader is directed to these and other publications cited for critical, analytical overviews of both early and contemporary attachment theory and the directions it is now taking. There is also a journal, *Attachment and Human Development* (published by Taylor and Francis), devoted entirely to attachment research and practice.

The focus of this book is attachment during the infancy, toddler and preschool periods. However, adult attachment representations (that is, how we as adults view or represent our own early attachments and their impact on our development) are discussed at some length because research has shown that these influence how we care for and respond to the attachment needs of children. They impact on the security of the attachment relationships children form with us. Research on this topic is important as well, because it shows how adult attachment representations may also impact on our professional relationships with other adults, including parents and colleagues.

Beyond this, there is now a large body of research on adult romantic attachments (e.g. Hazan and Shaver, 1987) and research on patterns of attachment in adolescence. Given the specific focus of this book, these latter topics will not be considered in any detail.

Misunderstandings about attachment and attachment theory

In discussing human attachment, Colin states that 'misunderstandings about the propositions, empirically established facts, and implications of attachment are common' (1996, p. 26). In Colin's view there are three major misconceptions that hopefully this introductory chapter has clarified for you. To summarise, firstly, it is now clear that even young infants usually become attached to more than one person. Secondly, although attachment experiences during the first 12 months are very important, they do not irretrievably set the path of later development. If we reflect on our own lives, it is very clear that experiences in later childhood, adolescence and adulthood do shape the people we become. Thirdly, child care, and separations from the attachment figure associated with it, do not inevitably lead to insecure attachments. However, as will be discussed later, attachment theory has important things to say about how the separation experience is best managed in early childhood settings.

QUESTIONS FOR REFLECTION

How and what we think about topics like attachment are determined by many things. Our ideas are inevitably influenced by the particular values held in our own family and cultural group, by media coverage, community attitudes and our own early attachment experiences. As a starting point, think about your response to the following questions based on your current understandings. You may like to jot your responses down in a journal and revisit them later. As you read through this book, reflect on whether and in what ways your ideas and understandings have changed. In what ways will you develop your practices to reflect these new understandings?

In your view:

- How early in life do interactions have an impact on emotional development?
- Can young children become 'too attached' to their professional caregivers? How would you know that a child is becoming attached to you?
- Are attachments to professional caregivers just as important as attachments to parents?
- What qualities of caregiving underpin secure attachments? Insecure attachments?
- What qualities in children reflect their attachment history? Which challenging behaviours in child care and preschool can be best understood from an attachment perspective?
- What is 'felt security' and how does it influence a child's behaviour? What is a 'secure base'?
- Do all cultures prioritise secure attachments?
- Does child temperament influence attachment quality?
- How are separations between child and parent best handled?

Part II

The significance of attachment relationships

2

Attachment theory

In the next four chapters, the significance of attachment relationships for psychological development is described. We begin with an overview of the theory, first developed by John Bowlby in the 1950s (but with origins back to the 1930s; see Karen, 1994) and later expanded by Mary Ainsworth and others until the present time. We consider the pioneering work of Bowlby and Ainsworth in detail because of the groundbreaking insights contained in these early writings, and then explore how the theory has evolved since. While some argue that we now have multiple versions of the theory rather than a single theory (see Goldberg, 2000), commonalities abound.

The psychoanalytic origins of attachment theory

The basic tenet of attachment theory, that social and emotional development is linked to a child's early relationships with primary carers, is firmly founded in psychoanalytic theory. Holmes (1993) describes attachment theory as 'a child of psychoanalysis' (p. 127). However, from the outset attachment theory reflected dissatisfaction with the prevailing views, based on both psychoanalytic and learning theory, that the child's tie to the mother arose from feeding and the pleasure associated with it.

Bowlby's views on these matters stirred great controversy within his own discipline of psychiatry. He emphasised the importance of actual experiences within the parent–child relationship for current functioning and later development, in contrast to internal, unconscious conflicts and fantasies as stressed within traditional psychoanalytic perspectives. He situated attachment theory within three disciplinary fields, all of which he drew upon as he developed his ideas about the infant–caregiver bond. These fields were ethology, control systems theory and information processing (cognitive science). We will consider the contribution of each in turn. Those interested in a detailed discussion of the relationship between attachment theory and psychoanalytic theory should consult Holmes (1993, chapter 7) and Fonagy (1999).

The contribution of ethology to attachment theory

Attachment theory is termed an ethological theory because, in Bowlby's view, the attachment relationship forms due to behaviours in the child and behaviours in the adult caregiver that promoted the survival of the species in much earlier times. He calls this historical period our 'environment of evolutionary adaptedness' (1969/1982, p. 58). What he is referring to is the primeval environment inhabited by members of the earliest human species, about two million years prior to the development of agriculture and the modified habitats and more 'civilised' society that this precipitated. Natural adaptation, in Bowlby's view, must always be about how and why a particular behaviour or behaviours promoted survival in these very early and presumably highly dangerous and challenging settings.

Ethologists are interested in, amongst other things, the evolutionary function of behaviours. It was Bowlby who first conceptualised the bond that develops between the infant and caregiver in this way. He theorised that human infants are born with a set of behaviours that act to keep a caregiver close (that is, maintain proximity between the infant and the caregiver) and signal the infant's needs, especially in times of danger or uncertainty. If the caregiver is sensitive to these signals and responds or reacts in a way that satisfies the infant's needs (including for protection), the infant's chances of survival are enhanced. Ideally, the attachment figure is also proactive (Goldberg, 2000). This means having routines in place that reflect the child's developing biological rhythms and needs (for rest, nutrition, social interaction and so on), making the environment safe, and being watchful for and anticipating potential hazards before even the child is aware that a danger exists.

Bowlby's position (1969/1982) was that the attachment bond is primarily about achieving protection at a time of life when, due to immaturity, self-protection is impossible. Put simply, without an attachment figure in early life, survival is impossible.

Infant behaviours

Infant behaviours of significance for attachment include what are termed signalling behaviours (Bowlby, 1969/1982). These include crying, smiling, babbling, calling and gestures such as raising the arms in the presence of the attachment figure. The function of these is to bring, and keep, the attachment figure close. Crying, for example, is a particularly potent signal for the attachment figure, and some types of cry, such as the sharp, loud cry of pain, are considered to be particularly potent in bringing the attachment figure to the child. Smiling and babbling, which occur in very different circumstances and when the baby is content, elicit caregiving of the kind Bowlby terms 'loving behaviour' (p. 246) in the adult, including reciprocal smiling, talking, gentle physical contact and picking the infant up.

Other behaviours are those that result in the infant approaching the attachment figure, in contrast to those just listed which act to bring the attachment figure to the infant. These include locomotion towards the attachment figure (seeking and following) and clinging. These approach behaviours only occur once the infant is mobile, although following the attachment figure visually through direction of gaze can be seen in young infants before the onset of crawling.

Infant characteristics such as the ability to signal clearly his or her needs may be compromised by genetically based or other abnormalities. These may impact on the nature of the attachment relationship that forms, as may other infant characteristics, including temperament (see Goldberg, 2000).

Caregiving behaviours

Attachment theory considers the caregiving behaviours of the attachment figure in detail. Bowlby termed this 'maternal caregiving' but, as has been noted in Chapter 1, from the outset and in each volume of the attachment trilogy he makes it clear that the term 'mother' is used as shorthand for that person who 'mothers the child' (1969/1982, p. 29), whoever that may be. Primary amongst caregiving behaviours is 'retrieval' (1969/1982, p. 240) which involves approaching, picking up and holding the infant. Like the infant's attachment behaviours, this is strongly elicited when the infant is in danger, is distressed or is perceived to be too far away.

From its inception, attachment theory has acknowledged the complexity of feelings experienced by mothers around attachment, particularly in modern industrialised societies where women may continue paid employment on a part-time or full-time basis throughout their childbearing years. The theory also acknowledges the fact that many infants and young children are cared for by 'mother substitutes' when the parents are in paid employment.

In the first volume of the attachment trilogy, Bowlby wrote 'most mothers experience a strong pull to be close to their babies and young children. Whether they submit to the pull or stand out against it depends on a hundred variables, personal, cultural, and economic' (1969/1982, p. 241). From his analysis of research data available at the time (e.g. Schaffer and Emerson, 1964), Bowlby concluded that multiple attachments were no cause for concern. In fact, drawing on Schaffer and Emerson's findings, he concluded that 'in the early months of attachment the greater number of figures to whom a child was attached the more intense was his attachment to mother as his principal figure' (1969/1982, p. 202).

As we will explore in later chapters, a key feature of adult caregiving from an attachment perspective is the extent to which it is sensitive and responsive. Various terms are used to describe these and other related features of caregiving, including 'interactional synchrony', 'attunement' and 'contingent responsiveness'. A key concern of attachment theory is thus not only the *presence* of an attachment figure but *the nature of the caregiving behaviours shown by this figure*, and how well it meshes with the needs of that particular infant or child.

Just as there is variability in the expression of attachment behaviours amongst children for a variety of reasons, so there is variability in the expression of attachment behaviours by caregiving figures. How these come together in each attachment dyad determines the nature of the relationship that forms. There are many complex, interacting factors that determine the quality of a caregiver's response to a child's attachment needs. For example, the caregiver's ability to be responsive will be compromised if they are highly stressed, as may occur in situations of acute financial need or chronic poverty, domestic violence, substance abuse and/or mental illness. If the attachment figure's own caregiving history was one of abuse or neglect, he or she may not understand and/or respond appropriately to the child's need for care and protection, particularly under stressful circumstances. However, it must be stressed that not all adults with less than optimal attachment histories recreate this history for the children in their care (the intergenerational transmission of attachment). An important factor is whether or not the adult has psychologically resolved their feelings about these early attachment experiences (Main and Goldwyn, 1984), something we return to in later chapters.

A final contribution of ethology to attachment theory concerns the role of separation experiences. Not surprisingly, the ethological, survival-based focus of attachment theory led Bowlby to the view that major separations between the young child and their attachment figures are highly detrimental. However, the sorts of separations that concerned him were those arising from the experience of bereavement in childhood, institutionalisation and extended hospitalisation (so poignantly captured in the films of Bowlby's colleagues Joyce and James Robertson; see Robertson and Robertson,

1971). These are in many ways very different from the brief and predictable separations children encounter in child care, something also returned to in later chapters.

Attachment and control systems theory

Bowlby also drew on control systems theory to develop his ideas about the infant–caregiver relationship. He conceived of attachment as a 'control system' (1969/1982; p. 235) best understood in relation to other forces operating within the child, such as the need to explore. Attachment behaviours are sensitive to prevailing conditions in the attachment relationship, and according to Bowlby act to maintain equilibrium in the attachment system. This means that at any point in time, the intensity of a child's attachment behaviours and those of the attachment figure will vary depending on the circumstances. For example, the child's attachment behaviours are very sensitive to the extent of physical distance away from the caregiver. Attachment behaviours are likely to be activated or will heighten if and when infants find the increasing distance between them and their attachment figure uncomfortable, or if the attachment figure has been absent too long. Attachment behaviours will activate when an attachment figure is departing, or acts in a rejecting way towards the child. How the child is feeling (for example, unwell, fatigued or frightened) is also an important factor in the appearance and intensity of attachment behaviours. The child who is unwell or tired may show more intense attachment behaviours, such as resisting the departure of the attachment figure, than might otherwise occur.

The control systems perspective underpins one of the fundamental concepts of attachment theory, that of the 'secure base'. The sensitive, responsive attachment figure becomes for the child a secure base from which to explore. What this means is that during infancy and toddlerhood in particular, children's exploratory behaviour is more likely to occur when an attachment figure is nearby. Exploration that takes the child too far from the attachment figure activates behaviours such as return and approach, or calling and crying if the infant is unable to achieve the required proximity quickly enough, or is prevented for some reason from doing so at all.

As Bowlby describes it, the 'system' works in the following way: 'So long as a child is in the unchallenged presence of a principal attachment-figure, or within easy reach, he feels secure. A threat of loss creates anxiety, and actual loss sorrow; both, moreover, are likely to arouse anger' (1969/1982, p. 209). Bowlby's words remind us not only of the importance to the young child of the accessibility of a trusted attachment figure, but also indicate the complex relationship that exists between attachment and various emotions, including anxiety and anger. This is discussed further in later chapters.

The contribution of cognitive science: The concept of the 'internal working model'

So far attachment theory has been discussed from ethological and control systems' perspectives. Drawing on concepts in cognitive science, the theory also emphasises that attachment relationships are the vehicle by which children develop a sense of self, that is, of who they are and how they can expect the world of people around them to respond. It is in the second-by-second, minute-by-minute, hour-by-hour interactions between the child and the attachment figure(s) that children construct what is termed an internal working model. This has been defined as a 'set of expectations about the availability of attachment figures, their likelihood of providing support during times of stress, and the self's interactions with those figures' (Berk, 2000, p. 423).

The internal working model, formed from interactions with a small number of significant attachment figures, is of great importance to ongoing development because it generalises to other close interpersonal relationships as they form over time. If the internal working model is based on caregiving that is sensitive, responsive and consistent, then the view of the self that develops is positive— *I am lovable and the world of people is generally a place that can be trusted and that has my best interests at heart.* If the internal working model is based on caregiving that is insensitive, unresponsive, harsh, rejecting and/or inconsistent, then the view of the self that develops reflects this and is less positive—*I am less lovable (or at the extreme, unlovable) and the world of people is generally a place that is not to be trusted and that may not have my best interests at heart.* This aspect of the theory, which describes the mechanism by which early experiences impact upon later development, particularly in the social–emotional domain, draws heavily on information-processing perspectives as well as cognitive science.

In total then, attachment theory embraces psychoanalytic, ethological, control systems and cognitive science/information-processing theories in its view of early relationship formation and the influence of these relationships on the subsequent life-course of each individual.

Different kinds of attachment relationships: The contribution of Mary Ainsworth

It was Bowlby's colleague, Mary Ainsworth, who first began to untangle the characteristics of different kinds of attachment relationships, termed 'secure' and 'insecure'. In the first volume of the attachment trilogy, Bowlby acknowledges the work of Ainsworth, first conducted in Uganda and then in Baltimore in the United States. This work broke new ground in the understanding of how different patterns of adult caregiving lead to different patterns of child attachment behaviour and, ultimately, to different types of attachment relationships. Ainsworth completed her doctoral dissertation at the University of Toronto, her area of research being based on William Blatz's security theory. She already had a strong background in the study and significance of parent–child relationships when she began work as a researcher with Bowlby in London in the 1950s, a position that continued for some three years or so.

In 1954, Ainsworth moved to Uganda and began her pioneering observational research on infant–mother interactions, amongst local Ganda village families, with a small grant from the East African Institute of Social Research (see Karen, 1994). Research on a sample of 28 infants formed the basis for her idea that there were different types of attachment relationships, the difference being observable mainly in the infant's response to separation and reflecting, in Ainsworth's view, more or less security in the relationship. Ainsworth attributed these differences to different patterns of maternal caregiving.

Ainsworth's study of Ganda families, *Infancy in Uganda*, was published in 1967. This book has been described as 'a unique document, rare in its meticulous attention to detail, original in its mixture of longitudinal and cross-sectional techniques, and the first to demonstrate the development of attachment, making sense of infant behaviours and developmental sequences that were poorly understood before' (Karen, 1994, p. 144). It is indeed worth careful attention, not least for its detailed observations of interactions between young children and their families. These observations are considered further in a later chapter.

The Strange Situation procedure

Ainsworth subsequently moved to Baltimore where she took up a position at Johns Hopkins University. It was there, some years later, that she began the research program within which the well-known assessment procedure, the Strange Situation, was first used. This procedure is detailed in most child development texts. It is usually conducted in a university laboratory playroom and consists of seven three-minute episodes including a play period in which both the infant and adult attachment figure are present, separations and reunions between them and episodes in which an unfamiliar adult is present (with and without the attachment figure). Infant–caregiver interactions as well as the child's response to separations, reunions and the unfamiliar adult are observed and recorded. The assessment usually takes place in a room with a one-way mirror for observation purposes and sessions are videotaped.

Secure and insecure patterns of attachment in infancy

Using this procedure and based on detailed observations from her Baltimore sample, Ainsworth identified three major attachment categories which she termed A, B and C. After further data had been collected in other settings and correlated with the laboratory-based observations, the terms 'avoidant' (A), 'secure' (B) and 'resistant/ambivalent' (C) were applied, although controversy has arisen when these labels have been used in a value-laden way, something that Ainsworth had not intended and that Bowlby had warned against (see Chapter 12).

In the Strange Situation procedure, infants in the secure category, consisting of four subgroups, use the attachment figure as a secure base for exploration, generally show some distress on separation, but are readily soothed by the attachment figure on her/his return, and usually become settled enough to return to play. Those in the resistant/ambivalent category are generally very distressed on separation and have difficulty settling on reunion, sometimes showing angry, resistant behaviour mixed with contact-seeking to the attachment figure. Those in the avoidant category show little contact-seeking either before or after separation, minimal sharing of affect with the attachment figure, often little distress during separation and marked avoidance (ignoring, moving away, gaze avoidance) during reunion.

A fourth category, termed 'disorganised/disoriented', has more recently been identified (Main and Solomon, 1986; 1990). Infants coded as disorganised show confused, contradictory behaviours in the presence of their attachment figure, particularly during the reunion episodes. They may show approach combined with gaze aversion, there may be signs of fear, stilling and/or behavioural stereotypies. This pattern is most often associated with a history of frightening behaviour on the part of the attachment figure, such as occurs when there is child maltreatment. It is also associated with the exposure of children to 'frightened' behaviour by the attachment figure. It is hypothesised that this frightened behaviour on the part of the attachment figure occurs when he or she has involuntary memories of unresolved trauma or loss in the presence of the child, which lead to sudden and unexpected displays of fright (see van IJzendoorn et al, 1999).

Main and Hesse (1990) note that these displays of fright on the part of the attachment figure, as well as other frightened behaviour by them in the presence of the child, may be subtle and not necessarily overt. They may be directly frightening, or may result from the adult's fear of the infant, or may simply be so 'disturbing or inexplicable to frighten and therefore "disorganize" the infant'

(Solomon and George, 1999, p. 13). Based on observations of mother–infant interactions, Solomon and George (1999) provide examples of the sorts of behaviours that may be involved: 'sudden looming into the infant's face, movements and postures that seem to be part of a pursuit–hunt sequence . . . [parent] appearing to enter a trance-like state, unusual vocal patterns, such as simultaneously voicing and devoicing intonations' (p. 13).

The various attachment categories are discussed in more detail in later chapters. The Strange Situation procedure revolutionised research on attachment relationships (Karen, 1994) and outcomes of studies using the procedure in the years since its development have added important insights about individual differences in attachment relationships and their role in development.

Assessing attachment security in older children and the home environment

Because the Strange Situation was designed for use in the infancy and toddler periods only, and in structured settings, other measures have been developed in recent years to assess attachment relationships in the home environment and with older children. Techniques for home-based, naturalistic observations include the Attachment Q-Sort (see Waters et al, 1995). This technique can be used to describe secure base behaviour in children aged one to five years at home, or in other indoor or outdoor settings. It consists of 90 items (behavioural descriptions) that are sorted by an observer into piles depicting how representative they are of this child with a particular attachment figure. Observations on two or three occasions, each of about three hours' duration, are recommended before doing the sort. Items include 'Child puts arms around mother or puts hand on her shoulder when she picks him up', 'If held in mother's arms, child stops crying and quickly recovers after being frightened or upset', and 'Runs to mother with a shy smile when new people visit the home'. The way the items are sorted (that is, which behaviours are considered to be highly descriptive through to not at all descriptive of the child) is used to determine a score from which the child's security of attachment can be assigned. There is good correspondence between attachment classifications from this technique and the Strange Situation procedure (Pederson et al, 1998).

Other methods for use with older children who have moved into symbolic ways of representing their inner world include story-completion tasks acted out with family figurines, for children aged three years and older (Bretherton et al, 1990; Oppenheim, 1997), and children's narrative responses to drawings and photographs of family and attachment-related events, such as separation. Main et al (1985) recorded the verbal responses of six-year-olds to drawings of children and their parents in separation-related situations, and to family portraits. Children's responses were found to differ according to their attachment security. Secure six-year-olds gave coherent, open and elaborated responses whereas those classified as insecure gave responses indicating they were unable to say what the child might do to cope with such a situation, or that were irrational or bizarre in some way. Secure children looked at, talked about and smiled in response to the family portrait, whereas insecure children avoided looking at it, dropped it or handed it back to the experimenter. Bretherton et al (1997) presented three-year-olds with attachment-related story beginnings ('stems') acted out with family figurines (mother, father and two child dolls). Stories included a situation in which a child accidentally spills juice during dinner, falls and hurts their knee on a family walk and is faced with the departure of their parents on an overnight trip. The child was then asked to describe and act out using the dolls what happens next. Of the 29 children tested, 19 gave responses indicative of security in which attachment figures were depicted as protective, non-punitive and empathic. The other children's responses were indicative of various kinds of insecurity, including descriptions of punitive or non-empathic responses by the attachment figure (for example, the attachment figure leaves the child who had hurt their knee behind at the park, or physically punishes them for falling over).

Finally, there have been studies of how school-aged children represent attachment relationships in their family drawings. Fury et al (1997) studied the family drawings of 171 children aged eight and nine years. Drawings were coded for major attachment categories (secure, avoidant and resistant) by specific signs, such as whether the child is presented alone, based on earlier work by Kaplan and Main (1986, as cited by Fury et al, 1997) and according to seven global criteria including vitality, family pride, vulnerability, tension and role reversal. These criteria were found to be significantly related to the child's early attachment history. According to the authors, the results support the use of drawings as a measure of children's representational models of attachment. They conclude that family drawings are 'especially effective in accessing the more subjective, personal, and possibly unconscious aspects of representational models of the self in relationships . . . especially during middle childhood' (p. 1162). These and other techniques have been described, discussed and critiqued elsewhere (e.g. Oppenheim and Waters, 1995; Colin, 1996; Cassidy and Shaver, 1999; Goldberg, 2000).

'History of care' and the organisation of attachment behaviours

The nature of individual differences in the quality of attachment relationships and their impact on later development is a very important topic within attachment theory and research (Weinfield et al, 1999). Bowlby's writings outlined the normative nature of attachment formation, that is, that almost every infant (even those who have been subjected to maltreatment by their attachment figure) becomes attached. In his view, a child will only remain unattached under gross distortions of normal conditions of rearing, such as might occur in an institutional setting where there simply is no stable caregiving presence, that is, where no one person is sufficiently available to the child for a relationship to form. In cases where the attachment figure is neglectful or abusive, the infant may well form an attachment to this person, although the nature of the attachment will likely be insecure. It is the 'history of care' (Weinfield et al, 1999, p. 68) built up from the thousands of interactional experiences the child has had with that particular attachment figure that determines the nature of the attachment that forms.

Ainsworth's research and that of many others since has demonstrated that it is not the *quantity* of attachment behaviour shown that is important in understanding attachment relationships (that is, how much the infant approaches the attachment figure, how long proximity is maintained, and so on) but how these behaviours are *organised* (that is, when the infant is most likely to approach the attachment figure and under what circumstances proximity is maintained).

What this means is that it is patterns of interaction, not individual behaviours, that show what a relationship is really like. Patterns of behaviours reveal expectations the infant has built up from their care history, particularly in regard to how they expect the attachment figure to respond to their attachment bids (when seeking comfort, reassurance and/or protection). While there is a continuum from security to insecurity, and somewhat blurry distinctions between attachment classifications, secure attachments generally reflect a history of caregiver availability and sensitive responsiveness to the infant's attachment needs. Avoidant attachments reflect a history of caregiver rejection of infant attachment needs, and resistant attachments a history of inconsistent, erratic responses. Rather than building confidence over time in the responsive availability of their attachment figure, infants with insecure attachments are therefore anxious about whether this person will provide comfort and/or protection when sought. They may be fearful and angry in the presence of the attachment figure, rather than confidently trusting, as observed in securely attached children.

Recent attachment research and theorising

Following Ainsworth's pioneering studies there have been many further studies of attachment quality and development. These include major longitudinal research programs drawing upon samples of disadvantaged families in the United States (Egeland and Farber, 1984), middle-class families in the United States (Belsky et al, 1984) and families in Bielefeld, Germany (Grossmann et al, 1985). Summarising the outcomes of these and other studies, it has been concluded that they each support the view that 'the mother's sensitive responsiveness made a significant contribution to the infant's developing a secure attachment to her' (Colin, 1996, p. 87), although Goldberg (2000) notes that none of these subsequent studies have replicated the size of the effect found in Ainsworth's original Baltimore sample.

Other research has widened the focus on caregiver sensitivity to include the father. For example, van IJzendoorn and DeWolff (1997) found that the sensitive responsiveness of fathers is related to security of attachment in their children, particularly if they are more, rather than less, involved in their caregiving. It follows that other caregivers, including early childhood professionals, are potentially very important attachment figures, and research has been conducted on the nature of attachment relationships between children and their child-care providers and teachers (see Howes, 1999). Summarising a large and complex literature, Howes (1999) has concluded that 'The construction of attachment relationships between children and their alternative caregivers appears similar to the construction of infant–mother attachment . . . When alternative attachments are formed outside the family (i.e. in child care settings), the process of attachment formation appears similar to the processes within families' (pp. 684–5). While noting that there is still much to be learned about how these attachment relationships impact on later development (and how the various attachments a child forms interact together in terms of later social–emotional development; see also Rutter and O'Connor, 1999), Howes concludes that 'Particularly for children with difficult life circumstances . . . it seems possible that alternative attachment figures can provide children with a "safety net" for their future development' (1999, p. 685).

Adult attachment representations

Another important development within attachment theory relates to the growing understanding of how adults' mental representations of their own early attachment experiences impact on their caregiving behaviours within attachment relationships with their children (see Main and Hesse, 1990) and on their romantic attachments to other adults (see Crowell et al, 1999). In the 1980s, Mary Main and her colleagues Carol George and Nancy Caplan developed a semi-structured interview protocol, the Adult Attachment Interview (AAI) (Main et al, 1985), which has now been used extensively to assess adult attachment representations. Interviewees are asked to describe the caregiving qualities of their childhood attachment figures and to provide examples that demonstrate these qualities. They are questioned about how they believe their own attachment experiences have affected their development, and parenting if they have children. The interview narrative is carefully transcribed verbatim and coded, amongst other things, for coherence and consistency.

On the basis of very detailed analyses of the transcripts, for which there are very stringent training requirements, coders classify participants into one of three possible categories: autonomous/secure, preoccupied/entangled or dismissing/detached. Autonomous adults present a coherent account of their childhood attachment experiences and, if these were problematic or traumatic, they present as psychologically resolved in relation to them. They show insight, and are realistic, acknowledging the effects—negative and/or positive—of attachment experiences on their adult personality. Preoccupied adults present a confused and incoherent account, and their narratives indicate they continue to be psychologically enmeshed and preoccupied with past negative attachment experiences, remaining angry and unresolved in relation to them. Dismissing adults tend to have short narratives, often state they cannot remember attachment-related experiences, and deny the impact of these experiences on their adult personality. Idealisation of childhood attachment figures, unsupported or contradicted by actual memories, is common. Individuals can also be coded into a fourth category, termed unresolved: they show marked confusion and disorganisation in their transcripts and have usually experienced a profound early attachment loss or trauma (such as abuse).

AAI categories have been consistently found to be correlated with parenting behaviour and the quality of attachments formed with children (van IJzendoorn, 1995). Autonomous adults are most likely to have secure attachment relationships with their children. A dismissing state of mind is associated with insecure/avoidant attachments, a preoccupied state of mind with insecure/resistant attachments and an unresolved state of mind with disorganised attachments. Fonagy et al (1991) found that maternal AAI categories as assessed during pregnancy predicted the quality of infant–mother attachment when the infant was one year of age.

While research using the AAI (and other measures of individual differences in adult attachment; see Crowell et al, 1999) has advanced new understandings of the adult contribution to the attachment relationship, there are those who consider that attachment theory has yet to embrace the true complexity of individual differences in adult caregiving behaviours. Focusing on the maternal role, George and Solomon (1999) have rejected the descriptions of mothers—such as sensitive, rejecting or inconsistent—contained in attachment theory and research, and argue for a perspective that attempts 'to understand the mother as an individual in her own right' (p. 665). In their view, this involves acknowledging the 'complex interplay of developmental factors and challenges' (p. 665) that each caregiver faces as they tend to the attachment needs of a child. These include other competing demands, roles, social and cultural factors.

Another interesting perspective on the effects of early attachment experiences is that of Belsky (1999a). Applying an evolutionary perspective, Belsky argues that people differ in terms of how susceptible they are to the effects of environment on their development. He considers that for most infants the quality of the attachments they develop will be strongly influenced by the kind of caregiving received, thus supporting an attachment perspective. Belsky termed such infants as 'environmentally reactive' (p. 157). He argues, however, that other infants 'may be strongly predisposed to develop secure, avoidant, or resistant attachments almost regardless of the quality of care they experience' (p. 157). This view is highly speculative, and is yet to be tested empirically.

Attachment over the lifespan

In later chapters, the process of attachment formation over the first three years of life is described in some detail, from the pre-attachment phase during the first few weeks after birth to the phase of clear-cut attachment at six to eight months, and on to the 'goal-corrected partnership' of the two- to three-year-old. Once an attachment exists, the frequency and form of attachment behaviours change with age. For example, attachment theorists consider that attachment behaviours decrease in urgency and frequency after the third birthday. From this time, attachment behaviours are generally not elicited as readily, and when activated they are less intense. In addition, what the child needs to terminate their attachment behaviours changes from close physical contact to other forms of contact that are less direct, such as a reassuring look or a gentle, brief touch. Attachment theorists also recognise that attachment is a lifelong process and that older children, adolescents and adults continue to have attachment needs. In adolescence and adulthood these are met through friendships and romantic attachments, although the significance of attachment relationships with primary carers from the childhood years remains. As Bowlby described it, 'attachment behaviour never disappears completely' (1969/1982, p. 261). He also wrote: 'human beings of all ages are found to be at their happiest and to be able to deploy their talents to best advantage when they are confident that, standing behind them, there are one or more trusted persons who will come to their aid should difficulties arise' (1973, p. 359). We can all relate to this sentiment, in both our personal and professional lives.

Implications and applications

CASE SCENARIO

In our first case scenario, we will rejoin one-year-old Eli and her caregiver Zamia, introduced at the beginning of chapter 1. Zamia has carefully recorded the following observations of Eli's behaviours over the first couple of hours one morning at child care. As you read her descriptions, think about the material we have covered in this chapter, particularly around what constitutes attachment behaviour (in the child and the adult attachment figure) and the conditions under which these behaviours are most likely to be elicited.

Eli comes into the centre in the arms of her mother, Anna. Anna appears flustered, and more rushed than usual. She comments that the family had a late night and slept in. Consequently she had to wake Eli, breakfast was a 'disaster' and now she is running late for work. She thinks Eli may be coming down with a cold.

Eli appears rather more quiet than usual, and she strongly resists going into my arms when her mother begins to leave, something that I haven't observed for some time (Eli has now been at this centre for eight months). Eli cries loudly when her mother leaves, again an unusual occurrence, and she takes longer than normal to settle.

During the morning she seems to relax, but three aspects of her behaviour are notable. First, she appears far more sensitive than usual to the comings and goings of adults in the room. When the door opens she often notices and looks, carefully checking out who it is. She seems more aware of minor disruptions to routine, such as when an unfamiliar adult comes in to talk to one of the caregivers. Secondly, she is more 'clingy' than usual, following me around, wanting to be held and showing strong distress when I leave the room for my break. My colleague Carla comments that Eli did not want anything to do with her while I was gone, despite her attempts to hold and comfort her. Thirdly, Eli doesn't seem as interested in play activities today. It is as if her need for my comfort and reassurance is getting in the way of her exploration and enjoyment of the toys and activities around her.

At around 10 a.m., Eli's mother telephones the centre and asks to speak to me. She is in tears. She is anxious to know how Eli is, and says on days like today, she just wants to forget work and be with Eli, to hold her close and care for her. In all, Anna calls the centre three times before lunch.

QUESTIONS FOR REFLECTION

- Which behaviours in Eli may be considered attachment behaviours?
- Why is Eli finding it more difficult to separate from her mother this morning?
- Why is Eli more 'clingy' than normal?
- Why does Eli watch the door?
- Why won't Eli settle for the other caregiver, Carla?
- Why does Eli explore less today than usual?

- How should Zamia respond to Eli? What does Eli need?
- From an attachment perspective, why is Anna's response so understandable?

DISCUSSION POINTS

Zamia's observations of Eli are consistent with a heightening of Eli's attachment needs. Eli may be more tired than usual or, as her mother suspects, may be a little unwell. She may also be unsettled by events at home in the morning. Under these circumstances attachment theory would predict that Eli may be more anxious about separation from her mother, and Anna more anxious about separation from Eli.

Eli's initial reluctance to go to Zamia, her strong distress at the departure of her mother and the time taken to settle make sense from an attachment perspective. Eli's need for the nearness of her mother as her primary caregiver is a normal, secure response. In the absence of her mother, Eli's need for the nearness and reassuring presence of Zamia as her main attachment figure at child care is also a normal, secure response.

Eli's rejection of attempts by caregivers other than Zamia to settle her and her sensitivity to change show that Zamia needs to be even more conscious of and sensitive to Eli's needs today. They show how important Zamia is to Eli's feelings of security at child care and the secure nature of the emerging relationship between them. Eli needs frequent cuddles, gentle talking and touching, and careful attention to routines.

Anna also needs extra comfort today. Attachment theory reminds us that it is natural for primary attachment figures to be more concerned about their child if he or she is unwell or unsettled. Given the circumstances, Anna's response does not mean she is unhappy with the centre, dissatisfied with the carer or questioning Zamia's ability to look after Eli. She is just seeking reassurance and making contact with her child in the only way possible for her at this time.

Further readings

Bowlby, J. 1969/1982 *Attachment and Loss: Vol. 1. Attachment* 2nd edn, New York: Basic Books

Weinfield, N.S., Sroufe, A.L., Egeland, B. and Carlson, E.A. 1999 'The nature of individual differences in infant–caregiver attachment' *Handbook of Attachment: Theory, research and clinical applications* eds J. Cassidy and P.R. Shaver, The Guilford Press, New York, pp. 68–88

3

Why interactions matter

As we have seen in the last two chapters, attachment theorists emphasise that caregiving interactions not only promote basic survival but, just as importantly, influence aspects of the child's psychological development in profound ways. In this chapter we explore the central role of attachment figures in the formation of the child's internal working model of self and others. The internal working model is considered in relation to two key, interconnected aspects of personality development: the emerging sense of self and the development of emotional self-regulation.

Everyday child–caregiver relationships and psychological development

Attachment theory ascribes a pivotal role to the caregiver–child relationship in the formation of human personality, including the sense of self. It is not the only theory to do so. Other writings on developmental processes that accord with this view include those of Erikson (1963), Freud (1965), Winnicott (1965), Mahler et al (1975) and Bronfenbrenner (1979). A common theme is the belief in the critical importance of affective synchrony or attunement (Stern, 1985; Hughes, 1997) in the infant-caregiver relationship. Attunement refers to the sharing of affect in mutually enjoyable ways. In relation to mother–infant interactions, it has been described as follows:

> When attuned to her infant's affective state, her response closely matches the intensity, duration, and shape of her infant's behavioural expressions. During the first 9 months, her response is most often in the same modality of her infant's. If he vocalises, so does she. When he makes a face or waves his hands, she immediately follows with a very similar expression. As he continues to mature, her responses increasingly use other modalities to express the same affective state. She may make a face in response to his vocalization or make a particular vocalization in response to a given movement. In this way she is leading her infant into more complex experiences of interpersonal enjoyment and union. Through these experiences he also is becoming more able to integrate his various affective states and activities (Hughes, 1997, p. 12).

Importantly, Hughes stresses that relationships thus develop out of 'small, ordinary moments—not dramatic, out of the ordinary experiences' (p. 13). Attachment theory emphasises this point too—that there are myriad opportunities for such moments during caregiving in the early years. This is a crucial thing to remember as we go about our day-to-day interactions with infants and young children. Hughes describes as 'living attachment' (p. 13) the unique feelings of emotional engagement for any infant–caregiver dyad during daily life. His words, and attachment theory generally, underline how special *every* interaction is in moulding the emergent personality. This includes interactions during everyday caretaking tasks like feeding and nappy-changing as well as interactions during play and other activities.

The emerging sense of self

Why are interactions between the child and attachment figures so significant in determining the sense of self that emerges? Essentially the answer to this question is that the 'self'—our concept of who we are—is not something we are born with. The young infant has no, or at most a very primitive, sense of self. The self—which Sroufe (1995) defines as 'an inner organization of attitudes, beliefs, and values' (p. 218) constituting what he calls the 'affective core of the self' (p. 219), can only develop in the social context of human interactions and relationships. Each of us is the product of our social and cultural milieu. The self emerges from how others respond to us and relate to us during the early years. Put simply, from an attachment perspective the child only becomes truly human through interactions and relationships. Without human relationships there is no opportunity to form a sense of self nor consciousness of that self.

According to Sroufe, these aspects of the self have become organised and coherent by the preschool period, at least for children whose attachment relationships have not been significantly disturbed or disrupted. Where such disturbances have occurred, the sense of self may be distorted. Thus, the developmental progression from early infancy to the preschool period, with the emergence of a true sense of self, is sensitive to what happens within the infant caregiving system during this time.

Attachment theory emphasises the particular importance of interactions we have within our earliest attachment relationships. Because the sense of self consolidates over time, attachment experiences in the early years are particularly potent in terms of later developmental outcomes. A major reason for this is that the quality of early interactions and relationships sets up expectancies about how the self will be responded to. These expectations can become a lens through which we view and interpret subsequent experiences. Our perception of events, including human interactions, is influenced by subjective interpretations. These may distort our perception of events so that they confirm existing expectations of ourselves and how others relate to us, based on our inner working model. This quite complex process is described by Goldberg (2000). In her view, internal working models

> exert strong (often automatic and unconscious) influences on feelings, thoughts and behaviours. By directing attention to some

actions and events instead of others, guiding appraisal of information, and selecting what is and is not remembered, internal working models shape behaviours towards others and hence the reactions that one engenders in others. In other words, internal working models of attachment serve as interpretive lenses that focus new experiences (p. 169).

The concept of the internal working model

As we have already discussed, the concept of the internal working model is central to attachment theory. Drawing on cognitive psychology and the work of writers such as Craik (1943) and Young (1964), Bowlby distinguished between the cognitive map or model that humans (and animals) build up of their environment on the one hand, and models of the self in relation to the world that he referred to as 'organismic' models (Bowlby, 1969/1982, p. 82) on the other. The latter model is in essence a working model of the self, consisting of a set of expectations about the social world of relationships and the individual within it.

Sroufe (1990, 1995) has written extensively on this topic. He integrates attachment theory with the work of theorists such as Erikson (1963) and Mahler (e.g. Mahler et al, 1975). In his view, there are two major developmental tasks for infancy and early childhood, and each feeds in crucial ways into the developing sense of self. The first is trust, built from dependency needs. The second is autonomy, which grows from independent strivings.

Sroufe considers Erikson's notion of basic trust (the psychosocial task or crisis of the first year of life) as the core element of the self. He describes it as 'the individual's fundamental sense of others as caring, the self as worthy, and the world as safe' (1995, p. 221). This fundamental sense of security or trust emerges from a history of caregiving relationships characterised by sensitivity, consistency and responsiveness to the infant's dependency needs in the first year.

Once the child becomes mobile, and during the first to the third years (in Erikson's formulation, the period during which children face the psychosocial crisis or task of autonomy *vs* shame and doubt), a second layer of the self emerges via attempts at autonomy or independent striving to obtain a goal. Optimal outcomes at this stage depend not only on current caregiving which sensitively supports the child's movements towards autonomy, but also on the quality of caregiving that the child experienced during the earlier dependency stage. In other words, the development of autonomy and dependency go hand in hand. The child with a well-developed sense of trust based on smooth, well-functioning and close relationships with the attachment figures in infancy, somewhat paradoxically is best placed to become successfully independent at the later stage. This is because the sense of trust in the reliable presence, and responsiveness, of the attachment figure as a secure base allows the child to practise independence with confidence and hence to move more effectively out into the wider world.

A true sense of what Sroufe terms 'instrumentality', or autonomous functioning in the absence of adult involvement, only emerges in the preschool period. This is when peer friendships that are relatively free from adult direction first develop and the child assumes rudimentary self-responsibility. Feelings of competence and self-esteem are the end-products of caregiving experiences that nurture each of the two phases of trust and autonomy. Unresponsive, inconsistent and/or insensitive care lead to predictable negative outcomes on the developing self-concept. These include vulnerability to feelings of insecurity, low self-competence and lack of self-esteem.

It is in the second volume of the attachment trilogy (1973) that Bowlby discusses the concept of an internal working or representational model of the self in detail. According to Bowlby, the working model that develops influences three important aspects of the child's world view, namely perceptions (how the child 'perceives events'), expectations (how the child 'forecasts the future') and how to respond in the future (how the child 'constructs . . . plans') (p. 203). In his analysis a central feature of the child's world view is the identification of key attachment figures, and their likely behaviours and responses. The internal working model of the self incorporates the sense of self as acceptable/lovable or unacceptable/unlovable based on this world view. The world view in turn reflects whether attachment figures are experienced as consistently available or unavailable—sometimes, often or all the time. The child's emotions, social behaviour and cognition thus are all affected by and effect their own unique attachment system.

Importantly, according to attachment theory, the child generalises the view of self that is developed from early attachment experiences to the world of people in general: 'an unwanted child is likely not only to feel unwanted by his parents but to believe that he is essentially unwantable, namely unwanted by anyone. Conversely, a much-loved child may grow up to be not only confident of his parents' affection but confident that everyone else will find him lovable too' (Bowlby, 1973, pp. 204–5).

Howe (1995) summarises a large and complex literature in the following way:

> It is in our relationships with others that the self forms, the personality takes on many of its characteristics, and we develop mental models which seek to make sense of people and social situations. The key features of this thesis are that the formation of the self and the individual's personality take place within a matrix of social relationships; that these relationships will vary in quality for each individual; and that the quality and character of the self and personality which emerge will therefore reflect the quality of that person's relationship environment. Individual differences in relationships, therefore, lead to different developmental experiences (p. 24).

One or many models of the self? Enduring or not?

Bowlby acknowledged that children may, and probably do, form more than one working model of their attachment figures and therefore of the self. His position is that the earliest models, especially those formed in infancy (prior to language), may be the most resistant to change. In his view, however, the sensitive period in which expectations about attachment figures are formed extends from birth through to age five and beyond, diminishing but not ending during the adolescent years. He stated that the expectations formed during those years 'tend to persist relatively unchanged throughout the rest of life' (1973, p. 202).

However, work using the AAI (introduced in the previous

chapter) shows that people with less than optimal early attachment experiences can nonetheless develop into autonomous, secure adults. Categorised as 'earned secure', it has been found that these individuals constitute around 40–70 per cent of adults categorised as autonomous on the AAI (Pearson et al, 1994; Phelps et al, 1998). However, in line with Bowlby's sensitivity hypothesis, Pearson et al (1994) found that those in the 'earned secure' category were more likely to experience depression than those autonomous individuals whose early attachment experiences were positive. Every experience of relationship with another person—be they friend, romantic partner, counsellor or mentor—is potentially transforming but caregiving history is not thereby erased (Weinfield et al, 1999).

Attachment and fear

Another central proposition of attachment theory is that the presence of a sensitive and responsive attachment figure (and his or her predicted availability at times of perceived or actual threat) reduces fear. For Bowlby, fear is a central emotion. The child who is not confident of an attachment figure's availability is susceptible to intense and/or chronic fear, while such feelings may be quite foreign to a person with a history of secure attachment relationships. Additionally, the securely attached person's pervasive feelings of security may be just as foreign to the person whose attachment relationships have been insecure. Indeed, the feelings associated with security, such as contentment and wellbeing, can only occur in the absence of alarm or fear. Even at this basic level of what could be called our 'affective resting state' (the normal level, intensity and latency of our emotions), the role of attachment relationships in the development of unique personalities can be seen to be in play.

Brain research is helping to make the process by which this happens clearer. It has revealed a link between the intensity of emotions experienced in the early years and the development of areas of the brain such as the limbic system, which is the site of emotionality in the central nervous system. The work of Bruce Perry and others (e.g. Perry et al, 1995; Joseph, 1999) has been directed to a better understanding of how early experience in the emotional domain impacts on brain development. It focuses on how childhood trauma, such as witnessing domestic violence, can have long-term impacts on an individual's emotionality by sensitising areas in the limbic system. Research has found that when exposed to chronic over-arousal during early childhood (such as through chronic fear caused by ongoing domestic violence), these brain areas require increasingly less stimulation to become highly aroused. This can lead to a child or adult who is chronically over-aroused (in this example, fearful even in the absence of fear-provoking stimulation). A brief overview of this work is provided in Rolfe (2000).

Emotional self-regulation and personality formation

A final and crucial way in which the nature of attachment relation-ships impacts on the self and personality formation is through their contribution to the development of self-regulation of emotions. Emotional self-regulation refers to our ability to manage emotional experiences and to keep emotional arousal at comfortable levels so that we can accomplish our goals. Without this ability, an individual is always at risk of being over- or under-aroused, or fearful about becoming overwhelmed.

As adults, it is important that we are able to use a variety of strategies to help maintain focus and motivation, overcome anxiety and keep ourselves reasonably happy much of the time. From an attachment perspective, how, and how well, we can do this is dependent on qualities in our earliest caregiving relationships. Reflecting this position, Sroufe (1995) states that a child's current pattern of emotional regulation is built on previous patterns developed within the child–caregiver relationship. His early work in this area (e.g. Sroufe and Waters, 1977b) was pioneering in its analysis of attachment theory as a theory of emotional regulation. He sees the evolution of the attachment relationship as change in the regulation of emotion within the caregiver–child dyad, with children becoming increasingly self-regulatory as they move towards and into the preschool stage.

Over the first months after birth, emotional regulation is not something that the infant can achieve alone. Infants can self-soothe, but they do need the help of their caregiver to modulate their level of arousal if it escalates too much, and to keep it within a range that is not so intense that they are over-aroused or overwhelmed, especially not repeatedly so. Again, one is reminded that what counts are simple, ordinary, moment-by-moment interactional experiences. Imagine two scenarios. In both, a young baby is beginning to cry in response to escalating arousal due to being afraid. In the first scenario, the baby's cries quickly bring the caregiver, who talks in soothing tones then calmly picks up the baby and holds him or her to the shoulder, gently swaying from side to side. The infant immediately begins to settle, emotional escalation ceases and de-escalation of arousal begins, bringing the infant's emotional state back within comfortable bounds. In the second scenario, no caregiver comes, at least not for many minutes. The infant may attempt to self-soothe but without effective adult intervention moves further and further into uncomfortable-feeling states of high arousal.

According to Sroufe (1995), the first baby is better placed to learn about emotional regulation, and in time to engage in the process with more independence. He states that during the period up to about six months of age, it is the adult caregiver who essentially achieves regulation, not the infant. It is only after repeated experiences of arousal escalation and de-escalation within the attachment relationship that the young child eventually develops the ability to self-regulate his or her emotional state. That is, experiences accumulate, and as infants' cognitive abilities develop they learn from experiences such as this whether the caregiver can be trusted to help them achieve a comfortable emotional state, defined as a level of tension or arousal that is not aversive—or as Sroufe terms it, 'disorganising' (1995, p. 189). This expectancy, both of the caregiver and importantly, of the child's own role in the process, is central to the internal working model that develops.

If the child's dyadic experiences lead to confidence in the caregiver, and the self, in terms of achieving emotional regulation, the child becomes able to tolerate increasing levels of tension, initially in the presence of the attachment figure and later without that person being nearby. These experiences also have positive impacts on the child's repertoire of emotions and associated behaviours, shown during social interaction. For the child whose experiences have led to lack of confidence in the caregiver's role in emotional regulation, there is the risk of negative impacts on their ability to manage tension and arousal.

Sroufe draws attention to the importance of joint attention interactions in this process. These occur during interactions in which the infant and caregiver jointly act upon and share attention to an object or event. Most often this is seen during play, when adult and infant interactions revolve around one or more toys that they both attend to. Sometimes joint attention interactions begin with the infant, who recruits the adult's attention so play can begin. Sometimes it happens the other way around, with the adult caregiver initiating the play interaction. In either case there is a sharing of experience, normally associated with positive affect including smiles, vocalisations and other communicative acts. Sroufe (1995) underlines the significance of joint attention interactions when he describes them as 'the reservoir of positive experiences that underlies the affective bond between most infants and their caregivers' (p. 174). However, research conducted on joint attention in child–care centres suggests that infants may have limited opportunities to experience this type of play because caregivers spend so little time in focused one-to-one interactions with the children in their care (see Smith, 1996, 1999; Rolfe et al, 2002). This is a serious concern from the perspective of attachment theory as well as other theories of social and cognitive development.

Linking caregiving experiences and patterns of security and insecurity

The child who has built strong feelings of assurance about the availability of others when needed is able to openly and directly express emotions, is curious and actively explores the environment, and is well able to cope with arousal escalation independently or with the help of others. Sroufe (1995) and others (e.g. Cassidy, 1994) have also discussed expected developmental outcomes when the history of caregiving has not been positive. If caregiving has been such that the child is unable to trust the caregiver for effective help in modulating arousal and emotional tension, these experiences lead to less honest emotional expression, either through minimisation or exaggeration of feelings. Children may also be vulnerable to feelings of fear, and their willingness to engage in the full range of emotional experiences available in the normal course of human life may be diminished. They may develop views of inadequacy about the self since they have repeatedly failed to gain through their own efforts the comfort and support sought.

Howe (1995) has referred to this important aspect of the inner working model as the child's 'subjective experience of self as potent' (p. 74). This sense of being able to exert influence over what happens in one's close relationships, and beyond this, to influence what happens in the wider world of experience with the animate and inanimate world, is an important component of the psychologically healthy self-concept. Without this, the child or adult can feel that what happens to them is due largely to chance, and not directly influenced by their own efforts.

The secure and insecure patterns of attachment that Ainsworth and later attachment writers have described, and which were briefly introduced in the last chapter, may be understood as a reflection of the child's strategies of emotional expression and control/regulation developed in response to particular caregiving styles. Securely attached children openly express their emotions, both negative and positive; insecure infants either minimise (avoidant strategy) or exaggerate (resistant strategy) their distress and needs for comfort. These different patterns and why they emerge will be considered in detail in the next chapter.

Implications and applications

CASE SCENARIO

In our second case scenario, we will observe an interaction between two-and-a-half-year-old Ryan and his caregiver Jung, who were first introduced at the beginning of chapter 1. Ryan has just woken from his afternoon nap. He is lying on his mattress, looking around and kicking his feet up and down. As you read the description of the ensuing interaction between Jung and Ryan, think about the material we have covered in this chapter, particularly around what impact Jung's behaviours will be having on Ryan's emerging sense of self.

Jung approaches Ryan's bed and smiles at him, reaching down to gently stroke his hair. She sits down, and begins to talk quietly. He gazes at her, rubbing his eyes occasionally in a sleepy fashion. Jung continues to talk quietly, then starts humming a tune, beginning to gently tap the side of Ryan's bed in time to the beat. After a few moments, Ryan giggles and begins to imitate Jung's movements. Jung reaches over, places her hand on his, and begins to tap to the beat with Ryan's hand, helping him keep in time. Soon they are both clapping in time and they begin to laugh together. Their play finishes with a big hug.

Ryan, now wide awake, sits up and reaches for his shoes. He gives them to Jung, who places them on the ground, smiling and chatting to Ryan as he begins to put them on. She allows Ryan lots of time, praising him for his efforts and providing a helping hand just as much as needed. With both shoes on, Ryan gives a broad smile, and walks towards the middle of the playroom. He stands there quietly for a few moments, then joins a small group of children in the block area. He turns back to look at Jung, who is folding up his bed, then sits down and begins to play.

QUESTIONS FOR REFLECTION

- This scenario describes the end of nap time. What aspects of Jung's behaviour would promote Ryan's feelings of security? Of autonomy? His self-regulation of emotions?
- In your view, how important are everyday caretaking routines as opportunities for promoting feelings of security, autonomy and emotional self-regulation?

- Think about other routine caretaking tasks like meal times and nappy-changing. Based on the descriptions of nap time interactions, how do you think Jung might interact with Ryan at these other times?
- In your view, what impedes sensitive, responsive caregiving interactions with infants and toddlers in early childhood settings? What can you do to change these?

DISCUSSION POINTS

The interaction between Jung and Ryan reveals caregiver sensitivity and responsiveness. The observations are consistent with an engaged and highly involved style of caregiving. This sort of caregiving is characterised by joyful interactions, gentle touching, sustained conversation and attunement. Jung is in tune with Ryan and Ryan is in tune with Jung. Together they create harmonious, happy interactions. These sorts of interactions have been found to be related to secure attachment between young children and their professional caregivers (Howes et al, 1992). They support feelings of security and autonomy in the child. They assist in the development of emotional self-regulation. Think about how different the early childhood experience would be for children in the absence of involved caregiving, if days are filled with highly routinised, inflexible, chaotic or emotionally distant care.

Further readings

Edwards, C. and Raikes, H. 2002 'Extending the dance: Relationship-based approaches to infant-toddler care and education' *Young Children* vol. 57, pp. 10–17

Sroufe, L.A. 1995 *Emotional Development: The organisation of emotional life in the early years* Cambridge University Press, Cambridge

4

Quality of attachment

In the previous chapter, the reasons that early attachment relationships are so important for child development were described. The concept of the internal working model was introduced to explain how and why the nature of caregiving by key attachment figures sets up expectancies about the self and the social world. In this chapter, we consider in detail two concepts central to attachment theory—security and insecurity, and the continuum between them. The work of various attachment theorists will be detailed and discussed, beginning with the pioneering work of Mary Ainsworth.

The concept of emotional security

It is widely understood that interpersonal experiences contribute in critical ways to the development of emotional security or insecurity. Attachment theory emphasises the role of attachment figures in this process, and that the roots of security (or insecurity) lie in the experience of caregiving by attachment figures particularly during the early years. Being responded to promptly, sensitively and consistently builds up the infant's sense that the world of people is predictable, can be trusted to meet one's needs and that one can feel safe and secure in this knowledge. Thus assured, the child is well placed to concentrate energies on other activities, including exploration, that enhance all the developmental domains including cognition. Security, then, as understood within an attachment perspective, has important implications not just for social and emotional aspects of functioning, but intellectual aspects as well.

From the outset, it is important to underline that the concept of security does not imply that securely attached children never experience anxiety or feel afraid. It is normal—and adaptive—for every person to feel these emotions from time to time, just as sadness, disappointment and anger are inevitable parts of life. Indeed, it is the experience of these sorts of emotions that motivates the expression of attachment behaviours in the child. What differs between securely and insecurely attached children is how they respond to these arousing feelings. This includes their perception of the availability of their attachment figure(s) at these times (available *vs* unavailable or unpredictable), their beliefs regarding the likelihood that care and comfort will be forthcoming (expectation of a caring, comforting response *vs* uncertain response or even rejection/ punishment) and how they respond (approach *vs* avoidance of the attachment figure).

It is this organisation of attachment-related behaviours (see Sroufe and Waters, 1977b) within the child–caregiver relationship, rather than the frequency of attachment behaviours per se, that reveals the essence of relationship quality. For example, consider two-and-a-half-year-old Ryan in the last case scenario. Secure and settled in his child-care room, he would normally explore enthusias- tically much of the time, with only periodic 'check-backs' to the caregiver. Imagine, though, that there is a potential threat to his safety, for example, the approach of an unfamiliar adult, or that he becomes anxious or afraid for some other reason. One would expect Ryan's behaviour to change quickly. We would not be surprised to see a series of intense attachment behaviours one after the other in rapid succession, including calling, crying and approach to his attachment figure, Jung, all designed to achieve proximity as quickly as possible. Once the perceived danger is past, however, and the child settles, a low level of attachment behaviour would likely again be observed.

The child with an insecure attachment to the caregiver shows a different pattern of behaviour to the child who is secure. Insecure behavioural organisation can take various forms. One example of insecurity is when the child characteristically explores very little, even in the absence of any perceived or potential threat to security. There may be constant monitoring of the whereabouts of the caregiver and anxious maintenance of proximity. In other children insecurity might be revealed by a very different pattern in which the attachment figure is apparently ignored, avoided or rebuffed, even when the child is, or could reasonably be expected to be, fearful.

The contributions of Mary Ainsworth

As introduced in chapter 2, Ainsworth's observations on the development of attachment relationships, first in Uganda and later in the United States, provided an empirical base to the newly developing understanding from attachment theory of how and why quality of relationships can differ between child–caregiver dyads. In Volume 1 of the attachment trilogy, Bowlby (1969/1982) refers to Ainsworth's longitudinal and cross-sectional field work in Uganda (1963, 1964, 1967), mainly drawing on the richly detailed, naturalistic observations it provides on mother–child interactions and the usual process of attachment formation. In Volume 2 of the attachment trilogy (1973), Bowlby discusses the outcomes of Ainsworth's later work in Baltimore, subsequently published in the late 1970s (Ainsworth et al, 1978). It is this important work, focusing on individual differences in attachment quality and the construct of 'security', that we first consider in this chapter.

Ainsworth's field study in Uganda

Ainsworth's initial observations of mother–infant interactions were made during a field study in Uganda during 1954 and 1955. The study had a small sample, 15 male and 13 female infants, but the observations were detailed and were to provide the foundation for the three primary attachment classifications introduced in chapter 2: secure, resistant and avoidant. The observations were made in village homes in Uganda and demonstrated how certain situations intensify the expression of attachment behaviours in children. As attachment theory predicts, the situations that evoke attachment behaviours vary according to the age of the child. But fundamental to them is always some threat to the child's sense of wellbeing or safety arising from either the absence, or threat of absence, of the attachment figure and/or the appearance of strangers.

For example, in her extensive case summaries Ainsworth (1967) provides the following description of a female infant, Aida, the youngest of three sisters in a family following traditional Ganda customs of the time:

> When we visited at twenty-four weeks, Aida had a bowel movement on the mat near the door soon after we arrived. She had had diarrhea for several days, and perhaps because of the excitement of our arrival her mother did not notice any signals. The mother did not fuss, but cleaned up the floor with leaves. Then she went outside to fetch water to give Aida a bath. The baby cried when her mother left but stopped as soon as she returned. Then she was bathed outside in a tub, just as before.
>
> Once back inside after the bath, Aida cried again when her mother left for a moment. Mrs. Kibuka [research assistant and interpreter] took her on her lap and tried to comfort her, but she continued to cry until her mother returned. Back on her mother's lap, she quieted, then became drowsy, and finally fell asleep. Her mother said that whenever she was left with someone else, even a familiar person, she cried for a while and then stopped, but when her mother was present Aida was friendly with other people, both men and women—and, indeed, she was friendly with us. She did not yet recognise her father for he was so rarely at home (p. 132).

This brief excerpt highlights a number of behaviours and situations which have subsequently emerged as highly important in identifying patterns of security and insecurity in attachment relationships. These include:

- the infant's response to her mother's departure and return (in the presence of familiar and unfamiliar people);
- her response to an attempt by the mother and others to comfort her; and
- her reported and observed sociability to unfamiliar people when her mother was present or absent.

In addition to the response of distress to separation from the mother, Ainsworth identified from her extensive observations 16 other behaviours characteristic of infants she concluded were attached to their mothers. These included differential crying, smiling and vocalisations, following, either with the eyes or locomotion, positive greeting behaviours, physical affection, use of the mother as a secure base and what Ainsworth describes as 'flight to the mother as a haven of safety' (1967, p. 332). She also identified the infant's response to strangers as important. Finally, Ainsworth used her naturalistic observations of Ganda families to begin her attempts at classifying infant–caregiver attachment security *vs* insecurity and the 'infant-care practices' (1967, p. 387) associated with each.

Sensitive responsiveness

Ainsworth's tentative suggestions at the time regarding caregiving practices that promote security included maternal warmth and affection, maternal availability, and a characteristic she termed sensitivity of response to infant signals—be they social signals or signals of need or distress. She defined what is meant by sensitivity and responsiveness: 'Sensitivity of response to signals implies that signals are perceived and correctly interpreted and that the response is prompt and appropriate' (1967, p. 397). The similarity of sensitive responsiveness, so defined, to the concepts of 'affective synchrony' and 'attunement' that we discussed at the beginning of chapter 3 are clear. Indeed, Ainsworth particularly noted that to be sensitive was to be 'attuned to the baby's state and mood—at the baby's own timing, not at the mother's timing . . . It is interaction that seems to be most important, not mere care' (1967, p. 397).

Subsequent work by Ainsworth

On her return to Baltimore, Ainsworth again conducted naturalistic observations in the home, augmented by structured observations in an unfamiliar university office/laboratory setting. These observations were an attempt to observe in a structured, time-efficient way an infant's reactions to the sorts of events commonly encountered in everyday life, reactions that had appeared so telling in terms of quality of attachment in her earlier naturalistic observations. These included brief separations and reunions with an attachment figure and interactions with a stranger.

The success of these structured observations led to the development of the Strange Situation technique (Ainsworth and Wittig, 1969) described in chapter 2. According to Weinfield et al (1999):

> The strange situation is so named because it is intended to be a mildly to moderately stressful experience for an infant, akin to an experience in a doctor's office waiting room. It introduces several strange and therefore stressful elements to an infant—a laboratory context that is unfamiliar, an unfamiliar adult who interacts with the child, and two brief separations from the mother. The premise of the situation is that the multiple increasing stressors will activate the infant's attachment behavioural system, and that individual differences in the child's expectations about the availability of the caregiver will thus be revealed (p. 71).

As Ainsworth herself described it, the technique was designed to expose infants to events that were 'unfamiliar' rather than 'odd' or 'peculiar' and which, based on her extensive naturalistic observations, were expected to 'activate and/or intensify infants' attachment behaviour' (Ainsworth et al, 1978, p. viii).

In Baltimore, Ainsworth also refined rating assessments of key aspects of caregiving behaviour—scales of Caregiver Sensitivity to Signals, Co-operation–Interference, Acceptance–Rejection, and Availability–Unavailability scales. Subsequent research was to reveal statistically significant correlations between infant–mother behaviour at home and that observed during the Strange Situation technique, thus confirming the validity of the laboratory-based procedure.

This was so despite Ainsworth's view that due to its stressful nature, 'one cannot expect behavior there [in the Strange Situation] to be precisely the same as at home' (Ainsworth et al, 1978, p. 311).

Different categories of attachment quality

In the remainder of this chapter, the four patterns of attachment organisation revealed by the Strange Situation procedure—secure (pattern B), avoidant (pattern A), resistant (pattern C) and disorganised/disoriented (pattern D)—are discussed in turn, followed by a discussion of the patterns of caregiving that have been associated with each category. The chapter concludes with a brief outline of patterns of security and insecurity identified in young children beyond the infant and toddler years. It is to be noted that extensive training is required in order to code accurately behaviours in the Strange Situation and to be able to reliably classify patterns of attachment quality from this and other assessment techniques.

The summaries that follow focus on the *main* dimensions of difference between the major secure/insecure classifications, based on behaviours observed in the Strange Situation procedure. Subgroups within each of these major classifications have also been identified and there is a continuum between them. Some secure infants, for example, show stronger tendencies than others to independent play. Some secure infants show distress at separation, some do not. Insecure patterns also show subtle and fine distinctions within categories. This appears also to be true for the disorganised/disoriented patterns (Waters and Valenzuela, 1999). The reader interested in these finer distinctions—which are used mainly in coding data from research studies—should consult Harwood et al (1995, pp. 8–9), who provide a helpful overview of the secure–insecure continuum.

Secure attachment

As outlined in chapter 2, the Strange Situation consists of seven three-minute episodes, always in the same order. These episodes are:

- adult attachment figure (parent or other caregiver) and child alone in the playroom;

- adult and child joined by a stranger;
- adult leaves the room and stranger remains with the child;
- adult returns and stranger leaves;
- adult leaves again and the child is left alone;
- stranger returns; and finally
- adult returns again.

During the Strange Situation procedure, the securely attached child uses the attachment figure as a secure base and is usually observed to explore the unfamiliar room, or at least the toys it contains, early in the procedure when the attachment figure is present, and before any separations have occurred. There may be 'check-backs' to confirm the continued presence of the attachment figure, but generally speaking the child appears interested and curious in the new environment and not overly preoccupied with the caregiver's whereabouts. While some interest is shown in the unfamiliar adult, especially when the attachment figure is still present, there is no indication of 'overly friendly' or 'indiscriminately friendly' behaviour. That is, the attachment figure is clearly preferred, and can comfort and settle the child more than the unfamiliar person. Whether distressed by separation or not, the securely attached infant will be noticeably and positively responsive to the return of the attachment figure, even after a brief absence. If distressed, immediate and unambiguous contact is sought on reunion, and importantly, the child maintains contact for as long as needed to achieve comfort. The secure infant is readily comforted by proximity or contact with the attachment figure and most securely attached infants eventually return to play. They also freely express their emotions, both positive and negative, in the presence of the attachment figure.

In discussing the securely attached pattern, Ainsworth et al (1978) have described the hallmark features of the child's interactions with the caregiver as 'harmonious . . . cooperative . . . positive and unconflicted' (p. 311). In considering why some secure infants are not distressed by separation, they state that this reflects the child's expectancy, built up from many prior experiences, of the attachment figure's ongoing accessibility and responsiveness even if she or he is out of sight temporarily. Such confidence results in a child who is 'bold' (Bowlby, 1988) in his or her exploration of the world.

Avoidant attachment

The avoidant child usually shows a strong focus of attention on the available toys during the initial phase of the procedure, but in contrast to the secure child there is little affective sharing or joint play with the attachment figure. There is usually little, if any, 'checking back' to the caregiver or, in attachment terms, little evidence of the use of that person as a secure base. There is generally little overt distress at separation, but again, the quality of this response differs from that of the secure child who does not cry, since in the reunion to follow there is little if any proximity-seeking by the avoidant child. This appears to indicate that the child is untroubled by separation (or even does not notice the attachment figure has gone). However, research measuring heart rate has tellingly revealed that avoidant children are in fact highly aroused by these events (Sroufe and Waters, 1977a) even though they do not show it in their overt behaviours.

The hallmark feature of behavioural organisation in the avoidant child is ignoring, turning or moving away from the attachment figure on his or her return. The avoidant infant may lean away from, or put a hand or toy between their own body and that of the attachment figure if picked up. The avoidant child may show fleeting expressions of anger towards the attachment figure (Waters and Valenzuela, 1999). This is something that may be noticed by the attachment figure (who makes comments like 'See, you're angry with me') and that some researchers suggest may act as a prompt to caregiving (Main, 1981, as cited by Waters and Valenzuela, 1999). The avoidant infant may appear to prefer the stranger over the attachment figure and often there is little that differentiates the child's behaviour to each adult. Avoidant infants appear to repress their emotions, particularly negative emotions of distress.

The reasons for this avoidant pattern in the child become clearer when considered in relation to the caregiving patterns that give rise to this form of attachment (described in detail later in this chapter). According to Ainsworth et al (1978) avoidance is a child's response to a history of unpleasant experiences around close bodily contact with their attachment figures (who, as we will see later, tend to be rejecting of their infants' bids for comfort) and an attempt to 'cut-off' (through averting their gaze, focusing on toys, etc.) from the experience of close contact. The avoidant response:

> short circuits direct expression of anger to the attachment figure, which might be dangerous, and it also protects the baby from reexperiencing the rebuff that he has come to expect when he seeks close contact with his mother. It thus somewhat lowers his level of anxiety (arousal). It also leads him to turn to the neutral world of things, even though displacement exploratory behaviour is devoid of the true interest that is inherent in nonanxious exploration (Ainsworth et al, 1978, p. 320).

Resistant (or ambivalent) attachment

A child classified as resistant (sometimes termed ambivalent) tends to be preoccupied with the attachment figure, anxiously seeking proximity and physical contact with him or her even during the first episodes of the procedure prior to any separations. Not surprisingly, the resistant child often becomes highly distressed by separation, but in contrast to secure infants is not fully comforted by contact with the attachment figure on reunion. The hallmark feature of behavioural organisation is the ambivalence shown by the infant to contact with the attachment figure during the reunion episode, often actively seeking contact, then angrily resisting it. In contrast to avoidant infants, there is an exaggeration, rather than minimisation, of negative emotions like distress. Ainsworth et al (1978) identified few infants as resistant, and described them as 'chronically anxious' (p. 314) in relation to the attachment figure.

These descriptions show that the secure, avoidant and resistant patterns are brought into stark contrast in the reunion episodes. The secure infant actively approaches the returning attachment figure, seeks contact and remains close until settled. The avoidant infant does not seek the comfort of the attachment figure on reunion, or does so minimally. The resistant infant approaches, but does not sustain contact long enough to become settled, leading to the characteristic alternation between contact-seeking and angry resistance of contact. In all cases, the child has been distressed by separation, and when the attachment figure returns a 'solution' to the problem is afforded (that is, contact for the purposes of being comforted). This 'solution' is only taken by the secure child (Waters and Valenzuela, 1999) for reasons to do with the history of caregiving behaviours, as discussed later in this chapter.

Disorganised/disoriented attachment

The A (avoidant), B (secure) and C (resistant) patterns all reveal behavioural organisation on the part of the child. That is, there is a coherence to the attachment behaviours shown. They are logical and strategic, whether secure or insecure (Main, 1991). Research has identified some children who, in contrast, show marked disorganisation or disorientation in the Strange Situation (Main and Solomon, 1990). This essentially refers to an inability by the child to maintain one organised, coherent behavioural strategy in the presence of the attachment figure, particularly under conditions of attachment stress. The sorts of child behaviours that may lead to the classification D (disorganised/disoriented) are stilling, fear behaviours (like putting the hands over the face) and behavioural stereotypies (such as rocking), all indicative of high level anxiety or panic. In the reunion episodes, the disorganised/disoriented child shows confused and contradictory behaviours to the attachment figure such as approach and avoidance at the same time (for example, looking at the attachment figure while backing away). It is generally considered that this attachment category represents the most extreme form of insecurity and is a risk factor for future emotional wellbeing.

Infants who are given a primary attachment classification of disorganisation are usually also given a secondary classification according to the underlying organised strategy (A, B, or C) that they show (van IJzendoorn et al, 1999). They are classified as disorganised because when faced with the attachment-related stress of the Strange Situation, any organised pattern they may have (and which may have been observed early in the procedure) breaks down, leading to the odd, contradictory and/or disoriented behaviours seen in the later episodes.

The disorganised behaviours shown are not only incoherent, they reveal the unresolvable stress and anxiety that the child experiences in response to the returning attachment figure. Disorganisation is usually seen in children who have been abused by their attachment figures, who have suffered major attachment disruptions (such as multiple foster placements and/or multiple failed reunifications following removal from parental care due to protective concerns) or whose attachment figures are themselves overwhelmed by previous attachment-related losses and whose caregiving behaviour, as described in chapter 2, is usually characterised as being 'frightened'.

When faced with this type of frightened or frightening behaviour by the attachment figure, the young child experiences contradictory attachment tendencies—they feel afraid and hence want to approach the attachment figure for comfort, but that person is at the same time the very source of their fear. This is what Main (1995) has referred to as experiencing fear with no solution—the attachment figure may have become a figure of intense fear for the child while at the same time being, paradoxically, their supposed source of comfort. This is the unresolvable dilemma that confronts these children in the Strange Situation reunion, and which causes any organised strategy they may have to break down, with resultant displays of incomplete, mistimed, interrupted and/or bizarre behaviours.

Solomon and George (1999) have added a further perspective on attachment disorganisation by underlining the importance of the context in which the young child experiences frightened or frightening behaviour by their attachment figure. They state that 'A key feature of this context should be whether or not the attachment figure engages in reparative behaviour once she has, intentionally or inadvertently, frightened or distressed the child' (p. 14). They note that inevitably, at times adults behave in ways that may alarm children, for example, if they become angry, distressed or alarmed for some reason. However, if the adult, noting the child's distress, acts quickly to reassure and calm the child (the act of repair or reparation), then 'the child's security is unlikely to be shaken; indeed, both the relationship and the infant's capacity for affect regulation may be strengthened' (p. 14). In infants who are disorganised, it appears there is likely a history of caregiving in which this act of repair and reassurance is absent, so that the infant or young child remains distressed, confused and/or afraid. There are thus repeated experiences in which the attachment figure does not act to repair the stressed relationship, and therefore, in the view of Solomon and George (1999), a failure by the attachment figure to successfully 'terminate' the attachment system (p. 14), which they conceive as an 'abdication of caregiving' (p.14).

Distribution of attachment classifications

North American samples typically show a distribution of attachment classifications as follows: avoidant 20 per cent, secure 60 per cent, resistant/ambivalent 10–15 per cent and disorganised 5–10 per cent (see NICHD, 1997). That is, about 60 per cent of children in non-risk samples show secure attachments, and about 40 per cent show insecure attachments.

Some differences have emerged between countries in the distribution pattern for the insecure categories. For example, in some Australian samples a relatively high percentage of resistant infants has been identified. Harrison and Ungerer (2002), classified attachment security in a sample of 145 Australian first-born infants and their mothers. The sample consisted primarily of Caucasian women (93 per cent were of European origin), with 7 per cent identified as non-European in origin (including Asian, Middle Eastern and South American women). At 12 months of age, 59 per cent of the infants were categorised as secure, 24 per cent as resistant, 8 per cent as avoidant and 9 per cent as disorganised. The authors report this distribution to be consistent with other Australian studies (e.g. Radojevic, 1996, as cited by Harrison and Ungerer, 2002).

Caregiving precursors of different attachment types

There have been many research studies conducted to investigate the kinds of caregiving experiences associated with these major attachment categories. In the main, Ainsworth et al's (1978) conclusions in this regard have been supported (see Weinfield et al, 1999). That is, secure attachments are associated with sensitive caregiving, and insecure attachments are associated with insensitive, less accessible and more interfering caregiving. DeWolff and van IJzendoorn (1997) found a statistically significant relationship between security and caregiver sensitivity in their meta-analysis of 66 studies.

The general conclusion in terms of the various insecure classifications is that avoidant attachment is associated with the experience of indifferent or rejecting caregiving, with infants learning that to 'make the relationship work' they must minimise their attachment bids since these generally evoke angry rejection by the caregiver. Avoidant infants view the attachment figure as unavailable, and they attempt to cope with attachment-related distress by themselves. Because of the nature of the strategies they adopt, avoidant children may appear precociously independent and emotionally autonomous.

Resistant behaviours are generally considered to be associated with inconsistent, insensitive and chaotic caregiving. Uncertain about caregiver availability (physical and/or emotional), the child develops the strategy of intensifying attachment behaviour to maintain caregiver interest and attention, but there is anger and resentment, and vigilance of the caregiver for any signs of impending unavailability. Caregivers of resistant infants may ignore the child's signals for attention at one moment, then become intrusive and demanding in the next. Howe (1995) states that the resistant child may have experienced little or no control of their emotional boundaries: [Caregiver] 'Responses come when they are not wanted and fail to arrive when needed. In interactional terms, the caregivers of ambivalently attached children generate confusion rather than co-operation' (p. 83).

In Bowlby's (1988) view, the separation anxiety, clingy behaviour and anxiety about exploring the world seen in resistant children also results from a history of threats of abandonment used by the attachment figure as a means of control.

Thus, despite their insecure nature, avoidant and resistant patterns are considered organised, strategic and adaptive in the face of the particular caregiving behaviours that underpin them. Marris (1991) has described this as 'working the system', by which he means 'understanding how to comply with the requirements of a relationship to achieve a desired result' (pp. 78–9). This 'desired result' is probably best conceptualised as the child's attempt to make the relationship work sufficiently well to ensure their caregiver maintains at least minimal care.

The D classification, as already discussed, is given when behaviours are not organised and is generally considered to develop in response to attachment figures who show inexplicably and frankly frightening or frightened behaviour in the presence of the child. There is no organised strategy that the child can use to stop the abuse or other maltreatment occurring; no way, as it were, to make this relationship 'work'.

Main and Solomon (1986) coined the term disorganised/disoriented and they were the first to describe the various behaviour patterns associated with this classification, including apprehension, fear and trance-like, dissociative states. Disorganised attachment behaviour is often subtle and difficult to observe, but with intensive training can be reliably scored. While it is relatively rare in non-risk samples it is observed much more frequently, at rates of 30–45 per cent in clinical risk samples (van IJzendoorn et al, 1999) of maltreating, abusive families.

Attachment disorganisation can have profound effects on personality and social development as well as other areas of psychological functioning, such as attention (see Lyons-Ruth and Jacobvitz, 1999). Children who show disorganised attachment patterns are at risk for childhood externalising problems (acting out and conduct disorders) and possibly psychopathology in later life (van IJzendoorn et al, 1999).

Intergenerational transmission of attachment quality

This discussion of caregiving precursors shows that the nature of attachment behaviour in children is in most cases best understood as a strategic response to the nature of caregiving received. The child's behaviour makes sense when viewed as his or her attempt to make the relationship work, to keep the attachment figure close or 'close enough' to ensure survival needs are met. It is not surprising, then, that links have been made between the attachment representations of parents themselves, as assessed using the AAI discussed in chapter 2, and the quality of attachment that their children develop to them (e.g. Steele and Steele, 1994). This is referred to as intergenerational transmission of attachment.

The mechanisms underlying intergenerational transmission of attachment are still not fully understood. However, research has indicated that autonomous adults tend to have children who are securely attached. Autonomous adults, as discussed in chapter 2, are resolved in relation to their own early attachment experiences. Sensitive responding to the expressed attachment needs of the infant is more likely therefore, than if unresolved memories of troubling early attachment relationships continue to intrude, especially when the child's attachment needs are strong. In line with this, Grossmann et al (1988) reported higher levels of empathy and understanding of the significance of attachment experiences in autonomous mothers.

Adults who are still enmeshed with negative emotions around their attachment history (termed preoccupied) tend to have resistant children. It appears that their memories of attachment experiences are so intrusive—especially when attachment issues are heightened by their children's dependency on them—that it is impossible for them to prioritise the child's emotional needs, at least in any consistent way. Dismissing adults tend to have avoidant children, since their own strategies of denial may lead them to be unresponsive to, or actively rejecting of, the expression of attachment needs in their children. Finally, it has been suggested that there is a link between disorganised attachment in the child and parental unresolved trauma or loss, categorised as Unresolved in the AAI.

Attachment quality in children beyond the infant and toddler stages

As children move beyond the infancy and toddler periods, their increasing cognitive development (including use of language, social understanding and skills of emotional control and emotional expression) allows for more sophisticated social relationships, including with attachment figures. Measurements of attachment must be subtle enough to detect what are, by then, mainly cognitive rather than behavioural indices of relationship quality. Measuring instruments also need to allow for the fact that as children become more independent, the circumstances that elicit the expression of attachment needs also change.

Despite these challenges, a number of assessment instruments have been developed to measure attachment during the preschool years. Some of these were discussed in chapter 2. Other measures have attempted to rework assessment criteria from the Strange Situation to make them more appropriate to older children, by including, for example, language interactions and more complex and sophisticated adult–child interactions, such as the ability to negotiate separations and reunions (e.g. Crittenden, 2000b). Crittenden's Preschool Assessment of Attachment includes the following categories: secure/balanced; defended (akin to the avoidant category); coercive (including threatening, punitive behaviour on the part of the child as well as charming, coy behaviour); defended/coercive; and anxious/depressed. In older children the disorganised/disoriented category usually includes elements of undue need for control, including role reversal (parentified behaviours), overly bright behaviour and/or rejecting, punitive or humiliating behaviour to the attachment figure. In chapter 8 we consider these categories in detail.

Links to the socialisation of emotions

The quality or nature of caregiving behaviours by attachment figures not only signals to the child their likely availability as sources of comfort and reassurance, it also provides the child with clear messages about how emotions may be expressed. Secure infants receive the message from their caregiver's behaviours and responses that both negative and positive emotions are accepted and will be responded to appropriately and in such a way that the emotions do not become overwhelming for the child (see chapter 3). In contrast, negative emotions and needy expressions by the child are not accepted in avoidant dyads, and are ineffective in gaining attachment figure support. They are therefore suppressed by the avoidant child. Resistant infants learn that the effects of expressing attachment-related needs and emotions are usually unpredictable, but that intense negative emotions are most likely to be successful in recruiting adult attention (Goldberg, 2000).

Some writers have argued that it is important to consider other factors in relation to attachment security and insecurity beyond internal working models and attachment strategies based on caregiving history. For example, Kobak (1999) has discussed other factors that may be disruptive to attachment, such as separations, conflict and loss-related trauma. He also emphasises that with older children and adults, the nature of communication between the dyad is highly significant and can influence how a disruptive event is understood. If there is open communication, disruptive events may be less likely to be perceived as threats of rejection. For example, parental anger accompanied by a clear explanation of what has led to this response allows the child the opportunity to make changes so that the likelihood of the same parental response in the future is reduced. However, if anger is expressed in hostile ways that do not identify why the parent is angry, and appear to be aimed at humiliation, it can be perceived by the child as a threat or an indication of rejection, abandonment or impending unavailability.

The notion that current circumstances interact with early and more recent attachment experiences to determine current functioning and development is consistent with Bowlby's position. For example, Bowlby (1969/1982) acknowledges that all caregiver–child inter-actions experience disruptions from time to time. Re-establishing a smooth interaction requires attention by each member of the attachment dyad to the cues of the other, and responsiveness to them. As Marvin et al (2002) state: 'It is this ability to repair a disruption that is the essence of secure attachment, not the lack of disruptions' (p. 109).

Implications and applications

CASE SCENARIO

In our third case scenario, we will consider how we might apply the material presented in this chapter to the naturalistic observation of child behaviours. To assist us, we will refer to the method used in a research study conducted by Stovall and Dozier (2000). The focus of this study was the development of attachment between infants and their foster carers, but for our purposes we will concentrate on the way in which naturalistic behaviours in the home were coded as secure or insecure.

All the infants studied in this small-scale case-study research project were in foster care due to maltreatment in their birth family. Foster parents were asked to complete daily diaries regarding the kinds of behaviours shown by their infants in attachment-arousing situations from the first day of placement, and recordings continued for 60 days of the placement. This included how the infants responded to being hurt physically (such as falling over accidentally), being scared, and being separated from the foster parent. The authors note that these are the prototypical conditions for the activation of a child's attachment behavioural system.

Secure responses included:

- proximity-seeking behaviours such as moving towards the foster parent, calling for the foster parent, and wishing to be held; and
- being calmed or soothed easily.

Avoidant responses included:

- acting as if nothing was wrong;
- looking at the foster parent only briefly, then looking away;
- not indicating that he/she needed the foster parent;
- crying without any attempt to approach;
- ignoring the foster parent; and
- acting cool and aloof.

Resistant responses included:

- acting angry and frustrated (stamping and kicking); and
- becoming quiet when soothed but then becoming fussy again.

See Stovall and Dozier (2000, appendix) for further behavioural descriptions associated with each category.

Think about these categories, and the material presented in this chapter, as we revisit a part of the description of Helina and her preschool teacher Malcolm, presented at the beginning of chapter 1.

Four-year-old Helina is playing happily with three of her friends in the outside play area of her preschool. They are laughing and making zooming noises as they ride their bikes around and around on the path. Unexpectedly, Helina and one of her friends collide. Helina bumps her knee and gets a fright. She starts to cry and, looking around, sees her teacher Malcolm standing not far away. She calls out to Malcolm, then runs to his side. Malcolm talks calmly to Helina and gently rubs her knee. Within a few moments, Helina wipes away her tears and begins to smile. Malcolm helps her back on her bike, and she is off again, calling out to her friends.

QUESTIONS FOR REFLECTION

- Which behaviours shown by Helina specifically indicate the security of her relationship with Malcolm?
- If this was an avoidant relationship, what would you expect Helina to do when she first gets a fright?
- If this was a resistant relationship, what would you expect Helina to do when she first gets a fright? After she sought comfort from Malcolm?
- What behaviours are shown by Malcolm on this occasion that are consistent with the development of a secure relationship?
- What sorts of behaviours would Malcolm need to show in response to Helina that would lead over time to an avoidant attachment? A resistant attachment?

DISCUSSION POINTS

Various behaviours shown by Helina are consistent with a secure attachment. First, she is observed to show a range of emotions openly. She cries when she is frightened, she smiles when she is comforted. Secondly, when Helina is upset she goes directly to Malcolm, and both seeks and accepts his support and reassurance. Thirdly, she is comforted by his presence, and in a short period of time has rejoined her friends in play. Malcolm is seen to be sensitive and responsive to Helina's needs. Helina's behaviours indicate she has built up over time an expectation that he will be caring, supportive and can be trusted when she is in need.

If Helina was avoidantly attached she may not show any distress at all, even if she is hurt or very frightened. If she was offered comfort by Malcolm, she may arch away or avoid his gaze or any physical contact. If Helina showed behaviours consistent with a resistant attachment, she may seek comfort from Malcolm, but she is unlikely to be soothed by it. She may go back to play, but would not be settled. She may begin to cry again, appear angry, then seek comfort again. This pattern may be repeated several times, interfering with her ability to join in preschool play and learning activities.

Further readings

Ainsworth, M.D.S. 1967 *Infancy in Uganda: Infant care and the growth of attachment* The Johns Hopkins Press, Baltimore

Ainsworth, M.D.S., Blehar, M.C., Waters, E. and Wall, S. 1978 *Patterns of Attachment: Assessed in the strange situation and at home* Erlbaum, Hillsdale, NJ

Harrison, L. 2003 'Attachment: Building secure relationships in early childhood' *Research in Practice Series*, Early Childhood Australia, Canberra

5

Attachment and resilience

In the preceding chapters, key concepts of attachment theory, including internal working models, security, insecurity and caregiver sensitive responsiveness have been described and explored. These concepts, together with associated research, reveal the importance of attachment relationships throughout life, and particularly in the early years, for psychological wellbeing. Developmental pathways cannot be predicted in any absolute sense from childhood attachment experiences because interpersonal experience is ongoing. However, the weight of evidence is that the expectancies of self and others set up during the early childhood period can have a significant impact on emotional and social functioning throughout life. There is much scope for attachment theory to inform a resilience perspective on development.

A resilience perspective

A resilience perspective prioritises knowledge about developmental experiences that have potential to help the child (and later the adult) cope effectively with the inevitable adversities that arise in life. Resilience has been defined as 'the ability to adapt effectively in the face of adversity' (Berk, 2000, p. 10) and it is a mechanism or process that helps the individual be resistant to stress. Fonagy et al (1994) have defined resilience as '*normal* development under difficult conditions' (p. 233). In this chapter, we explore links between attachment and resilience, emphasising attachment experiences that facilitate a positive, optimistic approach to life.

Although none of us is born resilient, there are some innate characteristics, including having an easy temperament, that seem to have a role in facilitating resilience. In the main, resilience develops as a result of particular kinds of interpersonal experiences, including those that promote high self-esteem, self-efficacy, optimism and coping skills during infancy and the childhood years. Signs of emerging resilience are apparent early in life:

> Six-month-olds who cry lustily to express hunger, or protest strongly when frustrated or angry, are showing that they expect a response and that they are developing a sense of their own agency and ability to impact on their world. Two-year-olds who assert their independence with confidence, who persist in the face of challenge, and who can turn to significant adults for comfort and support when needed, are showing they have a developing sense of trust in themselves and others. Four- and five-year-olds who tackle new learning tasks with curiosity, wonder and energy, and who explore new relationships with confidence or challenge traditional gender-based roles during play (see MacNaughton, 1998), are showing optimism at work (Rolfe, 2002, p. 3).

Resilience has also been defined in terms of competence, particularly in social relationships (see Howe, 1995).

Protective factors

Factors that promote resilience are termed 'protective' factors. Attachment theory provides an important perspective on the relationship-based protective factors that build resilience. From the outset, attachment theory linked the experience of secure attachment with the development of resilience. For example, Bowlby (1969/1982) described in his conclusion to the first volume of the attachment trilogy a model of how the resilient personality forms. In his view, when the young child experiences supportive, encouraging and cooperative caregiving, high self-worth and expectations of the helpfulness of others develop. Feelings of self-competence also grow, because this kind of caregiving enables the child to explore with confidence and respond effectively to the environmental demands encountered. Provided the quality of caregiving is sustained, he considers that 'personality becomes increasingly structured to operate in moderately controlled and resilient ways, and increasingly capable of continuing so despite adverse circumstances' (p. 378).

Bowlby also stressed that insecure attachments, resulting from insensitive, rejecting and/or inconsistent caregiving, compromised resilience and increased vulnerability to later adversity, particularly that associated with experiences of separation, loss or rejection.

Adversity and risk factors

Adversity is present in all aspects of everyday life, from minor disappointments and hassles through to major trauma. At some time or another most children are faced with challenging events like the birth of a sibling, moving house, or making the transition to a new child-care centre, school or teacher. Some children experience major adversity—significant environmental risks—including poverty, abuse, neglect, exposure to domestic violence, parental psychiatric illness, parental substance abuse, natural disasters such as floods and famine, war, or loss of loved ones. These may be short-lived or chronic but they act to put the child's wellbeing at risk. Risk factors rarely occur as a single or isolated stressful life event. More often multiple risk factors are present, and resilient children, by definition, have better developmental outcomes under such challenging circumstances.

Longitudinal research

One of the first studies to reveal a link between resilience and early relationships was conducted over a 40-year period beginning in the 1950s on the Hawaiian island of Kauai (see Werner and Smith, 1992). The sample consisted of about 700 children and their families and the study is notable for the high retention rate of participants over an extended time. The initial aim of the study was to focus on the negative effects of risk factors and document the long-term consequences of prenatal and perinatal stress on cognitive, emotional and physical development. However, over time, the researchers' interest became focused on the one-third of those individuals who were classified as high risk (including being exposed to parental mental illness, parental alcohol abuse, family breakdown and poverty) but who nonetheless developed into adults who were resilient. Resilient adults were those who 'loved well, worked well and played well' (Werner, 1989, p. 4) despite their exposure to multiple risk factors over their childhood years.

The researchers identified three major features present in the lives of these resilient individuals but missing from the lives of those in the high-risk group who were not resilient and who developed serious learning or behaviour problems, had delinquency records and/or mental health problems in adulthood. The first protective factor was that of childhood temperament, already mentioned above. The importance of an easy, outgoing temperament is that it appears to elicit positive responses from others and thus facilitates early positive relationship experiences. The other two protective factors were clearly relationship based. Resilient individuals had formed a close, positive relationship with at least one family member— although not necessarily the parent—who knew the child well and was committed to that child's wellbeing. They had also had the opportunity to link with outside-family supports that provided meaningful opportunities to be involved with others.

From an attachment perspective, the importance of at least one secure attachment within the family, or amongst the child's early caregivers (Fonagy et al, 1994) is its pivotal role in the development of trust, security and later autonomy and initiative. Outside-family supports are identified as important for their role in encouraging and reinforcing feelings of competence in the child and adding an extra dimension of meaning to life, particularly in the later childhood years. In both cases, the potential role for the early childhood professional in promoting resilience is clear, a point we will return to later in this chapter.

Recent research on resiliency

Recent research has supported and further underlined the important links that exist between resilience and early caregiving experiences that are the precursors of secure attachment (see Weinfield et al, 1999). For example, it has been found that caregiver sensitive responsiveness is a key protective factor promoting resilience (see Osofsky and Eberhart-Wright, 1992). In their discussion of results based on research with large samples of teenage mothers and their infants, Osofsky and Eberhart-Wright focus on the importance of affective reciprocity within the caregiver–infant dyad. They identify two types of reciprocity, the first what Stern (1985) has called affective attunement, and the second emotional availability (see Emde, 1980). Affective attunement, as we have already seen, is the ability of the caregiver to detect and understand the emotional signals of the infant and, in addition, to be 'resonant' with these cues. As Osofsky and Eberhart-Wright describe it: 'It is the parent's shared affective state that indicates to the infant that a feeling state is understood. If the parent is unable to share the infant's affective state, there is a lack of reciprocity, which we observe fairly often in risk groups. This lack of reciprocity can become problematic if it occurs consistently over time' (p. 27).

Emotional availability is the extent of caregiver accessibility to the infant and 'capacity for reading the emotional cues and meeting the emotional needs of the infant' (Osofsky and Eberhart-Wright, 1992, p. 27). Again, the overlap with the concept of sensitive responsiveness is clear. In their studies, Osofsky and her colleagues found that despite a variety of problems facing teenage mothers and their infants—including the mother's age and the extent of her own developmental needs, issues of poverty, limited educational opportunities, lack of positive role models and lack of community support—some dyads did well, or in other words showed resilience.

In the infant, characteristics associated with resilient outcomes included intelligence, positive mood and social approach, adaptability and supportive caregivers other than the mother. In the mother, factors protective for the children included 'the mother's always being there emotionally (even if she is negative or inconsistent); protection of the child from the mother's crises; the mother's ability to put her own life together and work on bettering herself; her ability to use intervention; her having goals for her life; and her ability to express negatives in her life and be positive with her child' (Osofsky and Eberhart-Wright, 1992, p. 33). There are clear links in many of these characteristics to predictions made from attachment theory about secure attachments as a principal source of resilience.

Other recent research has demonstrated the complexity inherent in this topic area and many writers have reviewed, discussed and theorised the concept of resilience (e.g. Anthony and Cohler, 1987; Fonagy et al, 1994; Glantz and Johnson, 1999; Howard et al, 1999; Luthar et al, 2000; Masten, 1999, 2001; Clarke and Clarke, 2003). Based on their critiques of many research studies, these authors have advanced challenging new ways of thinking about the concept. These discussions have identified, among other things:

- the impact of intelligence and metacognitive awareness on resilient outcomes;
- the shifting balance between risk and resilience.

Each of these is discussed in turn from an attachment perspective.

The impact of intelligence and metacognitive awareness on resilient outcomes

In their review of research on resilience, Fonagy et al (1994) identify high intelligence as one important characteristic of resilient children. This may help to explain how some children, whose relationship experiences appear pervasively negative, still achieve positive developmental outcomes. Discussing this from an attachment perspective, Howe (1995) links high intelligence to an enhanced ability to make sense of experiences, even those that are disturbed and traumatic. Drawing on the work of Grossmann et al (1988), Main (1991) and Fonagy et al (1994), Howe presents the view that the ability to reflect upon interpersonal experiences—including the thoughts and feelings of others—in an open and constructive way enables a more integrated model of the self to be constructed even if early attachments are insecure. This is because the nature of the relationship, and reasons why it has developed in particular ways, are conceptualised more accurately.

Within this view, resilience rests in part on an individual's ability to modify early internal working models based on insecure attachment experiences in the light of new, secure interpersonal experiences with significant attachment figures. Fonagy et al (1994) refer to this as 'ballast, a self-righting capacity' (p. 182). Such ballast appears missing when children (and adults) are unable to modify negative (i.e. insecure) working models despite the availability of attachment figures who are sensitive, responsive and consistent.

Main (1991) focuses in particular on the importance of meta-cognitive knowledge and abilities in determining how vulnerable a child is to the impact of negative caregiving experiences. Metacognition, or the ability to reflect on one's own thinking and thought processes, is a higher order mental function. Using an example based on an insecure working model, Main illustrates the distinction between cognitive and metacognitive understandings: 'the simple proposition "I am an unworthy person" is not an example of metacognition, whereas the thought that "I am a person who thinks that I am an unworthy person rather frequently" is' (p. 134). Such metacognitive awareness undergoes major development in the period beyond the age of three years, and this is true for social cognition as well as thinking about objects and non-social events.

Main (1991) draws attention to the crucial importance of the appearance–reality distinction (Flavell, 1986) to resilience, through the process of self-reflection. The appearance–reality distinction is essentially an appreciation that the same object, event or person can be experienced in different ways at different times, and that different people do not necessarily experience the same object, event or person exactly as another person does. The significance of this ability is that without it (before the age of around four years), 'the child is not usually equipped to query either her own representations of reality or those offered by attachment figures' (Main, 1991, p. 135). As Main describes it, the older child faced with negative caregiving experiences is advantaged over the younger child because: 'this child can "operate on" or meta-represent a proposition such as "I am a bad person" as follows: "I may be a bad person because my attachment figure seems to think so, but on the other hand, she has been found with false beliefs in other circumstances" ' (pp. 136–7). In other words, the older child is freer in a cognitive sense to query the self-image that is portrayed via the caregiving of attachment figures.

In summarising the links between resilience and metacognition, Fonagy et al (1994) note that secure attachments promote high-level reflective capacity, and that secure attachments are more likely when the caregivers themselves are high in this ability. Importantly, they conclude: 'As studies of resilient children suggest, even a single secure/understanding relationship may be sufficient for the development of reflective processes' (p. 258).

Older children, and individuals of any age with good meta-cognitive skills, are thus seen as more resilient to unfavourable caregiving patterns because they can reflect better on these experiences—and why they have occurred—and generate alternative explanations of their meanings for the worthiness of self and the likely availability and helpfulness of people generally. However, Main (1991) makes the point that children with a resistant attachment—the outcome of caregiving with the defining feature of inconsistency—may be particularly vulnerable because contradictory attachment-related experiences (e.g. unavailable one moment, intrusive the next) are especially difficult to make sense of or comprehend.

The shifting balance between risk and resilience

In writings on resilience, it is now generally agreed that terms such as 'invincible' are inappropriate. These terms imply a permanent state of invulnerability that is misleading. In other words, while the weight of evidence indicates that secure attachments early in life promote resilience, they cannot guarantee resilience for life. Even the most secure, autonomous and optimistic child or adult will be vulnerable and lose confidence in the face of major loss or trauma, such as family breakdown or a death in the family especially in the absence of ongoing emotional support. In other words, there is always a shifting balance between vulnerability and resilience, depending on the extent to which risk *vs* protective factors are present. In addition to their attachment history, how well children cope with adversity will be determined by the nature of the stressor or trauma, how long it lasts, its intensity, and the nature and availability of emotional supports at the time.

In his discussion of uncertainty and vulnerability, Marris (1991) argues that certain events, such as unexpected bereavement or major separations, are so traumatic that they break down an individual's ability to make sense of, or find a purpose in, them. Being able to prepare in some way for the loss means that the individual is less likely to be overwhelmed. He also makes the point that the availability of emotionally supportive relationships during times of trauma is essential. That is why many of the strategies developed to help children cope with adversity focus on providing extra comfort, in an attempt to reduce stress and increase feelings of support as soon as possible. It is important in times of high stress to achieve a rebalancing for children away from fear and towards feeling safe and protected.

From an attachment perspective, individuals with insecure attachment histories may be doubly vulnerable to experiences of grief and separation. Firstly, the interpersonal anxieties associated with feelings of rejection and/or abandonment will engender marked sensitivities to any subsequent loss. Secondly, the person with an insecure attachment history may continue to experience insecurities in later (adult) relationships, even if they are highly supportive. As Marris describes it, 'this underlying mistrust is likely to inhibit the relationship which could provide support in misfortune' (p. 83). In other words, not only is the person particularly vulnerable to experiences of loss, he or she is less likely to be able to utilise effectively the emotional support forthcoming from any current relationships.

The case of children removed from parental care

These considerations have particular implications for those who work with children who have experienced separation from their attachment figures due to protective concerns, such as maltreatment. When a child is abused or neglected, removal from the maltreating parent(s) can be seen as a protective mechanism insofar as it takes the child away from daily exposure to seriously disturbed family relationships and, hopefully, provides them with positive caregiving in the context of a foster or adoptive home (see Howe, 1995). However, there are many aspects of this experience with potential to be highly damaging. This is because the loss of the birth parent(s) is often sudden and unexpected with no time for psychological (or other) preparation. Many children in such circumstances already have a history of insecure attachment relationships consistent with the pattern of maltreatment that leads to removal. Therefore they are already particularly vulnerable to any experience of loss. Further, their pervasive mistrust may mean they are not well placed to gain from an experience of caregiver sensitive responsiveness in an alternative care setting, particularly in the short term.

The study by Stovall and Dozier (2000) introduced as part of the case scenario in chapter 4 found that if placed with foster carers after 12 months of age, young children often persist with insecure defensive strategies for 12 months or more, even if their carers are autonomous and hence well placed to provide sensitive, responsive and consistent care. In contrast, for children placed in foster care before 12 months of age, a secure pattern was observed soon after placement began if the foster carer was autonomous. In a later study with a larger sample of 50 infant–foster mother dyads (Dozier et al, 2001), foster-carer state of mind as assessed via the AAI was strongly concordant with the quality of attachment that formed for infants placed in foster care between birth and 20 months. The result from the earlier study with regard to infants placed after 12 months of age was not replicated. That is, the most important factor determining the formation of a secure attachment for all infants in the sample, regardless of age of placement, was an autonomous state of mind in the foster carer. The statistical effect size was similar to that found for samples of infants and birth mothers. Although there is a need for further research, these emerging results herald an increasing awareness of the significance of attachment state of mind, especially in those adults with a responsibility for the care of children.

Promoting resilience through secure attachments: The role of the early childhood professional

Honig (1998) has discussed at length the importance of secure attachment relationships for children and how early childhood educators can promote secure attachments with the children they care for. She stresses the special significance of early childhood professionals as caregiving figures, even if children already have one or more secure attachments within their family. For children with insecure attachment experiences, the role of early childhood staff in the development of resilience is even more crucial. Children can move from less positive to more positive internal working models if the quality of their caregiving becomes more sensitive and responsive, or they have opportunities to experience this kind of care for the first time with a new carer. The process is not automatic, however, particularly if children have experienced severe attachment-related trauma. Children whose emotional needs have been ignored or rejected may hide their feelings or refuse comfort. This can be confusing or even alienating to a responsive, sensitive carer.

Being responsive, sensitive and consistent to children requires a high level of commitment, self-understanding and self-awareness. As we have seen, from an attachment and resilience perspective, the balance of supports and stresses in our lives and our own history of early attachment relationships can each impact on the quality of the relationships that we develop. Early childhood educators bring to their work diverse attachment histories, and go through periods when they are more or less stressed, more or less supported. Honig (1998) wrote: 'Some of us received more nurturing than others. But all of us can reflect on our own past history. The more you know your limits, your fears, your joys, your abilities to act more maturely in the face of stressors, the more intuitively well will you handle challenges in relating to a particular youngster or in reaching through to create intimacy with a child who is difficult to reach' (p. 29).

There has been little research on attachment states of mind in early childhood professionals, so we cannot yet be sure whether or not differences in these mental representations are significant for the kinds of attachment relationships young children form with their caregivers and teachers in early childhood settings. In one study (Constantino and Olesh, 1999), 31 female day-care providers in two US centres serving low, middle and high income families participated in the AAI. Young children in the centre serving low income families had relatively frequent changes in caregiving relationships (every 8 to 12 months) whereas in the centre serving middle and high income families a primary carer model was followed with children generally cared for by the same caregivers for a two-year period. In addition to AAI classifications, observations were made of the quality of caregiving and adult–child play, predominantly between the caregivers and children aged under three years.

The study found no significant relationship between caregiver AAI classifications and their observed caregiving. In discussing their results, the authors note the discrepancy between the findings and the consistent link found between parents' AAI classifications and quality of caregiving/attachment. They suggest that the nature of centre-based care may promote a more competent, emotionally nurturing form of caregiving by non-autonomous adults than found in the home environment, or that training may lead caregiving to take a form that is not dictated by the underlying attachment state of mind. Finally, they suggest 'it is possible that the intergenerational transmission of attachment requires a level of emotional involvement that is more characteristic of parent–child dyads than day care provider–child dyads' (p. 145).

While many questions thus remain about the impact of attachment states of mind in the caregiving patterns of early childhood professionals, it seems safe to conclude that there is a role for self-reflection and self-nurturance amongst all those who work with children since the inner resources of the adult contribute in important ways to the development of resilience in the child.

Masten (2001) identifies several key factors associated with resilience. These are 'connections to competent and caring adults in the family and community, cognitive and self-regulation skills, positive views of self, and motivation to be effective in the environment' (p. 234). Positive relationships, new opportunities for support and positive new directions in life are all potential protective factors. Drawing on these frameworks, early childhood educators can promote resilience in three main ways:

* through secure relationships with children;
* through the positive emotional, social and cognitive experiences they provide for children; and
* through the support they provide to others who are responsible for the child's care (e.g. parents and other family members).

Each of these is discussed in detail by Rolfe (2002).

Implications and applications

CASE SCENARIO

In this case scenario, we learn more about four-year-old Helina's background. As you read her family circumstances, think about the material in this chapter and the potential contribution of her early childhood teachers in promoting her resilience.

Malcolm, Helina's preschool teacher, has written the following notes about Helina and her family:

Helina is the fourth child in a family of five children. Two of Helina's older siblings are currently in foster care due to protective concerns around issues of environmental neglect in the home and issues of parental substance abuse and domestic violence. The remaining three children, including Helina, spend every alternate weekend in a respite placement requested by their mother. Helina's parents separated two years ago, and Helina rarely sees her father. The family is well known to child protection services.

Helina and her younger sibling, aged two years, are required to attend a child-care program as part of their current court orders.

Helina's teachers at preschool have formed a positive relationship with Helina's mother, Renee. At the beginning, during Helina's first term of three-year-old preschool, Renee was very reluctant to come into the preschool room, and often someone else picked Helina up at the end of her session. Malcolm, who was Helina's teacher that year too, encouraged Renee to stay occasionally to see what Helina was doing at preschool. Over time, she indicated an interest in helping out once in a while with milk and fruit (morning snack) duties. Now, halfway through Helina's four-year-old preschool year, Renee is a regular helper.

Renee now also talks often to Malcolm and the other teachers about Helina's behaviour and development. She identifies them as amongst her main parenting supports. In the past couple of months she has started to mention that she might enjoy coming along occasionally to some of the parent evenings run regularly by the preschool. She is interested in sessions about child development, challenging behaviours, and the transition to school.

QUESTIONS FOR REFLECTION

- In what various ways is the preschool promoting Helina's resilience?
- What challenges confront Renee in becoming an active member of this early childhood community?
- In what ways have the early childhood teachers assisted and supported Renee?
- In what ways can they build even stronger relationships of support with Renee in the future?
- What is the likely impact of preschool on Helina's resilience?

DISCUSSION POINTS

In an earlier case scenario (chapter 4) we saw how Helina's behaviour shows security in her relationship with Malcolm. Malcolm is directly contributing to Helina's resilience as a figure of secure attachment. The case scenario in this chapter reveals another way Malcolm and his colleagues are promoting

Helina's resilience: by supporting her mother and, through this, helping Renee build a more positive relationship with her daughter.

Further readings

Dowlby, R. and Swan, B. 2003 'Strengthening relationships between early childhood staff, high needs children and their families in the preschool setting' *Developing Practice: The child, youth and family work journal* vol. 6, pp. 18–23. Belinda Swan is the manager of the NSW Benevolent Society's First Five Years Program. Robyn Dowlby is consulting psychologist to the Benevolent Society. The program described in this article has been evaluated. Children's behavioural problems were found to reduce significantly pre to post test (as measured on the Child Behaviour Checklist). Staff state of mind regarding the children moved from control preoccupying their thoughts to secure base themes as they reflected on their developing relationships with the children (Dowlby, 2003, personal communication). The day-to-day program was run by Belinda Swan and supported by Robyn Dowlby, who provided monthly consultations with staff.

Howes, C. and Ritchie, S. 1998 'Changes in child–teacher relationships in a therapeutic preschool program' *Early Education and Development* vol. 4, pp. 411–22

Rolfe, S.A. 2002 'Promoting resilience in children' *Research in Practice Series* Early Childhood Australia, Canberra

Part III

Attachment relationships through infancy and early childhood

6

Infancy: Developing trust

Emotional security—feeling safe and cared for—is something we all hope to experience as a normal, ongoing feature in our lives. But feeling secure is not the reality of every child and adult. Exposure to poverty, violence, war and/or famine poses serious threats to the safety of many people. Another form of insecurity has its roots *within* individuals and their interpersonal world. This is associated with a troubling and pervasive lack of trust in other people generally, and feelings of anxiety about the self. According to attachment theory, insecurity of this kind has its origins in difficulties experienced within the infant–caregiver relationship during the first year or so after birth. As Bowlby wrote in the second volume of his attachment trilogy:

> . . . just as we found that there is a strong case for believing that gnawing uncertainty about the accessibility and responsiveness of attachment figures is a principal condition for the development of unstable and anxious personality so is there a strong case for believing that an unthinking confidence in the unfailing accessibility and support of attachment figures is the bedrock on which stable and self-reliant personality is built (1973, p. 322).

In this chapter, we explore the development of the attachment relationship, focusing in particular on the development of trust during the infancy period. In subsequent chapters in this section, attachment during the toddler, preschool and early school years are explored. Issues of importance to the early childhood professional during these stages of development are identified, including the growth of autonomy, and links between security of attachment and cognitive competence.

Attachment formation

The attachment relationship takes time to develop. From the infant's perspective, attachment is not present at birth. It emerges over time. The process first involves the ability to discriminate between different people, then increasing preference for one or a small number of primary caregivers who thereby gradually assume the role of attachment figures. Achieving security and feelings of trust during this process is the primary developmental task of the first 12 months. As already discussed in chapter 2, both infant and caregiver contribute to the nature of the attachment relationship that forms. In essence it is how, and whether, the dyad achieves 'dynamic equilibrium' (Bowlby, 1969/1982, p. 236) in their attachment behaviours that determines the quality of the relationship, and hence its effect on the child's emotional development. By dynamic equilibrium Bowlby meant achieving a stable and presumably comfortable balance in the attachment dyad between closeness and proximity on the one hand, and the demands of competing needs on the other. In the infant these competing needs include exploration, and in the adult the pulls of other responsibilities, interests, feelings and desires.

In chapter 2, we considered how the infant is born with a set of behaviours that mediate the development of attachment, including crying, clinging and visual orientation. These are added to soon after by behaviours such as smiling and babbling, and later still by the emergence of locomotion and following. The young infant demonstrates an amazing range of sensory and perceptual capabilities. These include the ability to discriminate human stimuli, such as voice and face, from other auditory and visual stimulation, and a preference to orientate towards human stimuli. Infants of two or three months of age, if not younger, show rapidly learnt preferences for, or at the very least discrimination of, different people or human characteristics. (For recent overviews of the infant perception literature see Kellman and Arterberry, 1998; Muir and Slater, 2000; Lamb et al, 2002).

In sum, human infants have at birth, or soon after, the abilities required to signal their needs, orientate preferentially to other humans, discriminate between people and develop preferences quickly for one or a small number of people to whom signalling behaviours are then preferentially directed. The combination of these rudimentary abilities and skills provide the infant with the basic building blocks necessary for the beginning of attachment formation (Bowlby, 1969/1982).

Bowlby (1969/1982) described four phases in the development of attachment. These occur between birth and about three years of age. The phases he described were later elaborated by Ainsworth et al (1978) using slightly different nomenclature. In this book, Ainsworth et al's titles and descriptions will mainly be used. The first three phases occur during the first year of life and are therefore directly relevant to this chapter. The fourth, occurring in the third or perhaps fourth year, is mentioned briefly here and considered in more detail in chapter 7.

Initial pre-attachment

The first phase, from birth through the first few weeks, is called 'initial pre-attachment' by Ainsworth et al (1978) and by Bowlby (1969/1982) 'orientation and signals without discrimination of figure'. It is commonly referred to as the pre-attachment phase. The essence of this phase is that the infant can and does signal attachment needs (by crying, smiling, clinging and so on) and is responsive to human stimulation (being spoken to, smiled at, picked up, etc.) but does not show these behaviours preferentially—that is, they are no more or less frequent or intense in the presence of any particular person. However, even in this initial phase, attachment theorists consider that the infant is beginning to 'build up expectations (anticipations)' (Ainsworth et al, 1978, p. 24) based on how other humans respond to these signalling behaviours. This is a period, then, in which the infant's initial internal working model primarily reflects how his or her social world in its entirety (as represented by all those people who come into it) behaves. This phase ends when the infant shows consistent discrimination of the primary attachment figure or figures based on visual cues (rather than auditory or olfactory discriminations, which appear earlier and which Bowlby did not consider sufficient for the term 'attachment' to apply).

Attachment-in-the-making

Marked orientation and responsiveness to people continues into the second phase of attachment development, commonly called the 'attachment-in-the making' stage (Ainsworth et al, 1978). This phase usually occurs between about one month of age and six to eight months. What discriminates this phase from the one before is the infant's clear preference for one or a small number of persons to whom he or she directs attachment behaviours. Discrimination between familiar and unfamiliar people, and amongst familiar people, is a hallmark feature of this phase, referred to by Bowlby (1969/1982) as 'orientation and signals directed towards one (or more) discriminated figure(s)'. In this phase, physical proximity is sought selectively and comfort is most readily achieved by contact with one, or a small number, of preferred attachment figures.

Clear-cut attachment

Despite the evident preferences of the attachment-in-the-making phase, attachment theorists do not consider that the attachment bond has truly developed until the phase of 'clear-cut attachment' (Ainsworth et al, 1978) emerges when the infant begins to crawl or otherwise locomote, usually some time in the second half of the first year, around six to eight months of age. It continues through to about 18 months to two years or more. Bowlby and Ainsworth state that a clear-cut attachment is not evident until the infant maintains proximity to the attachment figure through locomotion as well as selective signalling.

This third phase is referred to by Bowlby (1969/1982) as 'maintenance of proximity to a discriminated figure by means of locomotion as well as signals'. Attachment-related locomotion includes following and greeting. It also includes a range of other behaviours that bring about or prolong physical proximity: intimate touching of the hands, face and body of the attachment figure; 'snuggling in', climbing onto and over him or her; and 'burying the face in the body of the attachment figure' (Ainsworth et al, 1978, p. 25). The hallmark feature of this phase is that the general friendliness towards people evident in earlier phases is replaced by awareness of and increasing caution towards unfamiliar persons. Bowlby's writings appear to conclude that most infants will select one primary attachment figure and some 'subsidiary attachment figures' (1969/1982, p. 267). As well as wariness of strangers, distress at separation from the attachment figure is observed during this third phase.

Another important characteristic of the clear-cut attachment phase is that the infant's attachment behaviours become organised on what is termed a 'goal-corrected' basis (Bowlby, 1969/1982, p. 267) for the first time. What this means is that the infant now has a goal in terms of what is to be achieved attachment-wise. This might be, for example, a certain level of proximity. The infant can then develop a plan in regards to how this might be achieved, often using a variety of interchangeable attachment behaviours. Even more importantly, the expectations or anticipations that form the infant's emerging internal working model become increasingly refined during this phase. Not only are babies able to plan how to bring about proximity, for example, based on their own behaviours, but it appears they are also able to take into account in those plans how the attachment figure might usually be expected to respond. The representational or working model of the self and the attachment figure thus appears to be well developed by this stage.

However, the intrinsic egocentricity of the very young child means that there are major limitations to how much the infant or toddler can really 'know' or understand the plans of attachment figures, and hence why those people behave as they do. This means that a truly goal-corrected or reciprocal 'partnership' (Bowlby (1969/1982, p. 267) in which both participants, including the child, have sophisticated insights into the other's needs, feelings and motives and can plan their own behaviour strategies accordingly cannot develop until later, usually in the third or fourth year. At this stage, the child is said to enter into the fourth phase. In this fourth phase egocentricity lessens, allowing the child to appreciate the mother's point of view and the feelings, motivations and plans that are influencing her behaviour. This final phase is described and discussed in the next chapter.

The development of trust

We have already noted that the major task for the infant during the first three stages of attachment formation is the development of trust. In order to appreciate why the development of trust is so central during the first year or so of life, it is necessary to truly comprehend the complete or almost complete dependency of the human infant during this period of development. It is quite difficult for adults, whose own autonomy is so well entrenched, to fully understand the total feeling of dependency that the young infant experiences. Try to imagine what it must feel like to be a young infant, totally dependent on others for your every need! Only then is it possible to appreciate why the first year or so of life is such an ideal time to learn about trust. Anyone who has experienced a debilitating illness or injury in adulthood can attest to how much this experience reveals about who can be relied on to be available consistently. This sort of experience of dependency also reveals how well other people understand our needs, even if we are unable to express them very well, and who can be trusted to attend to these needs in caring and sensitive ways, even when the going gets tough. This is essentially what the infant is learning about.

Many different words have been used to describe the kind of caregiving that supports the development of trust in infancy and promotes a secure attachment. In earlier chapters, key terms including sensitive responsiveness, attunement and emotional availability have been defined, and the overlap between them noted. In general, caregivers who are sensitive, responsive, cooperative, available, accepting, accessible, dependable and empathic support secure attachments. Important also is harmony in the dyad, variously termed mutuality or synchronicity. Emotional harmony scaffolds the child's developing understanding of the social and emotional world. It is these interactions that feed into the emerging internal working model. If the child feels secure, other people—generalised from a small number of attachment figures—are seen to be emotionally available and dependable (to be trusted) especially if the child is in need of comfort or support. 'Basic trust' (Erikson, 1968) is a sense of the self as worthy and lovable. The accompanying self-view is of oneself as 'the subject of interest and pleasure, concern and value to other people' (Howe et al, 1999, p. 49).

Not surprisingly, it has been reported that securely attached children are more friendly towards unfamiliar people, both adults and children, than insecurely attached children (Goldberg, 2000). This should not, however, be confused with what is termed indiscriminate friendliness, shown predominantly by children with disturbed attachment histories. Indiscriminately friendly children show no stranger wariness (e.g. Tizard, 1977) combined with a lack of appropriate social boundaries. Strangers may be approached, touched and their affection sought. The child may begin conversations about highly personal matters, and ask the stranger inappropriate questions about their personal life. There is no 'checking back' or use of an adult as a secure base. This form of interaction is very different in nature to that shown by the secure child who will engage with an unfamiliar adult provided the secure base of their attachment figure is present, providing information and reassurance every step of the way.

Feeling secure

Feelings of trust are the foundation of security. Trust emerges when one can count on someone else to be there when needed, and in order for this feeling to be confirmed it needs to be experienced time and time again. From an attachment perspective, caregivers become trusted attachment figures if they are *consistently* available, responsive and sensitive, and provide caregiving that soothes and comforts the infant, meeting whatever needs are there at the time. Trust develops because the infant is reassured repeatedly that the caregiver will generally provide a caring, responsive environment, and that he or she will behave in predictable ways.

Infants who receive sensitive, responsive and predictable caregiving also come to trust the attachment figure's ability to keep their arousal or tension levels within comfortable bounds, as described in chapter 3. As Sroufe (1995) describes how, in the first half year, the infant learns from a sensitive, responsive caregiver that 'in the context of the caregiver, arousal need not lead to disorganisation, and that when arousal does exceed the infant's modulation capacities, the caregiver will take action to recapture equilibrium' (p. 173).

In regard to the development of trust, what the infant also begins to learn as they move into the second half of the first year is their own role in successfully eliciting the support, assistance and availability of the caregiver. If their attachment behaviours (for example, actively seeking out the attachment figure when needed) consistently achieve the desired outcome, confidence in the efficacy of the self, and 'confidence in the relationship' (Sroufe, 1995, p. 173) develop. In other words, there is a direct link between the regularity with which the young child's emotional arousal has been successfully contained and regulated within the attachment relationship, and security. If emotional arousal regularly leads to infant behavioural disorganisation (over-arousal) because it is not successfully modulated or regulated within the relationship, security and trust cannot, and will not, develop.

The developmental issues framework of Alan Sroufe

How security and trust emerge through attachment relationships in the early childhood period has been extensively described and discussed by Sroufe (1995). His work provides a framework for understanding individual differences in emerging trust and security. He proposes six stages from birth through to age six years, with each stage building on the quality of interactions/relationships in the preceding stages. We consider the first three periods here.

Period 1

The first period is from birth to about three months of age. This corresponds to the earliest phases of attachment formation prior to the stage of clear-cut attachment. Even though discriminated attachments are only beginning to form, according to Sroufe even these first few weeks of the infant's life are important for the development of trust, particularly through the caregiver's ability to provide routines that are smooth and peaceful. This harmony lays a solid foundation for the interactions that are to come as the attachment relationship develops. He also notes that these early months are crucial for the attachment figure to learn about the infant, and to acquire what he terms a sense of 'investment and confidence . . . efficacy and satisfaction' (p. 161) in their caregiving role and relationship with the infant.

Period 2

The second period, from three to six months, revolves around the management of infant tension, or arousal. Whereas the first three months are about physiological regulation, and the task for the caregiver that of establishing smooth harmonious routines, in the second three months the task for the caregiver is to provide the infant with sensitive, cooperative interactions. Sroufe also notes the importance of brain development at this time and the crucial link between brain circuitry and social–emotional experience (see previous discussion of brain research, chapter 3). Effective tension regulation means avoiding overstimulation of the infant in addition to providing for the infant's needs—for example, feeding when hungry, comforting when distressed—as a means of relieving tension. Termination of distress is, however, only part of the complete picture.

According to Sroufe, infants also need to experience escalation of arousal within positive, affective interactions. This usually involves the sort of playful interaction in which gazing and touching lead to smiling and gross motor stimulation, and possibly then to laughter and often quite high levels of excitement (on the part of both adult and child). We saw an example of this in the case scenario of interactions after sleep time between Ryan and Jung in chapter 3. These experiences are important because they provide confirmation for the infant that high levels of arousal do not necessarily lead to distress and are not inevitably disorganising. They also provide wonderful opportunities for the matching of infant emotional states by the caregiver, or attunement, and the development of feelings of mutuality as the infant is drawn by the caregiver into a 'dialogue' and 'intimate social dance' (Sroufe, 1995, p. 164).

Both partners have an active role in these sorts of exchanges. They are not just about caregiver contingent responsiveness, that is, being quickly responsive to an infant's overtures or signals. They are about reciprocity, or synchrony, with each partner initiating and responding to interactions, albeit largely 'crafted' by the caregiver during the first six months or so. Routine tasks such as feeding, nappy-changing and play provide many of the infant's opportunities to engage in such exchanges, and they are opportunities not to be missed by the skilled caregiver. This sort of interaction may begin with gentle talking, to which the caregiver then adds more animation, using facial expressions and vocal intonations so that infant arousal builds. If the infant becomes overexcited, he or she may look away or start to show signs of distress. This leads the sensitive caregiver to reduce levels of stimulation, waiting until the infant is again ready to resume contact and play. Sroufe states that these simple exchanges provide the basis for the infant's growing understanding of mutuality and 'a primitive sense of give and take, social participation, and efficacy . . . Increasingly, the infant is not restricted to situations of moderate intensity, novelty, or complexity, but can cope with an increasingly rich and varied experience' (1995, pp. 164–5).

The importance accorded sensitivity and prompt responsiveness by the caregiver to the development of security does not mean that the infant must never wait, or experience any kind of frustration. These are inevitable occurrences in the lives of all humans, young or old. Sroufe stresses, however, that while normal and healthy, such frustrations should not be 'capricious and arbitrary . . . Sensitive caregivers acknowledge the infant's wishes even though not unconditionally acceding to them' (p. 166). When frustrations do occur, the infant's feelings should be acknowledged and in turn responded to sensitively.

Period 3

In the third phase, from six to 12 months, Sroufe describes the developmental issue as one of 'establishing an effective attachment relationship', which coincides with the beginning of the phase of clear-cut attachment. The role for the caregiver remains responsive availability, but Sroufe stresses that in this phase the infant becomes a more active participant in interactions, so that being responsive means 'co-operating with the infant' (p. 168) as he or she takes a greater role in initiating interactions. The caregiver now needs to be increasingly responsive to the infant's 'intentional bids' (p. 168).

Because the infant is now mobile, organisation of attachment behaviour to the caregiver as a secure base is important. The sensitive caregiver is aware of how much the infant relies on his or her reassurance and availability if exploration via locomotion leads to an experience of separation that is anxiety-provoking. This phase, then, marks the beginnings of the infant's transition to the wider world beyond the attachment figure(s).

Sensitive, responsive caregiving as the foundation of security and trust

As the foregoing discussion illustrates, the fundamental importance of a sensitive, responsive caregiver to the development of trust and security is a central proposition of attachment theory. And, according to those who have reviewed the empirical literature, there is acceptable research support for this proposition (see DeWolff and van IJzen-doorn, 1997; Belsky, 1999b). Reasonably small statistical effect sizes indicate that caregiving quality is not the only determinant of attachment security—but research does show that interventions promoting caregiver sensitivity generate an increase in secure attachments. This result supports a causal role for caregiver behaviour in the development of trust.

During the infancy period, the adult caregiver, by dint of his or her greater maturity, is seen as taking a leading role in the establishment of harmonious interactions that are sensitive to the child's needs. This means that there is no single form of sensitive caregiving. It must be flexible and adapt to the unique characteristics of each individual child at any particular point of time. Attachment theory thus recognises that the child also contributes to the quality of the developing relationship. The theory also acknowledges the role of the context in which the dyad is located and, in particular, the stresses and supports available to the caregiver as he or she carries out the caregiving role and all the demands that attend it. In the remainder of this chapter, the contribution of infant characteristics and contextual determinants are considered.

The impact of infant characteristics on security of attachment

Sensitive caregiving, by definition, implies an ability to respond appropriately to infant needs of any kind, regardless of what they are and how they are expressed. However, it is obvious that some infants present more of a challenge in this regard than others. Infants with a difficult temperament, or who have medical complications requiring extended hospitalisation at birth or during the infancy period, and infants with developmental disabilities or delays, have special needs in terms of sensitive caregiving. For example, children with a difficult temperament may have irregular bodily functions and biological routines, emotions may be more strongly or intensely expressed than would be the case in infants with an easy temperament, they may be upset or distressed more frequently, and new events or people may evoke very high levels of anxiety. Infants with medical complications, who were born prematurely, or who have other special needs, may signal their needs in atypical ways, and may respond to caregiving in challenging ways that reflect the compromised nature of their development in one or a variety of domains.

What constitutes appropriate care for one child may not be so for another (Seifer et al, 1996). One example of this is provided by the work of Marfo (1992), who found that higher levels of caregiver control or directiveness, normally considered to be indicative of caregiver insensitivity, may in fact be a sign of sensitivity in interaction with infants who have an intellectual disability or other special needs (for example, hearing impairment).

In relation to temperament and the other characteristics discussed above, it is clear that these impact upon, to a greater or lesser extent, the kinds of behaviours to which the caregiver must respond. For temperamental characteristics, there is evidence that behaviours may be modified by the quality of caregiving received (Sroufe, 1985). For example, by responding sensitively, the caregiver may find that infant irritability decreases, sociability increases and intensity of reaction settles. In other cases of profoundly compromised development, caregiver sensitivity may not so readily engender positive change or movement towards 'easier' behaviours on the part of the infant. Nonetheless, in reviewing research that has explored attachment in infants with medical conditions, including a meta-analysis of the literature by van IJzendoorn et al (1992, as cited by Goldberg, 2000), Goldberg (2000) concluded that these problems did not affect attachment security in any major ways and that most children developed secure attachments with their mothers.

Contextual determinants of security of attachment

Belsky (1999b) has presented a detailed overview of the contribution of both interactional and contextual factors in the development of secure attachments. In relation to contextual factors, his focus is on how the social context can promote or impede a caregiver's capacity to provide sensitive, responsive care. In such an analysis, sources of stress and support are central considerations. Attachment theory clearly acknowledges the negative impact of life stressors on any caregiver's ability to maintain sensitive care, and the positive impacts that pertain when a caregiver is well supported, both emotionally and practically. While social disadvantage does not necessarily and inevitably lead to insecure attachments between infant and parent or other caregiver (see Goldberg, 2000, chapter 8), it is very difficult for any caregiver to be sensitive, responsive and consistent if overwhelmed by too many competing demands or highly stressed by family violence, addictions, substance abuse or pressing, unmet financial concerns.

In his analysis of a number of studies examining attachment to professional carers, Belsky (1999b) concludes that the processes determining security of attachment in infant–mother dyads are similar to those between infants and early childhood practitioners. These attachment relationships, in his view, are just as sensitive to risk factors—such as insecure adult attachment representations, difficult infant temperament, high stress and low support—that predispose to insecurity between young children and their parents. Multiple or accumulating risk factors, not compensated by appropriate supports, are of particular concern.

Considerations such as these have clear implications not only for the importance of family support programs but also for the characteristics of settings in which infants are cared for by professionals. For example, there are many who would argue that provision of high quality infant care is totally incompatible with staff–child ratios in which one adult may have responsibility for five or more infants, and there is research evidence to back this up (see Howes, 1999). As just one example, Howes et al (1988) found that security of attachment to a non-parental caregiver in infants aged 12 to 24 months was lower when the caregiver was responsible for many children.

Implications and applications

CASE SCENARIO

In this case scenario we will look closely at the principles that guide and undergird infant care at the centre attended by one-year-old Eli. As you read this material, reflect on how the approach of this centre promotes secure attachments between infants and early childhood practitioners, and how, in the absence of this approach, secure relationships could be compromised.

Note: The material presented here draws on the approach outlined in Raikes (1996).

The early childhood centre attended by Eli bases its program on principles drawn from attachment theory. The approach can be summarised under three headings:

1. *Supportive relationships between early childhood professionals and children.*
2. *Supportive relationships between early childhood professionals and parents/families.*
3. *Supportive relationships between early childhood professionals and colleagues.*

Supportive relationships between early childhood professionals and children

A major guiding principle at this centre is that of 'primary care'. As far as possible, each child remains with the same primary caregiver until at least the age of three years. This means that as young children move through different age-group rooms during this period, one or a small number of caregivers move with them. 'Pairing' of child and professional is usually achieved very early, if at all possible at the time of enrolment so that even before an infant commences care, familiarisation and relationship-building can begin. That is, parents can get to know the primary caregiver who will be responsible for their child, and vice versa even before child care begins. As well, the infant and professional can get to know each other through a carefully guided introduction to the centre. As part of staff selection processes at this centre, Zamia's commitment to this approach, and to an attachment-based program, was considered.

Each early childhood professional at Eli's centre is responsible for making extensive observations and notes about each of the children for whom they have a primary responsibility—their strengths, interests, needs and development. Because they are with 'their' children for an extended period, caregivers get to know them very well, not just through their own observations but because, from the start, the child's parents and their unique knowledge of their child are totally integrated into the professional's understanding of the infant (see below). Using all this information, and their accruing experiences of interaction with the infant, caregivers are well placed to promote secure attachments. Involved caregiving, sensitive responsiveness and attunement are highly valued and well understood by early childhood practitioners at this centre, and the curriculum for the first three years emphasises these caregiving features. Prioritised are:

- careful attention to the needs of the child and parent during transition times (introduction to the centre, as well as daily separations and reunions);
- caregiving behaviours that promote a secure base for the child (frequent, sustained one-to-one interactions; infrequent, carefully timed and sensitively handled absences from the room);
- focus on the importance of physical comfort for each infant— gentle holding and stroking, based on a full appreciation of the role of emotion regulation in the formation of security; and
- use of all caregiving tasks as opportunities for respectful, harmonious interactions with the child.

Supportive relationships between early childhood professionals and parents/families

Positive, supportive links between the early childhood setting and each child's family are of the highest priority in this centre. It is recognised that the child's security at the centre will only be optimised if parents also know and trust the carer of their child, and the setting in which the child spends their time. Meetings are held between early childhood staff and parents before the infant commences care. A home visit is encouraged. This allows the infant to meet the caregiver in the infant's own special place, see him or her with their parents, and begin to form and then integrate an image of the caregiver as someone who is a meaningful part of their life, and valued by their family.

The early childhood professionals rely on parents to help them *understand the child, how he or she signals their needs, and what works best to comfort the child. Parents are encouraged to see and use the centre as 'a home away from home', to call in often and spend as much time as they can. A gradual, planned introduction of the child and family is required. There is a process of regular parent feedback. Zamia attends meetings every three months, during which parents provide feedback and raise concerns and where there is open, respectful discussion of issues. The centre prioritises cultural diversity and respect for all families.*

Supportive relationships between early childhood professionals and colleagues

This centre provides all professionals employed there with extensive guidance and support. A mentoring system ensures that all staff are assisted with the process of building secure, loving and security-promoting relationships with each infant in their care. It is recognised that supportive and harmonious working relationships are an essential foundation of the program. It is also recognised that some infant–caregiver relationships may need more support than others, depending on the temperament, needs and family background of the child, and the balance of stress and support in each caregiver's life at particular times. There is a strong commitment to adequate resourcing for staff development and support. This has recently included sessions on adult attachment representations and their effect on caregiving.

QUESTIONS FOR REFLECTION

- What is your response to the principles on which this centre's program is based? What challenges do they present?
- Are these principles followed at your centre? If so, are they achieved? If not, what impedes them?
- If any of these principles are not prioritised at your centre, what would need to change in order for them to be? How could these changes be introduced?

- What do you see as the most pressing change that needs to be made where you work in order to promote attachment-inspired principles?
- Think about your usual day at work. Think about each hour, and the caregiving activities that occur during that time. What will you now do differently in order to promote feelings of security for the children in your care? (If you are a student, think about centres you have visited or practicum placements for the last four questions.)

DISCUSSION POINTS

Zamia has been Eli's primary caregiver at child care for eight months now. She met Eli's parents as soon as a place for Eli was confirmed, and visited Eli at home before she started child care. At this home visit (when Eli was three months old), Eli's parents talked to her a lot about their daughter, her development, their relationship with her, what they had found unsettled or frightened her, and what they did to comfort her. When Eli began child care, she did so gradually, and Eli's mother and father stayed with her during her first visit of an hour or so. These visits gradually became longer, up to four hours or more, with Eli's mother or father staying for less time. By the time Eli was attending for a full day, Zamia was quite a familiar person for Eli, and since then has been a loving, involved caregiver whom Eli and her family have come to trust. Zamia is supported in her role by the other professionals in this centre. She in turn supports her colleagues actively.

At 12 months of age, there are clear signs that these various factors have successfully promoted Eli's security in her relationship with Zamia. Some of these signs are evident in the case scenarios in chapters 1 and 2. You may like to reread these as you reflect on the material in this chapter.

Further readings

Honig, A.S. 1998 'Attachment and relationships: Beyond parenting' Paper presented at the Head Start Quality Network Research Satellite Conference (East Lansing MI, 20 August 1998) (ED 423043)

Raikes, H. 1996 'A secure base for babies: Applying attachment concepts to the infant care setting' *Young Children* vol. 51(5), pp. 59–67

7

From one to three years: Becoming autonomous

If the period of infancy, with its high level of dependency, can be seen as the perfect opportunity to learn about security and trust, then the period between one and three years of age presents the ideal circumstances for children to begin to learn confidence in their own independent and autonomous strivings. Increasing mobility and burgeoning cognitive and language skills drive the child towards exploration and interactions beyond the immediate attachment dyad. However, these developments place the child into inevitable conflict with the caregiver who, realising the pitfalls and dangers inherent in such independent pursuits, somehow has to manage them while respecting and supporting the child's needs for initiative and autonomy. How attachment figures handle this will have important implications for whether the child moves into the preschool period with confidence in their own fledgling independence, or with pervasive feelings of doubt and shame (Erikson, 1963). In addition, providing the young child with reassuring support and comfort as her or his journey into the wider world begins reinforces feelings of trust engendered during the infancy period.

In this chapter, what happens within the attachment relationship during the period of approximately one to three years of age is described, and attachment perspectives on the development of autonomy and the implications for caregiving during this period discussed. The evolution of the goal-corrected partnership is considered. Finally, multiple attachment relationships are discussed, with reference to what is known about attachment hierarchies, particularly in the context of child care.

Dependent and independent

The toddler's movements towards independence occur alongside strong and enduring feelings of dependency. Sensitive caregivers at this stage of a child's development are aware of this complex mix of needs. They understand that it will still be some time yet before the child is fully and truly autonomous. Despite the obvious (and psychologically important) transitions towards independence during the toddler years, from an attachment perspective the urgency of attachment needs under certain conditions, and the child's ongoing need for the reassuring presence of an attachment figure, is something of which caregivers need to remain constantly mindful.

It is not until the age of three years or later that most children's attachment behaviours reduce in frequency and intensity. From this age it appears there are fewer situations that activate attachment behaviours, and when activated these behaviours are likely to be less intense. Attachment needs can be terminated by a wider range of conditions, including those that are mainly symbolic. But even adults under significant stress prefer the comforting closeness of their friend or partner over photographs, telephone calls and the like, however reassuring.

Individual variability in attachment behaviours

There is marked variability in the way attachment behaviours are expressed, how intense they are, and what activates them, both between children and for an individual child over time. The young child may appear content to explore the environment for a while, apparently unconcerned about the availability of the attachment figure. Then, quite suddenly, the child may become highly focused on re-establishing contact, desperately seeking comfort and reassurance. There are many factors that activate a young child's attachment needs and dampen enthusiasm for independence. These include being tired, uncomfortable, unwell or in pain. The location and availability of the primary attachment figure—whether he or she is near, leaving, absent or present but unresponsive or rejecting—have an impact. Other factors, including the occurrence of frightening events, or challenging interpersonal dynamics—like being rebuffed in an interaction with another child, or an adult—may also increase dependency needs. Therefore, in determining how much the child should be encouraged towards independence, the importance of being sensitive to each unique child's signals is clear.

Becoming autonomous

Since Bowlby's early writings, other attachment researchers have written about the stage of development in which children develop increasing independence. Sroufe's (1995) analysis of the development of autonomy is important to our discussion. Sroufe underlines the remarkable changes in various domains of development that take place in the years following infancy, including language and communication, social, physical, motor and central nervous system development, the development of self-understanding and movement from dyadic regulation of emotion to self-regulation. This is not achieved suddenly. Rather there is a gradual development over time. During toddlerhood, periods of self-regulation are interspersed with times during which the young child becomes highly reliant again on the attachment figure for help and support. These include occasions when there are demands on the child for impulse control (such as waiting one's turn), sharing, and dealing with anger, frustration and aggression.

Getting the required assistance and support may be initiated by the child, or by the caregiver in an anticipatory way. According to Sroufe, 'The caregiver's task is to anticipate frustration and to intercede should the child begin losing control, while at the same time allowing the child as much self-direction as possible' (1995, p. 193). As part of this process, the child learns about inhibiting impulses, and begins to develop skills in self-regulation. But it needs to take place under the caregiver's 'guidance, tutelage, and enforcement' (Sroufe, 1995, p. 193).

How this process unfolds, how challenging it is for child and caregiver, and what outcomes eventually pertain will depend on various factors, including the child's developing temperament and his or her earlier caregiving experiences. A lack of realistic demands and support for self-regulation in the child's caregiving history will hamper the process and may lead to negative outcomes. As Sroufe wrote, children 'not guided in establishing realistic standards for behaviour, or who are punished for even the slightest deviation of behaviour from a standard are vulnerable to overwhelming feelings of rage and shame (and later despondency and guilt)' (1995, p. 194).

The child is thus faced during this period with the dual tasks of expressing his or her emotions openly, directly and honestly, while at the same time doing so in a socially acceptable way, using developing skills of control. Feelings of security established earlier form the foundation of autonomy (Erikson, 1963) and provide a 'holding framework' (Sroufe, 1995, p. 194). That is, the secure child has learnt that strong emotions, both positive and negative, are accepted within the attachment relationship, but later comes to learn that they can, and must—at particular times—be contained.

Resolving the toddler–caregiver crisis

What has come before in the infant–caregiver relationship crucially affects how harmoniously the developmental 'crisis' (Mahler et al, 1975) of this phase is resolved. If the child has developed confidence in the attachment figure, attempts at autonomous functioning will be smoother. If the child's demands for independence are similarly responded to with sensitivity, positive outcomes are promoted and conflict more likely to be resolved harmoniously.

Mahler et al (1975) referred to the two-year-old period as the phase of 'rapprochement'. During this stage, the toddler shows an 'alternating desire to push mother away and to cling to her' (p. 95).

On the one hand the child is seeking autonomy, on the other, he or she is often overwhelmed with anxiety when trying to go it alone. The caregiver's ability to acquiesce to the child's demands and to go that one step further, 'to give him a gentle push, an encouragement towards independence' (Mahler et al, 1975, p. 79), is crucial. This includes genuinely enjoying the child's autonomous explorations, and sharing in the joy of the child's independent achievements and mastery (Ainsworth, 1984). Rapprochement, or the reestablishment of harmonious interactions between child and caregiver, is the desired outcome.

Sroufe (1995) presents an overview of research on individual differences in how well toddlers negotiate the challenges of this phase of development and the issues of interpersonal functioning it presents. This research was based on observations of how parents and toddlers responded during free play, clean-up and problem-solving sessions of increasing challenge. All children were faced with at least one task that could not be completed successfully without drawing on the adult's help (e.g. Matas et al, 1978). The clean-up session, in which parents were required to stop their child's play and get them to begin to put the play equipment away, was seen as most demanding in terms of potential for conflict. Those children who were most competent—more enthusiastic, happy, persistent and compliant—were more likely to have had a secure attachment history. Importantly, how the adult interacted with the child during the sessions was strongly related to attachment history. Providing clear, carefully timed and appropriate cues to help the child was important. So was finding the right balance between allowing the child to engage with and grapple with the problem on their own, and leaving them to get too frustrated. To Sroufe, the balance was right when children's capacities were 'stretched but not strained' (Sroufe, 1995, p. 211).

Other research overviewed by Sroufe, including Gove (1983, as cited by Sroufe, 1995), has demonstrated differences between infant–parent dyads with insecure attachment histories, either avoidant or resistant. In dyads with an avoidant history, the children showed less direct expression of negative emotions such as frustration and anger, were non-compliant but in passive rather than active ways (for example, pretending not to hear what their parents said) and their parents seemed emotionally uninvolved even if the child was having difficulty. In pairs with a resistant history, the children showed escalating distress, anger and frustration, and became more and more oppositional as their ability to solve problems independently was increasingly taxed. Although the adults were responsive to the child's difficulties insofar as they became more involved as a result, the quality of their involvement resulted in heightened, rather than reduced, conflict. This research reveals that despite the wilfulness evident at this age, toddlers in fact remain highly dependent on their attachment figures for help in managing their impulses and emotions.

The development of the goal-corrected attachment partnership

These changes in autonomous functioning are being established at a time when other important developments are taking place in the social and cognitive domains. Children of this age are becoming clearer about their individuality, that the self is separate from others. They are also beginning to understand that there are standards against which behaviour is judged, with resultant growth in the self-conscious emotions of guilt, shame and pride. At this time, the attachment relationship itself is also undergoing an important transition. As introduced in the last chapter, according to Bowlby and Ainsworth the fourth stage of attachment formation—the phase of a goal-corrected partnership—usually begins sometime in the third year, or perhaps a little earlier.

This development depends upon and reflects in large measure the growing cognitive competencies of the two- and three-year-old child. First, the child understands that the self is an independently functioning agent, and therefore that the attachment figure, too, is a separate entity. At first quite rudimentary and unsophisticated, through repeated observations of the attachment figure this emerging understanding becomes 'insight' (Bowlby, 1969/1982, p. 268). In turn, insights of this kind lay the groundwork for an even more sophisticated and reciprocal relationship, influenced by both members of the attachment dyad. It is a relationship in which the two are more accurately conceptualised as 'partners'.

Fundamental to this is the child's ability to understand the point of view of the attachment figure. This includes being able to infer the 'feelings and motives, set-goals and plans' (Ainsworth et al, 1978, p. 28) of the adult and how they will influence what the adult is doing. As this ability grows, so too presumably does the child's skill in negotiating the particular kind of attachment relationship—secure, avoidant or resistant—that he or she is experiencing. Since insecure attachment strategies—avoidance and resistance—are shown by young children as early as the infancy period (and as observed during the Strange Situation procedure), it appears that the ability to 'negotiate' the relationship begins earlier than the fourth phase. Ainsworth et al (1978) note this point, writing that Bowlby 'surely did not mean to imply that goal-corrected behavior did not emerge until Phase 4, for he is explicit in pointing out that such behavior is characteristic of Phase 3 and serves to differentiate it from Phase-2 behavior' (p. 28). What characterises the fourth stage, and demarks it as different, is the level of sophistication evident. As Goldberg (2000) describes it, the child now has an awareness of attachment figures 'as individuals with distinct goals and needs of their own . . . [and] that meeting his or her own needs and desires must be negotiated within this context' (p. 34). This is different from the very rudimentary understandings that may have been present at earlier stages.

Multiple attachments

The child's awareness of the unique characteristics and needs of the adult figure leads to the final topic area of this chapter, that of multiple attachments and their impact on development. Writing from the perspective of his own socio-cultural milieu, Bowlby focused on the mother as the usual primary attachment figure while acknowledging the attachment roles of others, and that these could substitute for the biological mother, a point also stressed by Ainsworth et al (1978). Furthermore, Bowlby argued against any interpretation of his writings as implying that shared mothering is inevitably harmful to the child (see Bowlby, 1969/1982, p. 303), although he did indicate that there are limits to the number of caregiving figures to whom children should be exposed.

Attachment theory has thus from the outset recognised that children form attachments to people other than the mother. For some children the birth mother may be entirely absent as a figure of attachment, due to her death, protracted illness or protective concerns that have resulted in removal of the child from parental care at birth or soon after. In many families, the mother may share the care of her child with others due to paid employment or other responsibilities. Primary care of the child may be taken by someone else, such as the child's father or another family member, a family friend or early childhood professional. In some families, the mother is the primary attachment figure, sharing child care with others only occasionally.

In the first volume of the attachment trilogy, Bowlby (1969/1982) considers the figures to whom a child's attachment behaviours may be directed. He raises questions about the possibility of multiple attachments, whether these develop simultaneously or not, whether all attachment figures are treated alike, and whether the birth mother necessarily has to be the principal figure of attachment. His answers to these questions are clearly stated: 'almost from the first many children have more than one figure towards whom they direct attachment behaviour; these figures are not treated alike; [and] the role of a child's principal attachment-figure can be filled by others than the natural mother' (p. 304). Indeed, he concludes from research results available at the time that for an infant of 18 months to have only one attachment figure is 'quite exceptional' (p. 304).

Hierarchies of attachment

Bowlby emphasises that most children form a hierarchy of attachments. Ainsworth's research suggested to him that children follow one figure primarily and, when the attachment system is strongly activated—as might occur when a child is ill, tired or frightened—the child seeks out that person in preference to others. He also underlines the error of labelling all approaches by the child to other people as attachment. In his view, approaches to peers, friendly but only slightly familiar adults and even some quite well-known adults have little in common, from an attachment perspective, with approaches to the attachment figure.

Bowlby considered that who becomes a primary attachment figure for a child depends on who assumes the role of primary caregiver, and how the child's household and family is constituted. Importantly, he also stressed that having multiple attachments does not weaken the child's attachment to the principal attachment figures: 'it is a mistake to suppose that a young child diffuses his attachment over many figures in such a way that he gets along with no strong attachment to anyone' (1969/1982, p. 308). Bowlby emphasised that it is in fact the child with a weak attachment who is most likely to concentrate all his social behaviours to that one person.

Attachments with professional caregivers

When infants and young children attend child care (whether family or centre based), or are regularly cared for by babysitters or nannies, attachment theory compels us to ask what similarities and differences exist between these relationships on the one hand, and the relationships that form between parents and their children on the other.

In her book on attachment and development, Goldberg (2000) reviews several studies addressing these issues. These studies show that young children do become attached to child-care providers. Further, the quality of attachment between children and their professional caregivers depends, as it does with other attachment figures, on the quality of the interactions experienced, and the extent and nature of the caregiver's involvement with the child (e.g. Goossens and van IJzendoorn, 1990; Howes and Hamilton, 1992). Goldberg concludes that infants usually do have a preferred caregiver, that this may not always be the mother, and that information on attachment hierarchies is very limited to date.

Characteristics of the child such as temperament impact on the quality of interactions with professional caregivers, just as they contribute to attachment quality in parent–child dyads. For example, Watson and Kowalski (1999) found that in a sample of 19 Australian child-care centres, caregivers responded in different ways to toddlers with easy versus difficult temperaments, and that temperamentally difficult children 'attracted the most attention (not necessarily positive)' (p. 53). They also found that in high quality centres there were more positive and less negative interactions with children overall, but particularly so with children of difficult temperament.

Howes (1999) presents another analysis of multiple attachment relationships, and asks the provocative question: Who is an attachment figure? In answering she proposes three criteria: '(1) provision of physical and emotional care; (2) continuity or consistency in a child's life; and (3) emotional investment in the child' (p. 673). By consistency of care, Howes meant persons who care for the child on a regular basis, and that this could certainly include teachers, child-care providers and members of the extended family.

In summarising research on the formation of attachment relationships with alternative caregivers, Howes concludes that the processes are similar to those that have been delineated for infant–mother attachments:

> Although the developmental context is different for relationships formed when children are toddlers rather than infants, children in both periods construct their attachment relationships on the basis of repeated interactions with caregiving adults. Children with prior relationship difficulties, when moved to settings with sensitive caregivers, appear to be able either to reorganize their attachment representations . . . or to construct independent relationships based on experiences with the new caregivers (1999, p. 678).

A systems perspective on attachment

Regardless of who becomes a child's attachment figure(s), it is important to note that no relationship ever exists 'in a vacuum' (Goldberg, 2000, p. 81). Goldberg draws on recent research to elucidate attachment within a systems perspective. All attachment relationships function within a mutually influencing social system. Interconnections between microsystems (such as family, neighbourhood or child-care settings) make the picture even more complex. For example, interactions between a child and professional caregiver will be influenced by the child's relationship with the parents and by the parents' relationship with the professional caregiver. And just as the quality of the marital relationship impacts on the quality of the child's attachment to each parent, so the professional relationships that exist within a child-care setting, and how stressed and/or supported the caregiver feels, will impact on the quality of a child's relationship to that carer, something we considered in the case scenario in chapter 6.

Goossens and Melhuish (1996) found that the sensitivity of a sample of 25 professional caregivers in their interactions with toddlers differed according to the context in which they were observed. Caregiver sensitivity was highest in one-to-one free play during a laboratory-based observation session, when there were no competing demands. It was significantly lower in the nursery (child-care) setting when interactions between the same caregivers and toddlers were made as the caregivers went about their normal duties, with adult to toddler ratios of 2:10. This result reminds us of other research (mentioned at the end of chapter 6) showing that attachment security in infants is lower at higher staff-to-infant ratios.

Implications and applications

CASE SCENARIO

In this case scenario we observe Jung as she helps Ryan learn about taking his turn and sharing with other children, and how she responds to his escalating feelings of frustration and anger.

Ryan is standing with three other two-year-olds. They are clustered around a wire cage that has been placed on a low table in the middle of their toddler room at child care. Inside the cage is a very large rabbit, called Bunny. Bunny was brought to the centre by one of the children in the three-year-old group, and for the past week Jung has been reading stories to the children about pets and pet care. Today the children have been talking about feeding pets, and each child has been given a small piece of carrot.

Jung is standing with the children and invites them to feed the rabbit. She says: 'So as not to frighten Bunny we will have to take turns. First Jasveen, then Shania, then Joseph, then Ryan.' She opens the cage door carefully, and asks Jasveen to offer Bunny a piece of carrot. This Jasveen does eagerly, and the other children watch with excited faces as the rabbit sniffs, then chews, the carrot. Ryan claps his hands and giggles. Jung comments, 'He loves his food, doesn't he Ryan?'

She then invites Shania, who is standing next to Ryan, to place her piece of carrot in the cage. As Jung begins to open the cage door again, Ryan moves forward and tries to put his piece of carrot in, pushing Shania's hand away as he does so. Jung speaks gently and calmly to Ryan, saying, 'No, Ryan, it is Shania's turn.' Ryan watches and frowns as Shania puts her piece inside the cage. He then quickly goes to put his piece inside. Jung immediately moves next to Ryan and repeats, 'No Ryan, next Joseph, then it's your turn.'

Ryan pouts, stamps his foot and then begins to cry. Jung immediately squats down, puts her arm around Ryan and gently holds his hand while watching and praising Joseph as he puts his carrot in the cage. Ryan's distress increases, and he starts to flail about. Jung calmly says, 'See, Bunny is still hungry. Now let's see him enjoy Ryan's carrot.' Ryan hesitates for a moment, and then throws his carrot into the cage. The other three children squeal with delight and run off. Ryan resumes tantruming.

Jung stays with Ryan, arms loosely around his body as his tantrum continues. She speaks gently, and continues to talk calmly with him about Bunny. It is some minutes before Ryan begins to settle, and at this stage he leans towards Jung, snuggling into her lap. Jung waits until Ryan is fully settled, a period of some minutes, then together they walk towards the door. She stands with him until he moves towards the outside water-trough. He approaches the teacher standing nearby (who is well aware of what has happened indoors) and stands next to her, saying nothing. She says, 'Do you want to join in, Ryan?' He nods his head and she offers him his plastic smock. Jung walks outside and joins a group of children playing in the sandpit area next to the water-trough, checking from time to time on Ryan's progress.

QUESTIONS FOR REFLECTION

- What did Jung do to help encourage Ryan's autonomy and that of the other children?
- What did Jung do to help Ryan manage his feelings?
- Why was it so important for Jung to remain with Ryan until he settled?
- What has Ryan learnt from this experience?

DISCUSSION POINTS

At the age of two-and-a-half years, Ryan has emerging needs for autonomy, combined with existing dependency needs. Maybe it was too much for Ryan to wait his turn behind three other children, and Jung might take this into account when planning for Ryan over the next weeks. She might consider providing Ryan with lots of opportunities to practise manageable sharing and waiting his turn, combined with lots of reinforcement for so doing in the months ahead.

It was important that Ryan experienced Jung as accessible, reassuring and calm as his own emotions escalated. It was also important that Jung maintained boundaries and insisted that Ryan take his turn, and that she remained with Ryan until he settled. She knew Ryan was settled when he moved off, ready to explore a new activity. She encouraged this independence, fostering Ryan's autonomy. Nonetheless, she wisely chose a place in the outside playground where she could monitor Ryan a little longer, just in case.

Further readings

Dowlby, R. 2003 'On being emotionally available' *Reflections: National Gowrie RAP Publication* Issue 12, pp. 4–6

Howes, C., Galinsky, E. and Kontos, S. 1998 'Child care caregiver sensitivity and attachment' *Social Development* vol. 7, pp. 25–36

McCartney, K., Scarr, S., Rocheleau, A., Phillips, D., Abbott-Shim, M., Eisenberg, M., Keefe, N., Rosenthal, S. and Ruh, J. 1997 'Teacher–child interaction and child care auspices as predictors of social outcomes in infants, toddlers, and preschoolers' *Merrill-Palmer Quarterly* vol. 43, pp. 426–50

8

The preschool years: Emerging instrumentality

In this chapter, we consider attachment in the preschool period, from three to five years, including peer relationships, and relationships with teachers in the preschool setting. First we consider the increasing sophistication of the attachment relationship as the child's conceptual abilities develop during this phase. Second, behavioural indicators of different attachment patterns—secure and insecure—during the preschool years are described. Finally, the link between attachment-related experiences and social competence are discussed as an introduction to more detailed consideration of emotional and behavioural problems resulting from unmet attachment needs in chapter 13.

Expectations of the preschool period

The preschool period is one in which most children begin to engage—if they have not already done so—in a social and emotional life beyond the family and primary attachment figures. Expectations of the child in regard to peer interactions, friendships, independence, impulse control and emotional self-regulation are generally much higher than before. In addition, the child is expected to be able to move away from attachment figures comfortably, to tolerate separations, and indeed to enjoy periods of play with peers and interactions with familiar adults without the continued presence of a primary attachment figure.

The organisation of attachment, and attachment relationships, undergoes change in line with these expectations and the developmental achievements of the preschool years. Nonetheless, children must remain strongly connected to their attachment figures. Although the nature of their 'secure base' transforms as children mature and become autonomous, its importance for optimal psychological health does not diminish. Because attachment is a lifelong process, the significance of warm, satisfying and reliable attachment relationships continues through the lifespan.

Bowlby's view (1969/1982) was that most children are probably ready to begin to move away from the principal attachment figures some time around the age of three years. By then children are generally less reliant upon the continual presence of their attachment figures and are psychologically ready to begin to cope independently—or assisted by less well-known adult caregivers—with everyday life. This includes new and developing peer relationships and novel learning situations, like the preschool, with all the challenges that these bring. However, reliance on others never ends. The secure child may indeed be more likely to seek out help and draw great pleasure from many close interpersonal relationships, but appropriate self-reliance is clearly a goal for those preparing the child to move into the world of school.

The attachment relationship in the preschool years

The publication of the edited volume *Attachment in the Preschool Years* (Greenberg et al, 1990) formally launched an important new focus of attachment beyond the infancy and toddler period. The contributors to this book acknowledged that as children grow they engage in a process of 'renegotiating the balance between being connected to others and being independent and autonomous as they encounter each new developmental phase' (Cicchetti et al, 1990, p. 3). Their reseach broadened the scope of attachment research beyond the infancy years, to what Robert Emde called, in his preface to the volume, the 'transition age' (Greenberg et al, 1990, p. x) from one to four years.

This broader focus required new techniques of measurement, since the Strange Situation was initially developed for use only with infants up to the age of about 18 months. It also drove conceptual advances in attachment theory. For example, the cognitive developments of the preschool period, and the increasingly sophisti-cated mental representations possible, demanded new understandings of the internal working model concept. How do children integrate into their working models the various views of self and others that are engendered by their different attachment relationships? What happens when a child has secure relationships with some attachment figures but insecure relationships with others? How do attachment relationships formed during infancy and the toddler years impact on the preschool child's relationships beyond the family? Are there differences between children with secure and insecure attachment histories in their peer relationships and relationships with significant adults (for example, teachers) during the early childhood period? As Greenberg et al state: 'Given the preschool child's rapidly expanding social understanding and social network, it becomes necessary both to conceptualise the attachment construct in accordance with these developmental transformations and to understand the relationship between the attachment construct and other developing systems of skills' (1990, p. xv).

Ten years later, Goldberg (2000) again stressed that the preschool period demands reconceptualisations of attachment relationships in line with the cognitive, communicative and motor advances of this stage of development. The essence of the preschool period is increasing representational skills, and the use of representational knowledge to organise attachment behaviours. Preschool children can think about and reflect on relationships, including attachment relationships, in quite sophisticated ways. They can understand explanations of why attachment figures may have to be away for a period of time. They have developing insight into why attachment figures behave as they do, and into ways in which their own behaviour can make the relationship work, or work better.

According to Bowlby this development of conceptual perspective-taking occurs some time between the third and fifth birthdays. From an attachment perspective, it enables the child to negotiate with the attachment figure in ways that may be convincing enough for the adult to accommodate, leading to a 'mutually acceptable compromise' (Ainsworth et al, 1978, p. 28). In Bowlby's view, these processes also characterised attachment relationships formed to other figures during later childhood and adulthood.

Categories of attachment security in the preschool years

Various measures, including adaptations of the Strange Situation procedure, are now available to measure the quality of attachment between preschool-aged children and their attachment figures. Several were mentioned in chapters 2 and 3. In general, measures of attachment quality during the preschool period and beyond have revealed behavioural patterns that mirror the secure and insecure categories described extensively for infants (see Goldberg, 2000, pp. 38–41).

Secure preschoolers are relaxed when reunited with their attachment figure after a separation, even if the separation has been prolonged up to an hour or so. Like secure infants and toddlers, they are able to achieve a comfortable balance between their attachment and exploration needs. Eye contact and relaxed, fluent conversations are characteristic. There is orientation towards the attachment figure after an absence, although actual physical contact is much less likely than in younger children.

Children showing the pattern of attachment termed 'avoidant' in infancy and 'defended' in the preschool and early school years (Crittenden, 1992) may be polite to the attachment figure on reunion after a separation. However, in contrast to securely attached preschoolers, minimal eye contact is shown. They *appear* too engrossed in their activities to include the attachment figure in the ways shown in secure dyads. As Goldberg (2000) notes, it is the attachment figure who must take the initiative to engage the child in relationship-focused interactions and he or she may have to work quite hard to draw the child into an interaction. The behaviour of the attachment figure may thereby appear 'inappropriately bright' (p. 38) or overly enthusiastic. The attachment figure may quickly become frustrated with this dynamic, making negative comments about the child's unwillingness or reluctance to join in. In some dyads, the child's behaviour may be interpreted by the attachment figure as an indication that the child does not like them and/or does not want to be with them.

The resistant pattern—during the preschool years termed 'coercive' by Crittenden (1992) and 'dependent' by Cassidy and Marvin (with the MacArthur Working Group, 1987, 1992, as cited by Goldberg, 2000)—is characterised by an almost exclusive focus on the relationship, with exploration and play limited as a result. Indeed, as the various terms connote, the pattern is one of apparent regression, distress and settling difficulties, conflict and/or sulky avoidance. These sorts of behaviours may have the appearance of non-compliance or behaviour-management struggles. Describing how a coercive or dependent dyad appears, Goldberg states that 'the episode is ridden with parent–child conflict. Such conflicts may arise over the child's repeated "testing" of the parent by engaging in inappropriate activities . . . or disagreement over minor details in attempted play or discussion' (p. 42). Feigned helplessness or immaturity in the child may be observed.

The disorganised attachment pattern when observed in preschool-aged and older children is characterised by controlling strategies, in which the child may assume a caregiving (parentified) style of interaction with the attachment figure, or be overtly hostile and punishing to him or her. In the former pattern, the child may appear overly bright, eager to please and focused on 'entertaining, comforting or helping' (Goldberg, 2000, p. 43) the attachment figure, who usually remains unengaged or subdued in response. In the hostile pattern, there may be rude, inappropriate behaviour that openly ignores the attachment figure's attempts at interaction or requests for compliance, which are often timidly or half-heartedly put. Indeed, it is often the child who demands or *commands* compliance by the attachment figure. All these insecure patterns—in comparison to the secure pattern—evidence an inability or unwillingness on the part of the child to openly, accurately and spontaneously express his or her attachment needs and related feelings.

Attachment and social competence in the preschool years

By the time they reach the age of four or five years, we expect a lot of children. We expect them among other things to be able to respond to frustration without aggression, to cope with high arousal without emotional disorganisation, while at the same time being 'spontaneous and exuberant' (Sroufe, 1995, p. 214) in their play. We expect preschoolers to be sociable and polite to adults, and are concerned if children of this age have ongoing difficulties separating from their parents, or are unduly dependent on their teacher.

A major developmental task for the preschool child is the ability to engage in positive interactions with peers and develop satisfying peer relationships. Peer relationships, as Dunn (1993) reminds us, take a variety of forms. They can be 'intense', 'intimate' and 'affectionate', or may be 'passing', 'detached' and 'problematic' (p. 58). An important aspect of attachment theory and research for the early childhood practitioner concerns the impact of earlier attachment patterns on peer relationships specifically, and social competence more generally. This is particularly so since the preschool period marks the developmental stage when 'personality' becomes consolidated, as represented in a child's unique, stable and coherent patterning of emotions, beliefs about self and others, and social adaptation.

Sroufe's (1995) thesis, drawing on attachment theory and the writings of Erikson (1963), Mahler et al (1975) and Sander (1975) and described in sections of the preceding two chapters, is that this personality, or affective core of self, is the outcome of interactions within and expectancies formed from the child's attachment relationships. At the innermost level is the individual's sense of trust and security, built from the experience of sensitive, responsive care in the infancy period and beyond. Around this is the individual's sense of autonomy and agency—the ability to achieve goals through one's autonomous actions—again built from the attachment figure's sensitive response to the toddler's efforts at independent functioning. In Sroufe's view, the preschool years are the time when these aspects of self—security, autonomy and 'acceptability'—become consolidated through a history of responsive care. The outcome of this is the development of a true sense of 'instrumentality' (1995, p. 221).

Attachment theory predicts that children with secure histories will be more self-reliant emotionally, have higher self-esteem, and be more empathic in social interactions. These predictions are supported by a substantial body of research, including long-term longitudinal studies. These have been reviewed elsewhere (see Sroufe, 1990, 1995; Colin, 1996) and reveal that children with insecure attachment histories have less rich play, with fewer emotional themes, and have problematic peer relationships. More aggression and less empathy is shown by children with avoidant histories. Children with a history of resistant attachment are more immature in their play and social relationships, more readily frustrated and tend to ambivalence in their relationships with peers. Whereas children with avoidant histories tend to bully other children, children with resistant histories are most likely to be their victims. The research also indicates that preschool teachers react to the behaviour of children with insecure histories in different ways. They may get angry with and want to reject avoidant children because of their 'cool defiance toward adults and their hurtful behavior toward other children' (Sroufe, 1995, p. 227). On the other hand, teachers were found to be more controlling with and 'infantalized' (Sroufe, 1995, p. 227) resistant children whose behaviour was needy and immature.

Summarising the research, Colin (1996) concludes: 'As infants, toddlers, or preschoolers, children who were securely attached to their mothers in infancy interact with peers more often than anxiously attached children do; during the preschool years, they show more competence and less conflict in interactions with peers, interact more positively, and are unlikely to be either bullies or victims' (p. 135).

Such outcomes depend, however, on the ongoing nature of the attachment relationship and whether or not the quality of attachment changes or remains stable. That is, if the child's relationship with attachment figures becomes less secure, the early attachment history is not likely to be predictive of later psychosocial functioning (see Thompson, 1999). There are many reasons why the quality of a child's attachment relationship may change. The adult may find it easier to be sensitively responsive to a dependent infant, but struggle with the demands of the two-year-old who is wilfully focused on asserting his or her independence. The preschool period marks a phase when fears and phobias peak, and these anxieties—and the way the child attempts to deal with them—may bring particular stresses to the caregiving relationship. As Cicchetti et al (1990) note, insecure attachments may develop (with new or existing attachment figures) in the preschool period. At any stage during the child's infancy and early childhood years (and beyond), life circumstances may change. Attachment figures may feel more or less supported, more or less stressed, with predictable effects on the quality of attachment.

This sort of analysis reminds us again that there is an amazing complexity in the answer to the question of whether, and how, early attachment experiences influence later development. Thompson (1999) concludes that while there is much research still to be done, the 'empirical landscape is both challenging and hopeful for attachment theory' (p. 281) in this regard.

Implications and applications

CASE SCENARIO

In this case scenario we follow Malcolm, Helina's preschool teacher, as he develops a professional development session for other teachers in his region. The topic is 'Attachment and Preschooler Behaviours'. As you read his plan for the session, consider ways in which you might use your growing understanding of attachment theory to contribute to an information session on the topic for colleagues and/or parents.

Malcolm belongs to an informal network of early childhood educators in his local community, an area comprising mainly poor families, with many parents out of work, and a majority of single parent families. Many families face multiple risk factors including domestic violence and substance abuse. Malcolm and his colleagues are committed to ongoing professional development and meet monthly for information sharing and professional support. They are all concerned about the problems facing many families in their community, and choose topics that they feel will help them support the needs of the children and families who use their early childhood settings. Each member of the support group facilitates one session per year on a topic of their choice. Malcolm has decided to facilitate an evening on attachment theory and research. He has decided to present information in two parts:

Part 1: Attachment security and insecurity in the preschool years.
Part 2: Cultural perspectives on attachment (this part of Malcolm's session is considered later, in chapter 12).

He develops the following plan for Part 1.

1. *Introduction—an overview of the concept of attachment and the usual process of attachment formation.*
2. *Secure and insecure patterns of attachment in infancy.*
3. *Secure and insecure patterns of attachment in the preschool years.*
4. *Responding to insecure behaviours (avoidant, resistant and disorganised) in the preschool setting.*
5. *Reflections based on professional experiences.*

QUESTIONS FOR REFLECTION

- In your opinion, how useful would a session like this be for early childhood educators?
- Given the particular needs of the local community, are there any additional areas that Malcolm might consider including, or areas that need a special focus?

- Would a case study approach be appropriate for such a session?
- How would you plan a session on these topics for *parents*?
- Reflecting on your own professional experiences, can you identify patterns of behaviour you have observed in children that 'fit' with the patterns described in this chapter?
- How might the early childhood professional support parents in maintaining/ promoting security in their relationships with their children in the face of the developmental changes of the preschool period?

POINTS FOR DISCUSSION

There are many factors that impact on a child's behaviour and development and it is important to acknowledge that attachment history is but one important part of the full picture. You may find it particularly helpful to reflect on your own responses to different patterns of behaviour in children, as well as thinking about ways in which you may be able to assist children with avoidant and resistant patterns to become more secure through their experiences in the early childhood setting. Preschoolers, like infants and toddlers, will learn better if the educational setting promotes feelings of trust and autonomy. Think about particular strategies you would use in the following situations:

- The preschooler who finds separation from the parent difficult and is refusing to allow the parent to leave the preschool room at the start of each session.
- The preschooler who is clingy and immature, and always following you around, needing frequent attention and redirection.
- The preschooler who is frequently bullying other children and who appears to take delight in upsetting the most sensitive children in your group.
- The preschooler who seems to want to control everything, and who appears very focused on pleasing you, more so than feels appropriate.

Further readings

Colin, V.L. 1996 *Human Attachment* McGraw-Hill, New York
Greenberg, M.T., Speltz, M.L. and DeKlyen, M. 1993 'The role of attachment in the early development of disruptive behaviour problems' *Development and Psychopathology* vol. 5, pp. 191–213

9

Attachment and cognitive competence

As our previous discussions of the internal working model indicated, attachment theory has from the outset recognised the central contribution of cognitive factors to the essentially affective bond that is attachment. The beginning of a true attachment, as we have seen in chapter 6, is dependent on the infant's ability to discriminate, and then to show preference for particular caregiving figures. The goal-corrected partnership discussed in chapter 7 that evolves some years later requires even more advanced cognitive abilities. These include the child's understanding of the motives and needs of the attachment figure and the ability to act strategically on this understanding to achieve attachment-related goals. The strategies used by insecure children in the context of rejecting or inconsistent caregiving can only develop through cognitive skills including learning, observation of the impact of one's own behaviours on the behaviour of another, memory, attention and so on. The development of attachment, and movement to increasingly complex attachment relationships during the early childhood period, can thus be seen to go hand in hand with a range of cognitive abilities of growing sophistication. However, this is not a one-way street.

The consequences of attachment security for cognitive competence

Research has demonstrated that the process of attachment formation not only *depends* on the emerging cognitive skills of the child, but also has *consequences* for cognitive competence. These are discussed in this chapter, in terms of differences in secure-base behaviour, exploration and learning.

Differences in secure-base behaviour

The secure child is much freer, in an emotional sense, to explore the wider world, trusting in the availability and responsiveness of the attachment figure should danger threaten. Children with secure and insecure attachments direct their attention in different ways to their secure-base figure. The securely attached young child distributes attention flexibly between the attachment figure and the surroundings, enabling a comfortable exploration of the environment without excessive monitoring of the caregiver, unless special circumstances of threat or danger warrant it.

In resistant children, attention is excessively focused on the caregiver to the exclusion of the environment. In avoidant children there is an excessive exclusion of attention to the attachment figure or, put another way, an apparent attentional preoccupation with the environment. This does not mean, however, that they are advantaged in terms of information processing. As Maslin–Cole and Spieker (1990) state:

> . . . whether the quality of object interaction shown by avoidant infants is consistent with that of secure infants and whether it meets the criteria for motivational behaviour are not known. For example, avoidant infants may use many toys quickly and simply without sustained persistence in the face of challenge. Avoidant infants' interactions with objects may lack effective engrossment, perhaps including tentative or cursory interactions or repetition which might suggest perseverance (p. 250).

Research by Sroufe and Waters (1977) has shown that although avoidant infants give the appearance of being very attentive to objects and ignoring or uninterested in the attachment figure, they are in fact highly anxious and aroused by their presence. This level of physiological arousal is likely 'incompatible with sustained attention or orientation' (Maslin-Cole and Spieker, 1990, p. 250) to the objects they appear so attentive to.

In the case of the disorganised/disoriented child, it appears there is no attentional strategy that is consistently applied or that can be maintained. Whether stilling, freezing and stereotyped movements in the disorganised/disoriented child 'represent lapses in access to needed information [or reveal] heightened monitoring and information processing that allow the infant subsequently to engage an organised strategy' (Goldberg, 2000, p. 155), something proposed by Crittenden (1995), is as yet unclear. Research has yet to establish the cognitive processes that occur when disorganised children dissociate, and why these dissociations occur. But there is no doubt that chronic dissociations pose a significant risk factor to ongoing mental health in later years (Carlson, 1998).

Beyond infancy, the same or similar strategies of selective attention apply in secure and insecure children, although the behavioural manifestations may change in line with increasing developmental maturity. Secure preschoolers and school-aged children flexibly and smoothly distribute attention between attachment figures and the world around them. The avoidant or defended preschooler or school-aged child continues to 'exclude or minimise attachment-relevant information' (Goldberg, 2000, p. 156). The dependent or coercive older child still focuses on the attachment figure to the exclusion of play and exploration. Put another way, defended children use strategies of *false cognitions* whereas coercive children use *false affects* (see Crittenden, 1995).

Exploiting opportunities for exploration and learning

In addition to these differences in secure-base behaviour between secure and insecure children, it has been argued by Maslin-Cole and Spieker (1990) that the cognitive development of secure children may be enhanced because secure children are better placed to exploit opportunities for exploration and learning. This is because they can quickly achieve, and then maintain, feelings of security in the face of novelty. This has to do with their enhanced ability to self-regulate their emotional state, as discussed at some length in chapters 6, 7 and 8. Novelty, new situations or unfamiliar challenges do not overwhelm the secure child, since they have many past experiences of dyadic regulation and self-regulation to draw on in response to the arousal they engender. Insecure children, on the other hand, are less able to deal with this arousal because of their past history and may indeed become very anxious, which is unhelpful to learning. Taken together, these and other outcomes indicate that there should be advantages to the secure child in terms of learning about the world since the acquisition of knowledge, skills and understanding proceed from and are dependent upon accurate perceptions and adaptive levels of arousal that allow focused, sustained exploration.

Despite this prediction, those who have reviewed the literature (e.g. Colin, 1996; Thompson, 1999; Goldberg, 2000) conclude that there has been little empirical support for a clear and consistent effect of security of attachment on cognitive achievement per se. As Thompson (1999) concludes, 'there have been few associations between attachment classifications and contemporaneous or subsequent measures of intelligence' (p. 279).

The role of socio-emotional factors in cognitive competence

These findings do not mean, however, that differences in the cognitive and emotional–cognitive domains do not exist when comparing children with secure and insecure histories. Outcomes obtained depend to a great extent on the nature of the cognitive tasks involved. For tasks that are more challenging for the child, and which by their nature call into play socio-emotional responses such as persistence, or the need to seek the help of others and cooperate with them to achieve a solution, clearer differences emerge. For example, an early follow-up study of 18-month-olds found that those categorised as secure were more cooperative, approached tasks more enthusiastically, showed less negative affect and persisted longer at age two years than insecure infants (Matas et al, 1978). This study also found that symbolic (make-believe or pretend) play was more frequently observed in secure children, an outcome which also emerged in a number of studies conducted in the 1980s (see Thompson, 1999).

These findings are all the more interesting since at least one study (Belsky et al, 1984) has found that secure children are advantaged in these aspects of their play even when the attachment figure is not present. For example, when the mother is present, it is possible that differences between secure and insecure children simply reflect more direct support, and encouragement of sophisticated, cooperative and sustained play, by the mothers of the secure children. But if these effects are found even in the absence of the attachment figure, differences observed between secure and insecure children must reflect instead the children's internalised understandings, their own cognitions and emotions.

Symbolic development

Many studies investigating links between pretend play and cognitive abilities have found that higher levels of symbolic play are associated with more advanced cognitive and also social skills. According to Piaget (e.g. 1926/1930), symbolic play emerges in the pre-operational period, between the ages of two and seven years, and is an example of the growing abilities of the child in the area of representational thinking. In his view, symbolic play allows the practising or exercising of representational schemes. Later research has found that sociodramatic play, for example, promotes a wide range of mental abilities, including perspective-taking, memory, reasoning, imagination and literacy (see Berk, 2000).

In relation to emergent literacy in particular, Bus and van IJzendoorn (1988) studied children in three age groups—1½ year-olds, 3½ year-olds and 5½ year-olds—in terms of the links between attachment and literacy development, observing them with their mothers while watching a children's TV program, reading a storybook and an alphabet book. Mothers of children who were securely attached showed a different style of reading to their child, thereby revealing one of the underlying reasons for the differences observed between secure and insecure children. They spent more time using book-reading tasks to instruct their child in reading, rather than simply narrating the story. In turn, children who received more of this type of interaction and instruction during reading time had higher emergent literacy scores. The secure attachment relationship, and the interactional harmony within it, allows the infant and young child to be particularly receptive to the attachment figure's guidance and tutelage in both the social and, it would appear, socio-cognitive domains.

Effects such as this of course depend upon the security of attachment at each age being maintained. As already discussed in chapter 8, secure attachment in infancy is unlikely to be associated with more positive developmental outcomes at early school age if the child's attachment has changed to insecure (Thompson, 1999).

Achievement motivation and ego-resilience

The ability to persist in the face of challenging cognitive tasks— termed achievement motivation—has been identified as one of the most important factors underlying academic success and positive learning outcomes in school. Research has found that by the age of four years, some children do not persist when the going gets tough (for example, when faced with a difficult jigsaw puzzle). This may be because they expect to fail, and that continued effort is therefore pointless, or perhaps because they fear they will be punished for failure (Burhans and Dweck, 1995; Cain and Dweck, 1995). These types of achievement-related attributions may have even more pervasive negative consequences in the later years of school when there is increasing emphasis on success, defined as obtaining the correct solution.

Ego-strength, or ego-resilience, refers to the ability to be flexible and persistent in response to problems and challenges. Ego-control refers to being able to manage impulses and emotions. Being moderate in this characteristic—that is, being neither too rigid in repression of emotions nor too impulsive or under-controlled—is clearly advantageous to successful problem solving. Both have been found to be higher in secure five-year-olds, whether assessed in laboratory problem-solving tasks, or during naturalistic observations in the preschool or school by teachers (e.g. Oppenheim et al, 1988; Grossmann and Grossmann, 1991).

For ego-resilience, the positive effects of secure attachment in infancy have been found to persist up to late childhood (Urban et al, 1992). In summarising the literature in this area, Colin (1996) concludes:

> The picture of securely attached children that emerges from all this research is a very positive one. They appear to be curious, self-confident about managing cognitive tasks, persistent in the face of frustration, and co-operative. On the average, avoidant children often perform as well as secure children on measures of cognitive development, but their responses to frustration and challenge are less adaptive. Resistant children also tend to show maladaptive responses when faced with cognitive challenges. The pattern of results is quite convincing. The same sorts of differences among groups with differing attachment histories show up in studies in Germany, Holland, Israel, and the United States (p. 138).

Sroufe (1995) has noted that positive or pleasurable feelings 'may be viewed at times as promoting, inspiring, or calling forth cognitive effort' (p. 129). This is important to an understanding of why sensitive, responsive caregiving (and resultant secure attachment) may set up quite long-standing, pervasive and positive achievement-related attributions. Within the context of an harmonious, supportive and trusting relationship, the young child's efforts in the face of any challenging task are more likely to be experienced by him or her as pleasurable, and as rewarded and valued. Over time, these feelings are reinforced again and again. As a result, the child is increasingly likely to approach challenges with curiosity and confidence, and with expectations of success if they persist.

The child with this kind of attitude to learning and problem solving is more likely to experience success than the child whose caregiving experiences have been discouraging, critical, punitive or inconsistent in the face of challenging tasks. And so a self-fulfilling prophesy—based both on earlier and current caregiving quality—is set up. The implications for early childhood teachers are clear.

Optimal learning outcomes are dependent on the emotional tone, and interpersonal interactions and relationships, surrounding the child's earliest and ongoing efforts to achieve. This is considered further in the case scenario at the end of this chapter.

Selective information processing

Drawing on the work of Hoffman (1985), Sroufe (1995) notes the pivotal role of emotions on information processing. Emotions like curiosity initiate and heighten information processing; fear and anxiety about failure disrupt information processing. Information processing embraces all the cognitive tasks that must be successfully undertaken in order to solve a problem—from attention, to cognitive encoding and memory, to making the required response. In explaining the information processing approach to cognition, an analogy is often drawn between the child or adult as an information-processing system and the workings of a computer. That is, information is taken into the information-processing system, then must be encoded and analysed in order that an appropriate response can be made.

Some of Bowlby's key conceptualisations of attachment and development (and in particular, the process of psychological defence) draw heavily on such an information-processing approach. For example, Bowlby makes the point that sensory information is always attended to selectively, and there is subsequent evaluation and interpretation before a response is made or before behaviour is otherwise influenced. This is a normal, adaptive process. However, some individuals come to deliberately (albeit unconsciously) exclude information over a prolonged period as a result of negative attachment experiences. Bowlby wrote:

> In the ordinary course of a person's life most of the information reaching him is being routinely excluded from further processing in order that his capacities are not overloaded and his attention not constantly distracted. Most selective exclusion, therefore, is both necessary and adaptive. Like other physiological and psychological processes, however, in certain circumstances selective exclusion can have consequences that are of doubtful or varying adaptive

value. For example, given certain adverse circumstances during childhood, the selective exclusion of information of certain sorts may be adaptive. Yet, when during adolescence and adult life the situation changes, the persistent exclusion of the same sorts of information may be maladaptive (1980, p. 45).

The process of psychological defence

It is beyond the scope of this book to detail the process of selective exclusion and psychological defence Bowlby developed, and which he outlined in Volume 3 of the attachment trilogy (1980). However, it is relevant to note that in his analysis Bowlby identifies two situations that lead to defensive exclusion of sensory/perceptual information. This occurs because, if not excluded, the information would bring the child into distressing conflict with the attachment figure(s). The first situation includes occasions when the child's bids for comfort and reassurance from the attachment figure are routinely ignored, rejected or punished. This, in Bowlby's view, leads to a deactivation of the attachment system, such that the child comes to defensively exclude, more or less completely, 'sensory inflow of any and every kind that might activate attachment behaviour and feeling' (1980, p. 70). This is termed detachment. Bowlby states that very young children are particularly prone to respond in this way, because at young ages vulnerability to separation, and the extent of suffering experienced when comfort and reassurance are denied, is probably greater than at older ages.

The second situation that is likely to lead to defensive exclusion due to potential conflict with attachment figures is when the caregiver behaves in ways to the child that are contradictory or inconsistent. The child may have difficulty accommodating these different images of the parent. Alternatively (and sometimes, in addition), there may be pressure from the attachment figure for the child to regard him or her in only a favourable light: 'On threat of not being loved or even of being abandoned a child is led to understand that he is not supposed to notice his parent's adverse treatment of him or, if he does, that he should regard it as being no more than the justifiable reaction of a wronged parent to his (the child's) bad behaviour' (Bowlby, 1980, p. 71).

In terms of the internal working model, the main negative effect of these sorts of defences is that they can become entrenched to such an extent that the adolescent or adult cannot change them. In the first case, accessing certain kinds of perceptual information may become chronically problematic, leading to constant emotional detachment. In the second, they are unable to do other than constantly attempt to 'placate' (Bowlby, 1980, p. 74) the parent or other attachment figure, leading to constant emotional vigilance.

Semantic and episodic memory, and the concepts of scripts and narratives

In discussing attachment and information processing, Goldberg (2000) draws together notions of semantic and episodic memory (see Tulving, 1972), 'scripts' and 'narratives'. Semantic memories are those that are generalised impressions of people or events ('Mummy is a happy person'). Episodic memories, which develop in the preschool years, are described by Goldberg as 'vivid, detailed, chronologically ordered memories of specific events based on direct experience' (p. 152), such as the child might develop around her grandfather's visit to preschool one day. Scripts are the encoded or symbolic representations of frequent rituals which may include the normal patterns of interactions that the child experiences with attachment figures. Narratives are our recounted experiences, and they 'build upon selective attention, integration of memories, and language and communication skills' (Goldberg, 2000, p. 153).

Narrative skills are largely developed in communication with others about joint experiences. If such 'co-construction experiences', as they are called, are disturbed, as would be the case when the child's direct experience is denied by another (see Bowlby's example above of the child constantly required to deny negative characteristics in the adult attachment figure), the child's ability to make sense of their experience is undermined. In relation to attachment experiences per se, Goldberg concludes that if such disturbances are pervasive, 'multiple inconsistent internal working models of attachment are retained without conscious awareness of discrepancies' (2000, p. 153).

Affirming the child's perspective

From a practical point of view, what this means is that children should be supported and affirmed in their perspectives on events. That is not to say that everyone's perspective on events is identical, especially when a child's view is compared to that of an adult. However, it is important that adults actively incorporate accurate descriptions of the child's point of view as well as their own in everyday interactions. This will support the child's ability to build coherent narratives of their lived experiences, retaining both their own perspective on events and those of others, including the attachment figure.

It is possible that young children are more vulnerable than older children to disturbances in co-construction experiences resulting from the attachment figure's denial or distortion of the child's perspective on events. This is because the meta-cognitive abilities required to retain an accurate, coherent memory of events under these conditions are not present in the very young child (Goldberg, 2000). This reminds us of earlier discussions of attachment and resilience (chapter 5), and how metacognitive skills underpin the child's ability to make sense of experiences, reflect on why certain events occurred, and how they are affected by them.

Beginning school

Children generally start school around the age of five to six years. Most have attended some kind of preschool program in the year or two before, so that by the time they begin school they have had some experience of a structured or semi-structured learning environment, albeit different in style and curriculum to that of the primary or elementary school.

With the transition to school comes a new level of independence. For many children, school may not represent their first foray into worlds beyond the family. Indeed, for those who have attended extended child care or other long-day programs, school may involve less time away from home than in earlier years. But the school context makes far greater demands on the child for independent functioning, emotional self-control and autonomous decision-making than these earlier settings. Preschool programs typically focus on moving a child towards sufficient independence by age five or six years to be able to cope with the learning focus of the classroom as well as the hurly-burly of playground life.

Children bring forward with them to this new setting their preceding attachment experiences—with parents, other family members, professional carers and teachers—and other social relationships with a widening circle of peers and adults. By the time they start school, most children will have developed a number of attachment relationships. Each will have influenced to a greater or lesser extent their internal working model of self and others. These will in turn influence their behaviour in, and approach to, the school setting and the people and learning tasks they encounter there.

The focus of this book is the early childhood period, but any discussion of attachment and cognitive competence would be incomplete without some comments on the early school years. Changes in cognitive-related abilities pervade all stages of the lifespan, from birth to old age. Even so, beginning school probably marks one of the most important transitions in cognitive-related demands. While the event itself does not mark any developmental shift in cognition per se, it heralds the start of a major new developmental context which, in contrast to those that have come before, has as its primary *raison d'être* academic learning. By its nature and focus, it faces the child with new challenges in relation to thinking and problem solving.

A great deal is now known about the cognitive processes that underlie the development of attachment, and how security of attachment in turn affects the way a child approaches learning tasks. Even in the school years, security affords the child considerable potential advantages. Tasks are approached with greater curiosity and optimism, help is sought more easily and integrated more harmoniously, and there is greater persistence, especially in the face of set-backs and frustrations. In addition, the secure child is more open to sensory and perceptual information in general, and social–emotional experiences in particular. Secure children are by definition less likely to engage in unhelpful and maladaptive perceptual exclusions as defences against previous hurts.

All these positive effects arise because the secure child's inner working model has developed from a history of sensitive, responsive, consistent caregiving. It has been moulded to be coherent through repeated co-constructions of experience during which attachment figures have affirmed, and accurately incorporated, the child's perceptions of events as well as their own. The advantages experienced by the secure child as she or he sets forth on their life journey beyond preschool are not due to chance. They reflect the knowledge, commitment, interpersonal resources and caregiving circumstances encountered by those adults who have had responsibility for the child's care during infancy and the early childhood years.

Implications and applications

CASE SCENARIO

In this case scenario we consider in more detail some of the ways in which early childhood professionals can support the developing achievement motivation and ego-resilience of young children. To do so we observe another interaction between Jung and Ryan, this time as Ryan faces some challenges with a jigsaw puzzle he is attempting. We also listen in on a conversation later that day between Jung and Ryan's mother, Siobhan, as Jung relates the incident to Siobhan when she arrives to pick Ryan up.

Ryan is sitting at the puzzle table with a number of puzzles in front of him. He reaches for his favourite, tips the pieces out, then methodically puts the pieces in, one by one. He completes it easily and repeats the process again. He then leans back on his chair, smiles, pushes the puzzle away, and looks around the room. Jung approaches, sits down by Ryan's side, and says, 'We have some new puzzles, Ryan. Would you like to try one?' Ryan responds eagerly and goes to the shelf indicated by Jung, selecting one of the new two-layer puzzles that the centre has just purchased. On the bottom layer are pictures of nocturnal Australian marsupials, and on the top layer, Australian marsupials that are seen during the day.

Jung first draws Ryan's attention to the two layers, talking to him about the different animals, and how some animals are active during the night, when he is asleep. At first she watches as he explores the different pieces, looking at them and turning them over. After a while, she suggests he may like to put the pieces in two piles—one for the bottom layer, then one for the top layer. She assists him to do so, talking with him all the while about the various animals, which ones he has seen, and what they are called. She then sits back as he begins to put the bottom pieces in.

At first Ryan struggles, but he remains intent. From time to time, Jung offers a piece for Ryan to try, or moves a piece chosen by Ryan to an angle that makes its place more obvious. Most of the time she just sits back and observes, gently encouraging Ryan's efforts and chatting with him about the animals. Ryan tells her he has seen some of the animals at home in the backyard at night. Others he has seen on family camping holidays.

When Ryan places the final piece in the bottom layer he sighs, smiles and then says, 'I don't want to do this any more.' Jung affirms his good efforts and asks if he would like to finish the puzzle tomorrow. Together they gather the pieces that are left into a stack and carry them, plus the completed section, to a cupboard. Ryan runs off, confident that he will have the opportunity tomorrow to finish his work.

Later that day, Jung tells Siobhan how well Ryan managed with the new puzzle. Ryan is keen to show his mother progress so far, so together they go to the cupboard and look at what he has done. Siobhan praises Ryan's efforts, commenting, 'That's a hard puzzle, Ryan. What great work you've done today!' She comments to Jung that Ryan's father, Peter, often sits with Ryan after dinner and they play together on some activity, including jigsaw puzzles. She says that she and Peter have always tried hard to encourage and support Ryan's efforts, and his attempts at new tasks. Peter is particularly patient, she says, especially if Ryan becomes frustrated.

QUESTIONS FOR REFLECTION

- How important to the outcome of Ryan's efforts was the supportive presence of Jung? Think about what this scenario might have been like in the absence of Jung.
- What particular aspects of Jung's interactions with Ryan supported his achievement motivation and ego-resilience? What things did you notice about Ryan's approach to the task that are suggestive of a secure attachment history?
- What aspects of Ryan's home life are supportive of his ego-resilience and achievement motivation? Think back to other case scenarios about Ryan (chapters 3 and 7). What else do we know about Ryan and his caregiving experiences that are indicative of secure attachments?
- How will Jung interact with Ryan if he chooses to work on the puzzle tomorrow? And after that, on other occasions when he has mastered it? Will Jung need to maintain the same level of support? Why, or why not?
- What has Ryan learnt from this experience?

DISCUSSION POINTS

In this case scenario we see a number of ways in which Jung sensitively supports and nurtures Ryan's emerging achievement motivation and ego-resilience. Firstly, she notices the cues that Ryan is ready for a challenge, and has followed his interest in puzzles at the right moment. Secondly, she offers him choices—to try a new puzzle, to select the one of his choice—and thirdly, she finds just the right mix for Ryan of direct teaching and encouragement of his independent efforts. Different children need different mixes, and over time Ryan himself will need less of Jung's involvement as his proficiency grows.

Finally, Jung has provided an important bridge between Ryan's efforts and achievements at child care and home. By sharing his accomplishments with Siobhan, Ryan has the opportunity to experience her supportive encouragement as well. Jung has also learnt important information about Ryan's home life, and insights into the precursors of Ryan's well-developing cognitive competence.

Further readings

Bowlby, J. 1980 *Attachment and Loss: Vol. 3. Loss, sadness and depression* Hogarth Press, London, chapter 4

Thompson, R.A. 1999 'Early attachment and later development' *Handbook of Attachment: Theory, research and clinical applications* eds J. Cassidy and P.R. Shaver, The Guilford Press, New York, pp. 265–386

Part IV

Attachment issues

10

Separation experiences

Separations between children and their attachment figures are highly significant experiences within attachment theorising and in much attachment research. Bowlby devoted an entire volume of his attachment trilogy to separation issues (Bowlby, 1973). How a child responds to a brief separation from the attachment figure (and perhaps more importantly to a subsequent reunion) has formed a central focus in research on individual differences in attachment security, as we have already seen. In this chapter we consider how children respond to separation from attachment figures, what factors influence the responses children make, and how children can best be helped to deal with separation distress.

Research about the effects of child-care attendance on development is also discussed. This is an area of great significance in our society where growing numbers of infants and young children are spending increasing amounts of time in non-parental care and hence experience repeated and sometimes quite lengthy separations from parental attachment figures during the day. How the parents themselves respond to this form of separation from their children is considered in chapter 11. Adults' feelings about separation, and how they deal with these feelings, can have important effects on how their children respond.

Attachment theory is not alone in considering the impact of separation, loss and grief on development, but it offers unique insights into how these experiences impact on social and emotional development. As Rutter and O'Connor (1999) note, attachment theory provides:

> . . . a compelling explanation for the feelings associated with the 'trauma' of separation and loss—fear, anxiety, anger, sadness, and despair—and for their disruptive effects on personality development. Thus from its first systematic formulation in the 1960s, attachment theory stood out from other theories in the ways in which it conceptualised the nature and importance of children's relationships with their caregivers (p. 825).

We first consider how children respond to major separations, then move to a discussion of short-term, or what might be called 'everyday' experiences of separation such as those that occur in the context of child care.

The response of children to major separations

In the first volume of the attachment trilogy, Bowlby details a number of studies current at the time that had as a primary interest the effects on infants and young children of separation from their mother or primary attachment figure. Most of these studies had observed the response of children to major separations in which children were placed in residential care (e.g. Heinicke, 1956) or were hospitalised for lengthy periods, often with limited access to their parents due to accepted hospital policies of the time (e.g. Robertson, 1953, 1962). In these studies, separations varied in duration but many of the children included in the samples experienced separations from the primary attachment figure(s) of a week or two, or even much longer, with at best brief and occasional visits. Ainsworth et al (1978) defined a major separation as one that is very long, or permanent, 'or one that is at least long enough to greatly exceed a young child's expectations of the likely period of time that must elapse before reunion' (p. 270).

Focusing on infants and young children before their third birthday, Bowlby described three phases in the child's response to major separations from an attachment figure to whom the child was securely attached. These phases are termed protest, despair and detachment. In developing a picture of how children respond to such separations, Bowlby drew extensively on the work of his colleagues, James and Joyce Robertson. Some of this work is captured in short films such as *A Two-year-old Goes to Hospital* (1952) and *Going to Hospital with Mother* (1958). This work led to radical transformations in hospital procedures as a result of the terrible distress revealed.

The first phase, *protest*, is characterised by strong distress, rejection of alternative caregivers, or clinging to them combined with distressed searching for the absent attachment figure. Bowlby interpreted these behaviours as indicative of the child's 'strong expectation' (Bowlby, 1969/1982, p. 27) that the missing attachment figure would return. In the Robertsons' studies this phase appeared to last from between a few hours to more than a week or so.

The second phase, *despair*, characterised by emotional withdrawal and lack of protest, indicates in Bowlby's view the 'increasing hopelessness' (1969/1982, p. 27) of the child as he or she fails to find, or be reunited, with their attachment figure. Bowlby stresses that the decrease in protest observed is not in any sense evidence for a reduction in the magnitude of the child's separation-related distress. Rather, it indicates that the child is beginning to give up hope of reunion. In learning theory terms, the child is ceasing to behave in ways that are not achieving the wished-for goal (re-unification with the attachment figure). During this phase, the child appears to recover insofar as he or she may begin to respond positively to other available caregivers. But importantly, from Bowlby's perspective, should the attachment figure return at this time, he or she is treated by the child with emotional detachment. The signs of detachment Bowlby identified were appearing not to recognise the attachment figure, being 'remote', apathetic and disinterested: 'He seems to have lost all interest in her' (1969/1982, p. 28).

Bowlby does not state how long this phase continues but it is succeeded eventually by the phase he termed *detachment*, if reunion does not occur. Again interpreting the observations of children experiencing prolonged hospitalisation under the conditions and policies prevailing at the time, Bowlby stated that if the child is exposed to a series of short-term carers (in this case, nurses) attachments may begin to form. However, if these are not sustained because of frequent staff changes, the child eventually stops forming attachments at all.

In the second book of the attachment trilogy, under the heading 'Prototypes of human sorrow', Bowlby explores the dynamics of separation experiences further. He states that the child's reaction to major separation from the mother or other primary attachment figure is a prototype for many pathological conditions later in life, and that while many children recover from such experiences without sustained ill effects, not all do.

Based primarily on the work of Heinicke and Westheimer (1966), Bowlby also describes children's responses to reunion with the attachment figure after long separations. Heinicke and Westheimer studied 10 children aged between 13 and 32 months who stayed at a residential nursery for periods of between two and 21 weeks, mostly because their mothers were hospitalised. Bowlby noted in particular the extent of the children's apparent detachment on reunion. Some children were observed to alternate tears with an expressionless face, but most ignored or appeared not to recognise the mothers from whom they had been separated so long. This detachment persisted for varying lengths of time, usually reflecting how long the preceding separation had lasted. A sequel of behaviours was identified: 'After briefer separations detachment gives way after a period lasting usually hours or days. It is commonly succeeded by a phase during which a child is markedly ambivalent towards his parents. On the one hand, he is demanding of their presence and cries bitterly when left; on the other, he may become rejecting, hostile, or defiant towards them' (Bowlby 1973, pp. 12–13).

In regards to how long this ambivalence continues, Bowlby's view was that this is determined by the reaction of the attachment figures. When parents respond in a calm, sensitive and reassuring way the child is able to resolve his or her feelings of rejection and/or abandonment more quickly than the child whose parents respond insensitively and/or with rejection in kind. Notable also in this study was the child's ongoing sensitivity to any further threats of, or actual, separations. The primary emotions aroused by extended separations thus are identified as fear, anger and anxiety.

The emotions that accompany major separations

From an attachment perspective, it should not surprise us that the child responds with fear and anxiety to major separations from the attachment figure. These two emotions are natural human responses to the perception of risk or danger. Being separated from the attachment figure is one of the 'natural cues' to danger (Ainsworth et al, 1978, p. 20). These cues not only elicit fear, they elicit and activate attachment behaviours as well because, in attachment terms, the role of the attachment relationship is to protect the child from danger. The child feels fear, and seeks the reassurance and security of the attachment figure's presence. If the attachment figure is absent, and the substitute carer is not yet a person the child trusts, the child's fear is compounded.

Fear can of course arise in the presence of an attachment figure if, based on previous experience, the child has built up an expectation that he or she will be insensitive or unresponsive to the child's need for protection, comfort and reassurance. Emotional availability, not just physical presence, is required to alleviate fear. Separation is not the only experience that elicits fear. Noise, heights, fantasy creatures and many other factors are associated with fear in young children. In every case, however, the presence of the attachment figure will be sought, and the secure child will be comforted by that presence.

Anger is another emotion aroused when children are separated from their attachment figure, or when there is threat of such separation. This is most likely to be expressed as aggression towards the attachment figure on reunion after prolonged separations. Bowlby construes this as an anger of hopeful reproach—that by being aggressive or expressing anger the attachment figures will 'learn' that their behaviour in leaving the child is not acceptable. It is an anger meant to discourage further separations, not disrupt the bond.

These forms of anger are different from the anger accompanying despair. According to Bowlby, the anger of despair is seen in response to repeated, prolonged separations, which are best conceptualised as an attachment loss. He draws attention to 'dysfunctional anger' (1973, p. 248) which occurs 'whenever a person, child or adult, becomes so intensely and/or persistently angry with his partner that the bond between them is weakened, instead of strengthened, and the partner is alienated' (pp. 248–9). In Bowlby's view, 'The most violently angry and dysfunctional responses of all, it seems probable, are elicited in children and adolescents who not only experience repeated separations but are constantly subjected to the threat of being abandoned' (p. 249). Strong and complex emotions accompany repeated or prolonged major separations, something that is well known to those working with children in child protection systems (e.g. see Fahlberg, 1994).

The response of the child to brief, everyday separations

So far we have considered how young children respond to major or so-called 'definitive' separations (Ainsworth et al, 1978, p. 18) that may continue over weeks or months. These are of course very different in nature from the brief separations that children may encounter frequently as part of their usual family routines. Ainsworth et al (1978) defined brief or 'everyday' separations as those that last up to several hours, occur in familiar environments and about which the child has built up 'a system of expectations' (p. 18). That is, they are separations which the child knows a lot about, such as when they occur, where they occur, with whom and for how long they last.

However, all these expectations take time to develop. Through a young child's eyes, any separation that does not follow a well-established, known routine has the potential to be major, and as such will likely be initially responded to as if it is. Any child faced with such a separation—at the moment when the attachment figure leaves, or later if expectations of an immediate return are not met—

will likely show intense attachment behaviours, and will protest strongly in trying to achieve a speedy reunion. These sorts of intense responses are most likely to be seen in the very young child whose cognitive abilities are insufficiently developed to allow him or her to understand verbal explanations from their attachment figures that they will return soon. They are also more likely to be seen in children who have received inaccurate information from their attachment figures in the past about the expected duration of separations, and who therefore do not trust the attachment figure to do as they say. The presence of caring, substitute attachment figures alleviates separation distress, if well known to the child.

These understandings based on attachment theory and research have led to many positive changes in the way children's major and more everyday separations from their attachment figures are handled. In hospitals it is not uncommon for parents to 'room in' with their sick child. In residential care settings, there is often a policy of assignment of one or a small number of primary carers to each child. In some child-care settings, the impact of attachment theory can also be seen. As we discussed in the case scenario at the end of chapter 6, the assignment of primary carers to infants and toddlers, and familiarisation periods in the presence of the parents prior to the first separation, are two ways in which attachment-guided principles have been applied in some child-care settings. Encouragement of toys and possessions from home is a third.

However, many working in the early childhood field know that the reality is often very far from the ideal. High staff turnover and other staffing-related issues mean that so-called 'primary-care' relationships are often disrupted or never really exist. Encouraged transition periods are not followed for many reasons, often having to do with the parents' desire to have the young child in their full-time care as long as possible (see next chapter in regard to parental separation anxiety) or because employment conditions do not allow it. Many young children begin child care with eight-hour days or longer, in a totally new environment, and with caregivers they have never met before. It may be very rare indeed for the ideal separation transition to be achieved.

The critical importance in the child-care setting of a transition period prior to actual separation is underlined in a research study reported by Rauh et al (2000), which makes the point that few studies of child care and attachment have controlled adequately for factors such as mode of introduction into a centre. In earlier work, Rottman and Ziegenhain (1988, as cited by Rauh et al, 2000) found that an abrupt mode of introduction into child care was associated with a change from secure to insecure attachment to the mother. They interpreted this as indicating that the infant in some way attributed the cause of their anger and anxiety to the mother who had left them behind in the child-care setting, and not to the caregiver with whom they were left, since the relationship with the caregiver showed no such disturbances. Since infants below the age of 12 months are unlikely to have the cognitive abilities to achieve this attribution, Rauh et al (2000) hypothesised that the mode of introduction to child care—whether abrupt or prolonged—would influence attachment relationships between infants and their mothers only when child care began after 12 months of age: 'We propose that coping with separation events, even when these involve high-quality day care, is a critical experience of paramount importance for young infants' (pp. 255–6).

In their study, introduction to child care was coded as lenient if attendance lasted two hours or less in the first days, and increased slowly after that, up to four hours per day after a month. It was coded as abrupt when the infant stayed at least four hours from the first days. They also coded the extent to which the mother remained with her infant during the introduction phase. This was coded as short ('abrupt') when the mother stayed with the child for no more than two hours in the first three or four days and left him/her unaccompanied for at least one hour. It was coded as long ('lenient') when the mother accompanied the child throughout the first week and did not leave the child for more than one hour each day. In their sample, 20 infants (37 per cent) experienced an abrupt entry in respect of both duration of daily attendance and amount of maternal company. Only three infants (5.5 per cent) attended for long hours from the start but were accompanied by their mothers. Sixteen infants (29.6 per cent) had short attendance on early days but were left by their mothers during these times, and 15 infants (27.8 per cent) experienced 'lenient' familiarisation and maternal company.

The study found that for infants who started day care between 12 and 18 months of age, those who were securely attached to their mother at 21 months had mainly experienced a lenient mode of familiarisation. Those who were insecurely attached to their mother at age 21 months had an abrupt mode of familiarisation. This effect was found to be independent of maternal sensitivity ratings prior to child-care attendance. The authors conclude that a sensitive mothering experience contributes in critical ways to quality of attachment. Child-care attendance, in and of itself, does not appear to directly influence the relationship. 'The kind of familiarisation, however, did make a difference for some of the children but only in later infancy' (Rauh et al, 2000, pp. 270–1).

These findings should not be taken to mean that child-care entry is not stressful for young infants under 12 months of age. But, according to the authors, it is unlikely that before 12 months of age infants have developed a 'working model' of their mother that enables them to attribute their experiences of separation distress to the attachment figure. They conclude that there are 'quite strong indications that from about 1 year of age, infants tend to put the "blame" for their unpleasant, abrupt familiarisation with day care on their emotional relationship with their mothers, and that these experiences can influence their future quality of attachment' (pp. 275–6). This research raises many interesting questions about the complexity of factors that determine how child care affects attachment relationships.

Factors determining the response of the child to separations

There are obviously many factors that influence how distressed a child feels in response to separation. Clearly, the nature, form and intensity of the child's reactions will be determined by the length of the separation, the familiarity of the environment, the familiarity of the substitute caregivers—including whether or not the child has met the carers previously while still in the care of the parent—

and the number of 'mother-substitutes' who care for the child. Less distress is associated with more familiar care environments, with the availability of one or a small number of alternative caregivers, and with having met the caregiver while still in the care of the mother or other primary attachment figure. Ainsworth et al (1978) also note that major separations cause more anxiety if the child lacks information about the separation, why it is occurring and how long it might last. Limited understanding might also contribute to why very young children are particularly vulnerable to separations.

Although attachment researchers initially expected that children with insecure attachment relationships prior to separation would show the most distress, and more disturbed behaviour following separation, this was not supported by subsequent observational data. Indeed, as we would now expect based on our clearer understanding of the attachment relationship, and how security and insecurity of attachment impacts on child behaviour and emotional expression, it was the children who appeared most securely attached prior to separation who showed the greatest distress during separation (Ainsworth et al, 1978).

Age is another factor influencing the response of a child to separation. Any separation from a primary attachment figure is usually more distressing for infants and young children than for the older child. Separation anxiety first appears around six months of age, and has long been considered to reach its peak at around 15 months of age (e.g. Kagan et al 1978). Reasons for the decreasing dependence of the older child on the physical presence of the attachment figure, discussed in earlier chapters, include the cognitive sophistication of the older child, and their growing independence in other domains. Indeed, by the age of five or six years, or even before, our society generally expects a child to be able to separate readily from the attachment figure and the attachment figure to be able to separate from the child. It is rare for children to experience significant distress to brief, and/or predictable longer separations, beyond the age of five or six years. School refusal is one example of this.

It is timely to note here that the absence of distress at separation, especially if the separation is brief and predictable, should not lead us to infer an absence of attachment to the departed figure. Ainsworth et al (1978), for example, found that crying in response to separation was prevalent in two-year-olds, less frequent in 2½-year-olds, and usually not seen in three- and four-year-olds.

Just as there are developmental changes in separation distress, so too are there changes in reactions to strangers. Thus, at the same time as many infants are first experiencing separations from their attachment figures, they are also at the stage of development in which fear of strangers grows. According to Bowlby (1969/1982) there is considerable individual variation in the age when stranger anxiety is shown, and how strongly it is expressed. This also depends on how the stranger behaves. Stranger anxiety can be seen as early as six months of age, but in some infants it may not be seen until the second year. When stranger anxiety peaks is also very variable, from seven months into the second year.

Finally, it is clear that other factors, such as temperament, how a child is feeling on a particular day, and events immediately preceding the separation and/or reunion will all impact on how the child (and indeed the adult) reacts and responds. Bowlby also noted how familiar possessions, toys or other items from home, can bring 'some measure of comfort' (1973, p. 16) during separation experiences.

How brief separations affect child development

The position of Bowlby and Ainsworth

While Bowlby, Ainsworth and other attachment theorists and researchers were clearly most concerned about major separation experiences on children's development, they did not consider brief separations to be totally innocuous. Drawing on observations of how Ganda children responded with distress when left with other caregivers for a few hours each day so their mother could tend the garden, Ainsworth et al (1978) state: 'Previous separation experiences may, however, make an infant or young child all the more alert to the likelihood of separation in a given situation . . . a child with a history of major (or even a series of seemingly minor) separation experiences is not likely to be as trusting as a child who has had no previous unhappy separations' (p. 271). In other words, in Ainsworth's view, young children who experience repeated separations, if they are not handled well, become 'sensitized to separation by their frequent, long absences from home' (p. 271).

In the second volume of the attachment trilogy, Bowlby directly discussed the effects of daily substitute care on the security of child–parent attachment. The data he had to draw on at the time were limited, and sometimes confounded by variables such as parental personality or mental health issues, and hospitalisation of the child. Sample sizes for children in child-care settings were very small. Based largely on clinical experience, Bowlby concluded that full-time child care before the third birthday should be cautioned against, noting however that: 'The more stable and predictable the regime [of substitute care] the more secure a child's attachment tends to be; the more discontinuous and unpredictable the regime the more anxious his attachment' (1973, p. 225).

Bowlby's early speculations about the effects of child care formed a very small part of his analysis of attachment, separation, loss and personality development. His analysis focused instead on experiences including hospitalisation, residential and foster care, parental threats of abandonment or suicide, parental suicide attempts and fear of parental desertion following family conflict. In fact, it was children receiving daily child care who in some cases formed the control group in those studies he could draw upon at the time. In his later writings (e.g. Bowlby, 1988) his position regarding the negative impacts of brief separations on primary attachment relationships was 'dropped' (Rutter and O'Connor, 1999, p. 827). This was largely because he had, by then, a more substantial empirical literature to draw upon. At the time he was developing his theory, there were only two main studies evaluating the effects of child-care attendance (Moore, 1969; Blehar, 1974). Since then there have been hundreds, maybe thousands, of studies and articles and books written on the matter.

The research literature on the effects of child care

Since the books of the attachment trilogy were written, many developmentalists have attempted to answer the question of whether relatively brief, predictable separations between young children and their primary attachment figure(s)—most usually associated with maternal employment and child-care attendance—are damaging to the emotional wellbeing of the child and deleterious to the security of the primary attachment relationship, and to subsequent attachment relationships with early childhood professionals. These studies have often generated conflicting results, some indicating negative effects on attachment associated with child-care attendance, some finding no effects—although studies without statistically significant results often go unpublished—and some reporting positive outcomes.

For example, Harrison and Ungerer (1997) studied child-care predictors of attachment security at one year of age in a sample of 145 infants and their mothers in Sydney, Australia. The study, part of the Sydney Family Development Project, found that more than 10 hours of non-maternal child care per week was associated with *increased proportions* of secure attachments compared to child-care attendances less than 10 hours per week, and that overall the percentage of secure attachments amongst infants in child care (62 per cent) was similar to most normative samples. They also reported that when care was based in government-regulated formal child-care services (particularly home-based), there was a higher incidence of secure attachments compared with the percentage for infants in non-regulated, informal services.

In discussing their results, the authors argue that minimal hours of care (less than 10 hours per week) may be more 'disruptive' and 'emotionally unsettling' (p. 44) than longer hours. It terms of the separation component of the experience per se, they state: 'Short, irregular periods of child care may be insufficient for the child to develop a sense of familiarity and mastery over the separation experience' (p. 44).

It is beyond the scope of this chapter to review the plethora of studies that have investigated the effects of child care on attachment security. The interested reader is referred to other published works that have undertaken this task (e.g. Belsky and Steinberg, 1978; Clarke-Stewart, 1988; Fox and Fein, 1990; Rutter and O'Connor, 1999; Goldberg, 2000). The area has been highly controversial, especially in relation to separation of infants and toddlers from their attachment figures. One reason for the emotionally charged nature of the debate has been that the topic often brings a juxtaposition of women's rights to be employed outside the home on the one hand, and children's rights on the other. Another is that the stakes are very high, since some studies have argued that child-care attendance puts infant–parent attachments at risk of insecurity (e.g. Belsky, 1986, 1989; Lamb and Sternberg, 1990). The controversy appears to have been most heated in Western industrialised nations, such as the United States, that may not have in place family support policies making it financially viable for parents to remain at home with their children during the infancy and preschool years if they so wish.

In an attempt to resolve the inconclusive and/or contradictory outcomes of studies in this area over more than 40 years, and the various interpretations based on them, a large-scale, prospective longitudinal study commenced in the United States in the late 1980s, under a consortium called the National Institute of Child Health and Development (NICHD) Early Child Care Research Network (1997). The consortium included many of the key researchers whose work, published in the preceding decade or so, represented various views and conclusions about the effects of early child care.

Over 1000 infants were included in the sample, which was 'large enough to allow examination of interactions between child, family and alternative care variables' (Goldberg, 2000, p. 103). This was important because in many previous studies it had been impossible to disentangle the respective effects of these factors due to small sample sizes. That is, if differences were found between those infants who attended child care and those who did not, it was not possible to establish whether the differences were due to child-care attendance per se, or whether they reflected the impact of other factors. These factors included variability in the way young children with child-care experience respond to assessment techniques like the Strange Situation, pre-existing differences in the family, and variations in the type or quality of the child-care environment attended.

In describing the study, Goldberg (2000) refers to it as the 'last word on the US controversy in the 1990s' (p. 104) and others reviewing the literature consider it to be the 'most rigorous, and most systematic evaluation of day care ever undertaken' (Rutter and O'Connor, 1999, p. 828). Infants and their families were visited at home at ages one, six and 15 months. If infants were in any form of child care, they were visited there as well at ages six and 15 months. Mother–infant attachment was assessed at 15 months.

In brief, the study did not find that child-care attendance during infancy in and of itself undermines secure attachment. In fact this major study found, as many other studies had reported before it, that there were no significant differences in attachment security according to child-care factors. Rather the quality of attachment to the mother was directly related to the quality of maternal caregiving, namely her sensitive responsiveness to the child. Summing up the results, Goldberg (2000) states that: 'Poor-quality alternative care, increased hours of care, and changes in care arrangements were associated with insecure attachment when combined with low ratings of maternal sensitivity/responsiveness' (p. 104).

Implications and applications

CASE SCENARIO

In this case scenario, Zamia reflects for us on Eli's first weeks at the child-care centre, noting in particular how important to her 'settling' was the extended transition to child care (see case scenario in chapter 6). We also hear comments from Eli's mother, Anna, regarding this transition phase.

Zamia: *Anna had enrolled for a child-care place during her pregnancy and I remember the first time I met Eli. She was just one month old and Anna and David (Eli's father) brought her to the centre so we could all meet her. Although it would be three months before Eli started child care full-time, Anna and David were committed to helping Eli feel at home in the centre before she started.*

At one month of age Eli didn't appear at all fazed by being passed around from adult to adult. I already knew I was going to be Eli's special caregiver when she started so I was keen to get to know her as well as I could. On that first day, Anna, David and I spoke for a while about Eli's temperament, her likes and dislikes, and so on. Over the next months, Anna or David popped in with Eli about once a week. When Eli was about three months old, I asked Anna and David if they would feel comfortable with me visiting their home, so that I could talk some more with them about Eli, and so Eli could see me in her home environment. They readily agreed.

During their first visits to the centre, Anna and David would only stay a short while, walking around the infant room with Eli, talking to staff, and showing Eli some of the toys. Occasionally they would change Eli on the nappy-change table, just so she could get used to this as well. During the month before Eli started full-time, Anna would leave her with me and go, at first for short periods, then for up to an hour or two. All this was encouraged by the centre, in line with its attachment-based program.

I guess because Eli was by then already familiar with me, and with her child-care room, she never cried when Anna left, although she did cry the morning she began full-time. Anna cried that day too. I feel Eli's transition to child care was handled very well. Not all parents can do it this way. I'm sure how well Eli has settled reflects the way she began child care.

Anna: I always knew Eli would be going to child care full-time from a young age. It was very hard, but I began looking at child-care centres as soon as I knew I was pregnant, and we settled on this centre after a lot of thought and asking around. I liked the way they encouraged us to visit the centre and get a feel for it before making up our minds. More than any other centre they seemed to understand just what a big decision this was for us. I thought this would be a good indication of what I could expect once we were enrolled, and I was right.

Taking Eli to the centre from a young age wasn't easy for me as there were days when I didn't want to even think about our impending separation. But in hindsight, I wouldn't do it any other *way. In fact, I've told several friends in the same situation to do it that way too if their centres allow it.*

There's no doubt in my mind that the gentle introduction helped Eli. I know it helped David and me. By the time Eli started full-time, she was quite familiar with Zamia, and so was I. I felt confident that Zamia had a good working knowledge of Eli's needs. It was still really hard leaving her that first day, and for some time later. But to be quite honest, I don't think I would have been able to go back to work at all if I'd done it any other way.

QUESTIONS FOR REFLECTION

- From an attachment perspective, what is achieved for Eli by the gradual transition to child care?
- In what ways might centres do more to encourage parents to introduce young children to child care more gradually than is usually the case?
- What impediments exist to the gradual transition to child care Eli experienced?
- What are the benefits to Anna, David and Zamia of the gradual transition? Who else may benefit?

DISCUSSION POINTS

From an attachment perspective, the transition to child care is crucially important. Getting to know new people takes time for any young child, and attachment theory warns that separation from the primary attachment figure is traumatic if there are no familiar, substitute caregivers present. The gradual transition allowed Eli and her parents to get to know the centre and its staff, to feel more comfortable with them and enabled Anna and David to form a relationship with those people who would be caring for their child. Eli had an opportunity to see her new carer and parents together, both in the centre and at home. It was very important to David and Anna that by the time Eli started child care, her caregivers had a good working knowledge of Eli's needs. This lessened their anxiety and distress in leaving Eli.

Further readings

Bowlby, J. 1973 *Attachment and Loss: Vol. 2. Separation, anxiety and anger* New York: Basic Books

Fein, G.G. 1995 'Infants in group care: Patterns of despair and detachment' *Early Childhood Research Quarterly* vol. 10, pp. 261–75

NICHD Early Child Care Research Network 1997 'The effects of infant child care on infant–mother attachment security: Results of the NICHD study of early child care' *Child Development* vol. 68, pp. 860–79

Sims, M. and Hutchins, T. 1999 'Positive transitions' *Australian Journal of Early Childhood* vol. 24, pp. 12–16

11

Adult attachment issues

Adult attachment representations and intergenerational attachment issues have been described earlier. In this chapter we explore the adult side of the attachment relationship further. Factors which influence the attachment figure's ability to provide sensitive, responsive care are discussed, with a focus on mental health issues, including maternal depression. How adults respond to attachment-related experiences, such as separation, discussed earlier in relation to the child, are also considered. Finally therapeutic interventions to increase sensitivity are reviewed, and the concept of the 'resilient' attachment figure introduced.

The adult's contribution to the attachment relationship

Bowlby considered the adult side of the attachment relationship in the first volume of the attachment trilogy. At its most basic level, the attachment relationship requires that sufficient physical proximity be maintained between child and adult to guarantee the child's safety in times of threat or danger. To ensure the attachment system works, the adult must remain vigilant to the whereabouts of the child, monitor his or her wellbeing and be motivated (and available) to respond if the child moves too far away, is in danger, or expresses anxiety, distress or need for comfort. Bowlby commented in particular on the critical importance of the caregiving behaviour he termed 'retrieving'. In essence this consists of the attachment figure approaching the infant, lifting and then holding the child in their arms.

Many factors impact upon caregiving behaviour. Amongst them are other tasks and responsibilities that compete with the caregiving role. However, Bowlby saw competing tasks, such as household duties, paid employment and other relationship responsibilities, as far less concerning than factors he described as 'inherently incompatible with care' (1969/1982, p. 242). These include feelings of aversion to physical contact with the child, and/or aversion to one or more of the usual cues to retrieval, such as crying or other signs of distress. Although all caregivers are likely to experience negative feelings to these things occasionally, and briefly, Bowlby's concerns were with those caregivers who felt this way all or most of the time.

Caregiving behaviour and caregiver mental health

Amongst the circumstances that might lead an attachment figure to experience these major bonding and caregiving difficulties are those associated with poor mental health. One such case that has been extensively studied is maternal depression. Depression in adults is usually associated with a range of symptoms incompatible with sensitive, responsive and consistent psychological availability to others, including children. In discussing the impact of maternal depression on attachment relationships, Radke-Yarrow (1991) states:

> Translation of the classic symptoms of depression into the role of mother suggests problems for the mother–child relationship: depression is characterised by feelings of hopelessness and lack of self worth, low involvement and low energy, disordered interpersonal relationships, episodic emotional dysregulation, and psychological

unavailability. Such impairments in the mother would seem to place the child in a perilous and uncertain caregiving environment (p. 115).

More recently, Teti (2000) has explored the outcomes of maternal depression for child–mother attachment during infancy and the early childhood period. The consistency of findings in the extensive research literature reviewed provide compelling evidence, according to Teti, that young children with depressed mothers are at an increased risk of developing an insecure attachment. Maternal depression is associated with lower levels of sensitivity, less warmth, flat affect and low levels of engagement with their children. Furthermore, Teti (2000) found that depressed mothers

> were often preoccupied and absorbed with worries about issues that had little to do with their relationship with their children; thus they appeared to tend to the needs of their children sporadically, when they had the energy reserves to do so. Indeed, the predominant theme characterising many of the depressed mothers in this sample was inconsistency and, for mothers of older children, an inability to cope with the demands their children placed on them. It is perhaps not surprising that, as a result, the proportion of anxious–ambivalent infants was greater among infants of depressed mothers (23.3%) than among infants of nondepressed mothers (10%), and among preschoolers of depressed mothers (38.8%) than among preschoolers of nondepressed mothers (21.8%) . . . This was especially true of children of mothers who were 'intermittently' depressed, among whom the highest proportion of Type C attachments were found (p. 208).

Disorganised and atypical attachments among infants and preschoolers were associated with severe and chronic maternal depression, probably because the behaviours shown by these mothers are at times 'frightened and/or frightening' to the child. As already discussed, Main and Solomon (1990) consider these to be the central elements of caregiving that predispose children to form a disorganised attachment. Caregiving may include violent and unpredictable outbursts of anger or distress directed to the child, or to other children or adults while the child is present. Particularly frightening would be the occurrence of such behaviours in direct response to the child's bid for comfort or reassurance.

Parental separation anxiety

In discussing different cultures of the time, Bowlby (1969/1982) noted that in contrast to non-industrialised societies, in which mother and infant often remain in very close physical proximity, in industrialised communities the mother may not be the person who cares for the infant at all times, making for a more complex situation. He states that even when the mother has arranged for another person to care for the infant, she is likely to still experience a 'strong pull' (p. 241) to be with her child.

Object relations theorists identify a process of separation or individuation that occurs gradually for both attachment figure and child as the child moves into the early childhood stage (Winnicott, 1965; Mahler et al, 1975). Furthermore, using a case-study approach, it has been observed that some mothers feel more comfortable with the demands of caregiving during those stages of their child's development requiring much physical and emotional closeness, while other mothers prefer stages in which the child is more autonomous (Mahler et al, 1975) and caregiving demands are more to do with managing independence rather than dependency needs.

Quantitative research measuring parental separation anxiety

There is much research confirming Bowlby's view, and that of other theorists, that attachment figures may experience anxiety about being separated from their young children. Most of the research has investigated these feelings in mothers, and the term 'maternal separation anxiety' has been coined. Ellen Hock's pioneering work in the United States (e.g. Hock, 1984; DeMeis, Hock and McBride, 1986; Hock, McBride and Gnezda, 1989) found that mothers differed in the extent of their apprehensions and concerns about being separated from their infant. Hock and her colleagues hypothesised that maternal separation anxiety is influenced by personality attributes (such as 'need to nurture') and role-related conflicts around motherhood and employment. They found that lower levels of separation anxiety in the mother were associated with higher adjustment to child care in the child, and that separation anxiety generally decreases from infancy to early school age (Hock and Schirtzinger, 1992). The initially high levels of anxiety needed to sustain careful maternal monitoring and physical closeness give way in the healthy mother–child relationship to separation–individuation and decreasing concern about independent activities as the child moves into the early childhood phase. Hock et al (1988) also found that the extent of maternal separation anxiety is related to the type of child care chosen, with mothers lowest in anxiety more likely to choose centre-based care rather than home-based family day care.

Hock and her colleagues developed a questionnaire to measure maternal separation anxiety, the Maternal Separation Anxiety Scale (MSAS) (Hock et al, 1988). Australian research using this instrument has confirmed a number of Hock's findings. For example, Rolfe (1997) reports the results of a nine-month, longitudinal study of 156 Australian mothers with a child aged two years or less. Questionnaires were completed at three-monthly intervals and participants categorised into three groups: those who used child care for their infant throughout the study (75 women), those who cared for their infant at home throughout the study (32 women) and those who started using child care for their infant while the study was underway (33 women). While there were some changes in the type of child care used, almost all mothers initially using centre-based care were still using this form of care, either solely or in combination with other forms of care, at the conclusion of the study.

The possible range of scores on the questionnaire is from 7 (no, or minimal anxiety) to 35 (very high anxiety). The range of scores obtained from the study was high. For example, on the subscale which directly measures feelings of sadness and anxiety about separation, scores ranged from 12–32 at the beginning of the study, and remained at 10–34 by the end of the study. Analysis of group means showed that sadness and anxiety levels were significantly lower in mothers using child care at all measurement points, and declined significantly over time for all groups. But this was not the pattern for all women. For example, one woman at home with her infant had a 15-point increase in her anxiety scores during the nine months of the study (compared to a mean decrease for the group as a whole of 2.7). The finding of such heightened anxiety over time supports earlier conclusions that some mothers 'grow comparatively more convinced about the value of caring for their infants or more resistant to or threatened by the idea of daily, employment-related separation' (DeMeis et al, 1986, p. 631).

In another Australian study, Davis (1997) investigated separation anxiety in a group of fathers using a modified version of the MSAS. She found that while paternal separation anxiety was lower than maternal separation anxiety, the spread of scores was similar to that of mothers. Mirroring outcomes for mothers, the data also revealed that not all fathers are distressed by separation from their infant. For some parents, separation in the context of infant child care is a straightforward, positive experience. For others, it is an experience accompanied by great distress, anxiety and guilt.

There is growing evidence for an important link between maternal attitudes and feelings, use of child care, and security of attachment (e.g. Stifter et al, 1993; Harrison and Ungerer, 2002). Stifter et al (1993) found that security of attachment was linked to lower levels of maternal separation anxiety. In their recent study of Australian mothers and their first-born infants, Harrison and Ungerer (2002) found that maternal attitudes to paid employment before their child was born, as well as when the mother returned to work, significantly affected attachment security. These effects were independent of other factors such as maternal sensitivity. Mothers who were more committed to paid employment, less anxious about the use of child care and hence less 'conflicted' (p. 769) were more likely to have infants who were securely attached. So too were mothers who returned to work earlier. The authors report the proportion of securely attached infants in dyads in which the mother returned to work before the infant was five months of age as 72 per cent. This reduced to 62 per cent in dyads in which return to work occurred between the ages of five and 12 months and to 45 per cent in dyads in which the mother did not return to work at all.

As Harrison and Ungerer note, the effect for dyads in which the mother returned to work is consistent with predictions from attachment theory (that is, that predictable separations established in the attachment-in-the-making stage may be less disruptive than separations begun after a clear-cut attachment has formed). However, this cannot explain the higher rate of insecurity in the dyads in which the mother remained at home. In interpreting this outcome, the authors advance the view that mothers who do not return to paid employment during their infant's first year, and who have insecure/resistant infants, may be those who are particularly anxious about providing close care and attention to the child's dependency needs, perhaps because they do not trust the infant's ability to signal, or do not trust their own ability to care for and protect the child. Harrison and Ungerer also suggest that in societies where maternal employment rates are high, those mothers who remain at home may feel isolated or lack emotional support. Data from their sample are consistent with this possibility.

Interventions to reduce parental separation anxiety

From a family-systems perspective (see chapter 7), it is not at all surprising that how the attachment figure feels about separation will affect how the child-care experience impacts on the child. That is, if an insecure relationship to the mother is found in children who attend child care, this may reveal direct effects of the child-care experience itself (that is, what the child experiences in that setting), but it may also reveal important indirect effects on the child, resulting from how the mother or other primary attachment figure feels about the experience. For example, highly anxious or distressed parents may become overly protective of their child during times they are together to compensate for periods spent apart, and may themselves show heightened levels of distress during separations. This would be expected to affect how the child responds as well, likely increasing their distress. This has clear implications for early childhood staff who support parents and children as they go through the early stages of child-care use.

There is only limited research on interventions designed to reduce parental separation anxiety. In one Australian study, Davison (1994) failed to reduce maternal separation anxiety levels through interventions such as providing factual information on the potential benefits of child care, and the provision of a mothers' support/ discussion group. However, as the author notes, her interventions were introduced about three months after child care began and may have had a greater impact if timed to occur earlier in the child-care experience.

Qualitative study of parents' experiences of separation

In an attempt to gain a better understanding of the complexity and diversity of mothers' responses to separation from their infants, Rolfe and her colleagues conducted two qualitative studies of mothers using infant child care. In the first study, 10 mothers whose infants had entered child care prior to 18 months of age were interviewed once (Rolfe et al, 1991; Rolfe and Richards, 1993). In the second study (see Rolfe and Richards, 1994), 16 mothers using centre-based day care for their first-born infant aged less than 12 months were interviewed four times, giving a total of 64 interviews, ranging from about one to four hours in length. The first interview occurred during the week prior to the infant's entry into the child-care centre, a second around two or three weeks later, and two further interviews at three-month intervals thereafter. In this study, diaries were provided at the first interview and were used by the women as they wished during the nine months of the study.

Women in each study were encouraged to reflect on their feelings about the child-care experience in general and about separation from their infant in particular. In line with results from quantitative studies, it was found that very high levels of sadness and anxiety were expressed by some (but not all) women, especially in the weeks before and immediately after child care began. One woman encapsulated the feelings of others with the words, 'It was heartbreaking. I felt just torn in two.' In part, these feelings were linked to attachment-related fears about the wellbeing and safety of their infants when they (the mothers) were not present and hence were unable to monitor the child for themselves. These sorts of anxieties are evident in the words of two of the study participants:

> JENNY: I'm absolutely convinced nobody is going to be able to care for him like I do . . . the best I can expect is that the people like children and are going to give him a bit of time . . . I'd hate to think that he's going into a centre and they just change his nappy and feed him when he wants to and leave him to do his own thing for the rest of the day . . . and really it's out of your control because you're not there.
>
> HANNAH: I have him with me all day and I know what he's like, so there are different things we do and I do to settle him or to entertain him or whatever and they are not going to know any of those things. I mean I know it's not supposed to be home, it's not going to be like home, but how are they going to know?

By the third interview, about four months after commencing child care, most women had achieved an apparent resolution of their grief and anxiety, in many cases born of their growing trust in child-care staff to meet the needs of their infant:

> INTERVIEWER: And so, would you say that being separated from Angela is becoming easier or harder?
>
> SANDRA: . . . I think it is easier in a way, because I know that, you start to accept that other people can do it . . . You tend to think, oh I'm the only one who can look after my own child. You tend to then realise no, that is not right. And then when you get the taste of being able to do what you want to do for a few hours in a day, it is quite, you don't mind, or I don't mind anyway.
>
> INTERVIEWER: You enjoy it?
>
> SANDRA: Yes, I do. I couldn't stay home all the time, not now.

A positive and unexpected aspect of the child-care experience for many women was the extent to which early childhood professionals became important and, in some cases, essential partners in the process of raising a child. The experience thus moved from one of anxiety, sadness and guilt to one of the reassurance afforded by shared care and parenting support. The child-care experience had the potential, therefore, despite issues to do with the pain of separation, to impact positively on the mother–child relationship through the support it provided the mother in her caregiving role.

Stress and support as determinants of caregiving quality

Earlier we considered how the amount of stress in a person's life, and the amount of support, will influence the kind of caregiving shown. Bowlby emphasised that attachment theory is not about blaming caregivers for insecure attachments in children. It recognises that the amount of emotional support available, and a caregiver's own attachment history, both influence caregiving style. And it offers a realistic, honest and thorough appraisal of why insecurities in children occur and how caregivers might be helped to promote secure attachment with children.

Attachment theory from the beginning underlined the challenging nature of caregiving in general, and of sensitive, responsive caregiving in particular. As Bowlby (1988) noted, 'To be a successful parent means a lot of very hard work' (p. 2). Despite a widespread view to the contrary, he did not believe that the responsibilities for caregiving should fall to the shoulders of one person, and he was highly critical of societies that allowed such a state of affairs to develop (see Bowlby, 1988, p. 2).

Learning to be sensitive?

Given the many factors that influence caregiver sensitive responsiveness, answering the question of how best to promote it is clearly very complex indeed. Parents and professional caregivers alike bring to their tasks a very diverse range of attachment experiences from their families of origin. As we have seen in earlier chapters, some of these experiences may have led them to develop psychological defences, such as denial, that are associated with avoidant attachments in children. The children of adults who remain enmeshed with their early caregiving experiences appear to be more likely to develop resistant attachments. Clearly, adults who have themselves experienced unhappy, psychologically damaging attachment relationships need opportunities to resolve their feelings in order to optimise the chances for secure attachments in their children. Sometimes opportunities for resolution come through the romantic relationships or close friendships that are formed in adolescence or adulthood. Sometimes further opportunities come through therapeutic interventions, including individual or family-based counselling.

According to Bowlby, if counselling occurs it must be directed towards the person's internal working models of self and others, allowing the person to 'reappraise and restructure' them (1988, p. 138). To do this, the therapist must provide a secure base, and be a 'trusted companion' (p. 138) for this exploration. There needs to be careful analysis, assisted by the therapist, of current relationships, and especially of problematic interactions, including those encountered with the therapist. Links between current social–emotional functioning and early attachment experiences need to be explored. Finally, there is a need for the old models to be revisited, and seen 'for what they are, the not unreasonable products of his past experiences or of what he has been repeatedly told' (p. 139). Importantly, there is a need for working models to be imagined that are more concordant with newly developing, more positive ways of feeling, functioning and relating.

The ultimate aim of attachment-focused therapy is thus to free a person from 'being a slave to old and unconscious stereotypes and to feel, to think, and to act in new ways' (Bowlby, 1988, p. 139). With children the process is probably quite similar, except that it is best undertaken within the child's current attachment relationships rather than with a therapist per se. Most attachment interventions with children involve the attachment figures in central ways, with the therapist taking the role of model and guide (e.g. see Randolph, 2000).

Since Bowlby's original formulations, there have been a number of research studies whose results support his view that it is through a remaking of representational models that a person is most likely to achieve greater sensitivity to others, including the children one cares for (e.g. Main and Goldwyn, 1984; Grossmann et al, 1988; Main, 1991; Fonagy et al, 1994). Of great importance is the ability to be able to reflect on past experiences constructively and achieve an honest and coherent understanding of early attachment relationships, including why they occurred and how they influenced one's own development. The process is well described by Howe (1995) for mothers, and it probably applies equally to other attachment figures.

> Mothers who hold coherent and consistent models of their own attachment history, whether that history was favourable or unfavourable, are more likely to develop integrated models of self and personality structures as well as enjoy secure attachments with their own children. Main and her colleagues believe that those who can access, process and organise all aspects of their relationship history, whether pleasant or painful, are likely to develop more fully integrated personality structures (Main, 1991). In turn this allows them to respond accurately and sensitively to the emotional condition of others, including their own children. Fonagy et al (1994: 245) also add that reflective mothers with a deprived childhood appear capable of more effective planning, finding a supportive partner, and learning from experience (pp. 181–2).

Work such as this has led to the coining of the term 'resilient parent' (see Howe, 1995, pp. 182–3) although the term 'resilient attachment figure' is more appropriate to the focus of this book. The above discussion has focused on the role of professional therapists in helping those with negative childhood attachment experiences achieve or 'earn' security in later life, but supportive relationships with sensitive, affirming partners and friends can also help to 'disconfirm' an insecure working model (Howe, 1995).

Despite his emphasis on psychological, often unconscious processes, Bowlby did not ignore the role of learning in the process of becoming a sensitive caregiver. He explicitly acknowledged the importance of opportunities to observe first hand how sensitive caregiving is 'done'. He was not at all confident that sensitivity could be taught by instruction, but emphasised an apprenticeship-type model, especially for young adults contemplating the tasks of parenting:

We seek always to teach by example, not precept, by discussion, not instruction. The more we can give young people opportunities to meet with and observe *at first hand* how sensitive, caring parents treat their offspring, the more likely are they to follow suit. To learn directly from such parents about the difficulties they meet with and the rewards they obtain, and to discuss with them both their mistakes and their successes, are worth, I believe, hundreds of instructional talks (1988, pp. 16–19).

Implications and applications

CASE SCENARIO

In this case scenario, Ryan's caregiver, Jung, reflects on her own early attachment experiences and how these, and her experiences later in life, have impacted on her ability to provide sensitive, responsive caregiving.

Jung: My family — Mum, Dad, my three older sisters and me — first came to Australia when I was an infant. My parents worked very hard, and spent many hours each day away from home. My sisters primarily cared for me, but they also helped out in the family business. So there was a lot of stress. My parents and sisters were always tired, and I remember being left on my own a lot. I also remember crying because I was lonely and afraid, but no-one came. It was a very sad time.

My mother died when I was 12 years old. This made our lives even more unhappy and difficult. I helped out in the family business, along with my sisters. My father wanted me to do well at school, and he was very strict, so I focused on my studies every opportunity I had. I knew I wanted to work with children, and was determined to become qualified to do so. School was actually a special place for me. It was often where I felt most secure. I loved the routine. I had good teachers, and in high school there was one special teacher. She helped me feel more confident in myself. She helped me to believe that I could achieve what I wanted in life. My earlier

*experiences had made me feel inferior to everyone else. I suffered
from low self-esteem, but my teacher made a difference. I began to
believe in myself.*

*My sisters and I are now very close. We have talked a lot about
our early family life, and how it has affected us. I know that for a
long time I found it difficult to talk about those times, but now I feel
like I've made sense of it. I realise how much my parents were trying
to make a positive life for their family. My mother's death affected
me profoundly, but with the help of my school friends and sisters,
I got through a difficult grieving process. I get along okay with my
father now. He hasn't changed much, and I accept that he probably
never will.*

*My early life has made me realise how much young children
need consistent, available caregivers who are there to respond to
their needs. In my work, I am very aware of this, and work hard to
put these aspirations into practice.*

QUESTIONS FOR REFLECTION

- What aspects of Jung's early attachment experiences, as she describes them, will have impacted in a negative way on her internal working model of self?

- Which resilience-promoting factors can you identify from Jung's description of her life history?

- What in particular appears to have helped Jung to reflect on her past experiences constructively, why they occurred, and what impact they have had?

- Do you believe that an understanding of internal working models and adult attachment representations would be helpful to those working in the early childhood field?

- How would you conceptualise your own adult attachment representations?

DISCUSSION POINTS

Jung's description indicates periods early in her life when she did not receive consistent, sensitive and responsive care. She identifies times when there was no-one to respond to her needs, and other times when stress and sheer exhaustion undermined the ability of her family to be responsive to her needs. In the absence of her parents, her sisters were probably far too young to care for an infant, and this, along with their other responsibilities, appears to have put a great deal of stress on them.

Nevertheless, Jung identifies school and her school friends and teachers as sources of comfort and security for her. They appear to have been very important sources of support at the time of her mother's death.

It is clear that her positive relationship with her sisters in adult life has helped bring a resolution for her in relation to early attachment experiences. Her honest and coherent account reveals insight into how her experiences have impacted on her development.

Jung has also used her own negative experiences to help strengthen her commitment to provide sensitive, responsive care to the children she works with. Earlier case scenarios of interactions between Jung and Ryan bear testimony to the success of her resolve.

Further readings

Benoit, D. and Parker, K.C.H. 1994 'Stability and transmission of attachment across three generations' *Child Development* vol. 65, pp. 1444–56

Berlin, L.J. and Cassidy, J. 2001 'Enhancing early child–parent relationships: Implications of adult attachment research' *Infants and Young Children* vol. 14, pp. 64–76

12

Cultural perspectives on attachment

Attachment theory and research are fields of endeavour with many and varied accomplishments. However, the study of attachment, and its theoretical underpinnings, is not without controversy, and there have been critics. Some argue that from its original, focused definition as a behavioural system designed to protect the young child from danger, the term attachment is now used as a catch-all for every aspect of child–caregiver relationships and for development beyond the social and emotional domains. There has been ongoing controversy about the Strange Situation procedure as a measure of attachment security, and criticism of the apparent deterministic view of development implied by the importance accorded early relationships in the formation of inner working models of self and others. There remain those who construe attachment theory as 'mother-blaming'. This is so despite the fact that from its inception, and as discussed in earlier chapters, the theory rejected any notion of blame, focused on understanding and reconciliation (see Bowlby, 1988, p. 146), and clearly embraced all caregivers whose role was to protect the child from danger— including mothers, fathers, grandparents, professional caregivers and others. While there *is* a clear preponderance of mothers, as opposed to other possible attachment figures, in the samples studied in attachment research, this is consistent with findings that the mother is still most often the primary caregiving figure (Goldberg, 2000).

Many concerns have been raised regarding cultural perspectives on attachment. There are different elements to this controversy, escapsulated in the three following questions:

- Is attachment theory a narrowly conceived view of relationships based on a limited Eurocentric perspective?
- Does attachment theory allow for the impact of culture?
- Is secure attachment necessarily the ideal?

These concerns and questions are the focus of the first part of this chapter. The aim is to present a range of current positions regarding these debates. In the remainder of the chapter, some of the results of cross-cultural studies of attachment are presented. Two recent reviews of the cross-cultural literature, van IJzendoorn and Sagi (1999) and Goldberg (2000, chapter 7) inform much of the material presented. Child rearing amongst the Aboriginal people of Australia is discussed based on the Aboriginal child-rearing strategy (Warrki Jarrinjaku ACRS project).

Is attachment theory a narrowly conceived view of relationships based on a limited Eurocentric perspective?

There are two viewpoints on this question.

There are those who view attachment theory as narrowly conceived from the one, Euro-American, cultural perspective, at one point in time:

> The metaphor of emotional security, so clearly a product of 20th century Euro-American notions of individual needs and inter-personal relations, is a remarkably recent and local concept on which to build a universal model of human development . . . In other words, judgements of secure and insecure attachment through Ainsworth's Strange Situation procedure, however reliable and

theoretically rationalised, might still represent the moral judgements of a particular society at a particular moment in history rather than indicate normality and pathogenesis for all humans at all times . . . The development of the mother–infant relationship is not a biopsychological process isolated from the cultural values and social patterns of the community; on the contrary, mothers and other caregivers are deeply influenced by culture-specific norms in the preferences that guide their interaction with babies and set goals for their behavioural development (LeVine, in Foreword to Harwood et al, 1995, p. x).

Others, however, stress that attachment theory has always been open to 'culture-specific influences and idiosyncrasies' (van IJzendoorn and Sagi, 1999, p. 714). The basic tenet that the *formation* of attachment relationships is universal across cultures, it is argued, does not deny that the particular culture into which the child is born influences the way the relationship is moulded and expressed. Van IJzendoorn and Sagi (1999) argue further that the theory does not imply that secure attachment would be the norm in every culture or community.

Does attachment theory allow for the impact of culture?

One possible reason for the controversy surrounding attachment theory and culture is that, until recently, the preponderance of research on attachment processes has been undertaken in Western, industrialised communities. This is so, despite, as we have already discussed, one of the earliest and most influential empirical studies of attachment that was undertaken by Ainsworth in Africa amongst the Ganda people (see chapters 2 and 3). In this 1967 study, only 16 of the 28 children studied were classified as securely attached (57 per cent). A total of 12 were insecurely attached, seven children behaved in ways characteristic of resistance, and the others (originally classified as 'unattached') behaved in ways consistent with what has come to be known as avoidance.

In chapter 4 we saw how in many samples since that time, most of them in the United States or Europe, securely attached children represent about two-thirds of the sample, although the distribution of the insecure categories has been found to vary. That this may reflect cultural expectations and child-rearing goals is now clearly acknowledged (van IJzendoorn and Sagi, 1999). What is needed, these authors argue, is an 'emic' approach in cross-cultural studies of attachment, where the focus is on understanding the culture from within 'its own frame of reference' (p. 714). This is different from an 'etic' approach, in which the assessments and hypotheses developed within the majority culture are applied universally in an attempt to study cross-cultural differences.

The study of attachment relationships and the process by which they are formed offers the potential for unique insights into the interface between the psychological and the social worlds, between the individual and the culture. Marris (1991), for example, argues that attachment can be viewed as 'the essential bridge' (p. 88) between the two

> . . . because it is at once the primary relationship through which personality develops, and the relationship through which we create our sense of order. Society, as I conceive it, is a structure of meanings embodied in patterns of relationship, and the attachment relationship is both a microcosm of those meanings—an expression of a culture as its child-rearing practices embody them—and the experience out of which each generation recreates a meaningful order. We do not, as some sociological accounts seem to suggest, passively absorb the values of society. We each create our own meaning out of a unique experience of attachment which is still also recognizably the product of a culture (p. 88).

From such a perspective, it is inconceivable that attachment relationships could develop and exist without the influence of culture. As Grossmann (1995) puts it:

> Beyond biological factors, parenting is anchored in cultural and subcultural settings with culture-specific control mechanisms, plans, prescriptions, rules, and instructions designed to direct and control human behavior. These prescriptive rules and attitudes are shared by all, or at least most, of a society's members and, via parenting

practices, are communicated to the next generation. Considered from an anthropological perspective, attachment relationships constitute the very foundation for the child's entry and socialization into the qualitatively specific type of engagements between people— emotional, communicative, and supportive—that is characteristic of a given culture (p. 86).

Grossmann underlines the importance of understanding how it is that different sorts of cultural norms become established, and the potential for attachment theory to explicate the process of trans- mission of these norms across generations. In Grossmann's analysis the norms of 'negligence, hate, indifference, anxiety, and destructive selfishness' are contrasted with those that 'allow loving relationships to emerge and thereby foster care, concern, and a sense of constructive meaning toward one's offspring—the preconditions for promoting their capacity for mutuality and for living well-balanced individual lives' (1995, p. 87).

Grossmann's use of the term 'offspring' connotes a focus on child-parent relationships. But what attachment theory makes clear is that any attachment relationship—between mother and child, father and child, early childhood professional and child, and between adult partners—has the potential within it for the promotion of peace, care and respect, or fear, anxiety and distress. The earliest of these relationships, those that occur during infancy and early childhood, appear most profound because, as has been noted elsewhere in this book, they set up a pattern of expectations and ways of interrelating that persist. In our endeavours to create a peaceful world for all, we must look carefully at what societies and communities teach their children through the way that attachment is 'done'.

Is secure attachment necessarily the ideal?

Writing pre-11 September 2001, Crittenden (2000b) stated that:

Those of us living in postindustrial, Western countries are fortunate enough to experience one of the most peaceful and safe periods in human experience. It is a period in which food is abundant, shelter available, and disease so rare that infant and child mortality are extremely low and most children do not lose their parents until well into the child's adulthood. Furthermore, in spite of crime and war, our cities and countries are safer for more people than ever before. Possibly it is these conditions that permit us to believe that safety and security are normative conditions and, therefore, that security is the normative and optimal pattern of attachment. A simple look at children outside this protected context suggests that most humans need other strategies for coping with danger and that flexibility in organising and varying these strategies is very valuable (pp. 382–3).

Crittenden also argues that children who have been classified as insecurely attached show positive characteristics, despite the view of some that there are primarily negative connotations attached to insecurity:

> For example, Type A functioning implies independence, predictability, and trustworthiness, whereas Type C individuals can be lively, persuasive and loyal. That, of course, was Bowlby's point when he recommended to Ainsworth that she not label the [attachment] groups until she knew the empirical meaning of the groupings. Although she followed Bowlby's advice with regard to her own data, others have applied the labels in preference to the letter codes [i.e. A, B, C, D]. Nevertheless, it may still be premature to presume that we understand the value of strategies in all cultural contexts (2000b; p. 370).

We must be alert to the possibility of inappropriate, value-laden judgements and open to the diversity and complexity inherent in a culturally sensitive appraisal of attachment processes. There is a logic to the position that to feel secure and be safe, regardless of the self-protective strategy underlying it, is what constitutes '*adaptive* attachment' (Crittenden, 2000b, p. 369). However, it is secure attachment—with all its positive developmental sequelae, including prosocial skills and empathy—that represents the ideal to which we should all aspire in our caregiving of children.

This approach is in no way at odds with the compassionate approach to insecure patterns that Crittenden (2000a) describes:

> To understand anxious attachment, I think we must both understand a child's situation and feel for him or her. When assigned with informed compassion, an anxious pattern of attachment does not describe inadequacies, but rather acknowledges a child's attempts to cope with the challenges of his or her world. Knowing what children can do to protect themselves is at least as important as knowing how 'securely' that child would act if they experienced no threat . . . The point is that I fear we have taken a deficit approach to thinking about 'anxious' attachment. No wonder no one wants their child, family, or culture to be associated with one of the anxious patterns. Recognising the accomplishment and adaptation implied in the non-B patterns and placing them in the ecological context of family, culture and history can help us understand human relationships better and change the negative value placed on the Type A and C patterns (p. 10).

Attachment across different cultures

We turn now to a consideration of attachment across different cultures. In their analysis of cross-cultural patterns of attachment, van IJzendoorn and Sagi (1999) and Goldberg (2000) draw upon research in both European and several non-European, non-Anglo societies, as well as in the United States. Attachment researchers have studied many different cultural groups, including societies in Africa, Australia, China, Germany, Israel and Japan. While it is impossible here to document this research in detail, several examples will provide a 'feel' for the sorts of outcomes that have been emerging.

Firstly, some studies have sought to extend Ainsworth's initial exploratory work in Africa. These studies have provided further insights about the formation of attachment relationships in multiple-caregiver contexts. Research has included the Gusii of Kenya, the Hausa of Nigeria and the Dogon of Mali (see Marvin et al, 1977; Kermoian and Leiderman, 1986; True, 1994; all as cited by van IJzendoorn and Sagi, 1999).

Among the outcomes of these studies are findings that:

- Gusii infants form secure attachments to their substitute caregivers as well as to their mothers.
- The attachment behaviours shown by the Gusii infants are culture specific (a handshake as a greeting) but their mode of expression of security or insecurity is similar to North American infants, in that secure infants anticipated the handshake with enthusiasm whereas the insecure infants showed avoidance.
- Hausa infants form attachments to more than one caregiver, usually on average three or four, but show a preference for the attachment figure who holds and interacts with them most.
- Hausa infants, whose caregivers generally restrict their independent locomotor exploration due to dangers in the wider environment, nevertheless still use the caregivers as a secure base, exploring the environment through touch and vision but only when a caregiver is present.
- The attachment behaviours shown by Hausa infants are culture specific (passive signalling such as crying rather than active behaviours such as following).
- Eighty-eight per cent of the Dogon infants—whose mothers breastfeed frequently and who keep infants in close physical proximity most of the time—were classified as securely attached, with none classified as avoidant (although there was a high percentage of infants classified as disorganised, possibly due to the high stress of separation in the Strange Situation procedure).

Studies of the !Kung San or Bushmen of Botswana and the Pygmies of the Ituri forest of northeastern Zambia (Konner, 1977; Morelli and Tronick, 1991; as cited by van IJzendoorn and Sagi, 1999) provide examples of attachment in hunter–gatherer societies. The child rearing of the !Kung is characterised by 'indulgence, stimulation, and nonrestriction' (van IJzendoorn and Sagi, 1999, p. 719) with infants breastfed frequently and on demand, during the night and day, when they are carried around in a sling by the mother. The Pygmies use a very dense, shared-care arrangement, with infants suckling from a number of females, and spending 60 per cent of their time with caregivers other than the mother by

18 weeks of age. Nonetheless infants aged between six and 12 months show a preference for their mother, and protest if separated from her, possibly because she provides care during the night, and this care includes both feeding and play. As van IJzendoorn and Sagi (1999) describe it: 'From the perspective of attachment theory, the night may be an especially stressful time during which infants in general need a protective caregiver most' (p. 719).

Other cross-cultural research has included samples from China, and from Israeli kibbutzim. Among the results to emerge from these studies are:

- Child development experts and parents in China 'found the concept of attachment applicable in their cultural context' (van IJzendoorn and Sagi, 1999; p. 720); experts and mothers were of the view that a child with secure characteristics was ideal; and these defining characteristics of security accorded with the views of experts from other Western and non-Western societies.
- Collective night-time sleeping arrangements when experienced by young children in a kibbutz are associated with insecure parental attachments, probably because the unavailability and inaccessibility of the parents during the night exposes the infant to inconsistent responsiveness, 'given that sensitive responding by a mother or caregiver during the day contrasted sharply with the presence of an unfamiliar person [only] at night' (van IJzendoorn and Sagi, 1999, p. 722).
- Socio-emotional aspects of development at age five years, including measures of empathy, independence and motivation, are significantly related to the security of the child's attachment to their kibbutz *metapelet* (caregiver) during infancy but not to the security of their attachment to their parents.
- Measures of attachment security across the three primary carers (mother, father and caregiver) are most predictive of later positive functioning for children reared in a kibbutz (as compared to measures of security to the parents, or to the mother only).

These outcomes provide further weight to an 'integration model' of attachment security (van IJzendoorn and Sagi, 1999, p.723) in which secure attachments may compensate for insecure attachments within a network of multiple attachments. A recent study using the Adult Attachment Interview (Sagi et al, 1997, as cited by van IJzendoorn and Sagi, 1999) has also found that intergenerational transmission of attachment security from mother to child is high in families who reside in kibbutzim where the parents cared for their infant during the night, but low when the infant slept in a communal setting at night (away from the parents). This means that intergenerational transmission of attachment is sensitive to rearing arrangements and contextual factors such as communal sleeping. These may 'override the influence of parents' attachment represent-ation and their sensitive responsiveness' (van IJzendoorn and Sagi, 1999, p. 724) or lack thereof.

Finally, the outcomes reported for the concordance between parent and expert views on secure attachment and the ideal child, reported above, were also found for samples from Columbia, Germany, Israel, Japan, Norway and the United States (see Posada et al, 1995). There was great similarity in these views across cultures. This does not mean that security, and the behaviours shown by secure children, are valued for the same reasons in all cultures. Research by Harwood et al (1995) with samples of Puerto Rican and Anglo mothers in the United States indicates that children who behave in secure ways—including being readily compliant, co-operative and appropriately sociable—may be seen as 'ideal' for reasons that are unrelated to attachment issues. The Puerto Rican mothers in this study emphasised the importance of respect, calm, obedience and politeness. Anglo mothers, however, focused on secure behaviours as indicative of an appropriate balance between dependency and independence. The views of the Anglo mothers thus embraced attachment constructs, where the views of the Puerto Rican mothers did not.

Summarising the various results of cross-cultural research on attachment, Goldberg (2000) concludes that although secure attachment is the most frequent pattern observed across cultures studied to date, there are 'shifts in the type of security and insecurity that are related to cultural expectations and interpretations of desirable child care and behaviour. In addition, although most cultures appear to value secure attachment, different cultures may value it for different reasons' (p. 113).

Child rearing amongst the Aboriginal people of Australia

The dispossession of Aboriginal people in the legal, social, political and economic arenas since the white colonisation of Australia in the eighteenth century has caused intergenerational and transgenerational trauma, associated with the weakening of families, family breakdown, mental illness, alcohol abuse and violence from generation to generation.

Despite these and other devastating effects of colonisation, Aboriginal cultural knowledge has survived, including the child-rearing practices it embraces. But there is to date relatively little written information available on the topic. In a recent review of the literature, only one report was located describing outcomes of research initiated and conducted by Aboriginal people rather than by non-Aboriginal anthropologists (Australian Department of Family and Community Services, 2002). This literature report and review was prepared as background and support to the project Warrki Jarrinjaku Jintangkamanu Purananjaku ('Working together everyone and listening'), otherwise known as the Aboriginal Child Rearing Strategy (Warrki Jarrinjaku ACRS). In this project, senior Aboriginal women from Central Australian desert regions are 'recording their child rearing and parenting practices with the aim of strengthening their cultures and improving the wellbeing, health and educational outcomes of their children, particularly those aged 0–5 years' (Australian Department of Family and Community Services, 2002, p. 14).

It is not possible to provide in brief summary form a respectful overview of the features of Aboriginal child rearing so far emerging from this work, and the original work should be consulted. However, using the words of the review document, some key features identified include:

When Yapa and Anangu look at babies and young children they see small adults . . . Young Yapa children are gradually introduced to their specific obligations and responsibilities associated with Jukurrpa. As part of these teachings young children have almost complete freedom to choose and demand what they desire . . . Anangu and Yapa children sleep, eat and play whenever and wherever they choose. If babies cry they are immediately picked up and held . . . Yapa children never sleep on their own, and it is rarely a quiet environment for sleeping because they are always with their mother and other family members . . . an important feature of Aboriginal child rearing is the emphasis placed on a child's ability to learn compassion for others and to share . . . There is no concept of 'mine' in regard to a plaything (p. 16).

The review also notes that Aboriginal children are taught the importance of relationships with others and responsibilities to the environment and everything it contains: 'They are taught to help and encourage one another; to keep each other safe and to work together' (p. 17).

Implications and applications

CASE SCENARIO

In this case scenario we return to Helina's preschool teacher, Malcolm, as he develops the second part of his professional development session on attachment. Recall from chapter 8 that the first part of Malcolm's session focused on attachment security and insecurity in the preschool years. The second part is directed to cultural perspectives on attachment.

Malcolm decides that he wants the second part of his session to be highly interactive, and to draw upon the knowledge and experience of his colleagues, many of whom work in multicultural settings. Therefore he sends the following questions and activities to those who will be attending the session, a month before it is due to take place:

Dear colleagues,

**Re: Upcoming professional development session on
attachment—a request**

*As you know I am preparing a session for our meeting in one
month's time. It will be in two parts, the first on attachment and child
development, the second exploring attachment from a multicultural
perspective. In order to facilitate a lively discussion during the second
part of the session, I wonder if you would think about the following
questions, and if you have time, follow up with some of the resource-
finding requests:*

- *Consider the various cultural backgrounds of the families you
  work with. How much do you know and understand about
  differences in parenting and views on child rearing in these
  families?*
- *Try to find out as much as you can about parenting beliefs and
  child-rearing patterns amongst your families by accessing relevant
  resources and talking with family members.*
- *Think about ways in which your centre's practices could be more
  sensitive and responsive to these cultural differences.*

  Looking forward to seeing you then.
  Kind regards, Mal

*Drawing on this preparation, Malcolm decides to use the time
available on the night to facilitate a discussion amongst his colleagues
on the following topics:*

1. *How might ideas about sensitive caregiving be influenced by
   awareness of cultural differences in parenting and views of the
   child?*
2. *How can we reconcile awareness of culturally specific child-
   rearing practices and goals with centre policies and practices
   that promote secure attachment as the ideal child-rearing
   outcome?*

QUESTIONS FOR REFLECTION

- How much do you know about different cultural perspectives on caregiving, attachment and child development amongst the families attending your early childhood setting?
- Where might you access more information on these topics?
- Are there ways in which the setting in which you work could be more sensitive to these issues? How might more inclusive policies be developed? What might they look like?
- How might your practice be developed to reflect greater sensitivity to cultural differences in parenting and views of the child?

DISCUSSION POINTS

This chapter has stressed that attachment theory neither denies nor minimises the impact of culture on the nature of the attachment relationship that forms. What is universal, the theory argues, is the *formation of an attachment*, and the reliance of the child on the attachment figure or figures for care and protection. Not all cultures prioritise secure attachment, and not all child-rearing customs promote it. An 'emic' approach attempts to understand culture-specific goals of child rearing from within the framework of the culture itself. This offers a unique opportunity to learn how different child-rearing patterns mould individual children to become members of a particular society, to 'fit in', and be adaptive to specific cultural demands and expectations.

The nature of attachment relationships in different cultures provides insight into how the personal and social worlds are linked. Attachment relationships cannot be understood in the absence of cultural values, beliefs and practices. Early childhood educators need to understand these values in order to work together, in respectful and supportive ways, with the families they serve.

At the same time, early childhood professionals must have a clear view of the goals of their own caregiving practices, the form of attachment they are aiming for through their caregiving, and the theory and research outcomes on which these goals are based. This book espouses the benefits to children and societies of secure attachment relationships—security, responsible autonomy, empathy and resilience.

Further readings

Australian Department of Family and Community Services 2002 *Warrki Jar-rinjaku Jintangkamanu Purananjaku 'Working together everyone and listening': Aboriginal child rearing and associated research: A review of the literature* Commonwealth of Australia, Canberra

Harwood, R.L., Miller, J.G. and Irizarry, N.L. 1995 *Culture and Attachment: Perceptions of the child in context* The Guilford Press, New York

13

When attachment needs are unmet

In one of his last publications, Bowlby (1991) reflected on the ways in which research based on attachment theory has contributed to an understanding of personality development and psychopathology. He stressed how an attachment-based approach can shed light on the importance of the human need for proximity and relatedness with others. And he emphasised the theory's ability to generate concern and insight about those individuals 'whose attachment needs have been and are still unmet' (p. 293).

This chapter explores the behavioural and emotional consequences for children whose attachments have been, or still are, significantly disturbed, disrupted or insecure. We consider ways in which therapeutic interventions and family support programs may assist the child with such an attachment history.

The developmental pathways approach

From the beginning, attachment theory has espoused a 'pathways' approach to development. That is, the potential life course of any individual is seen to consist of many possible trajectories or pathways, with new directions emerging in response to changing experiences encountered along the way. From a mental health perspective, some of these pathways are seen to be conducive to psychological wellbeing, others are not. As Bowlby (1988) described it:

> Children who have parents who are sensitive and responsive are enabled to develop along a healthy pathway. Those who have insensitive, unresponsive, neglectful, or rejecting parents are likely to develop along a deviant pathway which is in some degree incompatible with mental health and which renders them vulnerable to breakdown, should they meet with seriously adverse events . . . Although the capacity for developmental change decreases with age, change continues throughout the life cycle so that changes for better or worse are always possible (p. 136).

Writing some time later, Weinfield et al (1999) underline that this conceptualisation of development does not construe the experience of insecure attachment early in life as pathological in and of itself. Insecure attachment is not a disorder (Goldberg, 2000). Rather it is seen to be a predisposing or risk factor for pathology:

> In the pathways perspective, the hypothesis is that patterns of anxious attachment represent initiations of pathways that, if pursued, will increase the likelihood of pathological conditions. Thus, although anxious attachment is considered a risk factor for pathology, not all, or even most, anxiously attached infants will develop psychopathology. Psychopathology, like social competence, is a developmental construction involving a myriad of influences interacting over time (Sroufe, 1997). Similarly, secure attachment is not a guarantee of mental health, but rather is viewed as a protective factor (Weinfield et al, 1999, p. 81).

Secure attachment is one amongst many possible protective factors. Insecure attachment is one amongst many possible risk factors that increase psychological vulnerability to mental health problems.

As we have already considered, one of the ways in which secure attachments promote mental health is via their positive impact on emotional development and the promotion of effective emotional self-control strategies (see discussions in chapters 6 and 7). Adaptive management of emotions appears to lie at the heart of psychological wellbeing. As Greenberg (1999) notes, 'the management of anxiety, anger, and sadness through the healthy use of secure-base figures and mature defenses is likely to be an important protective factor against various forms of psychopathology across the lifespan' (p. 470). The relative ease with which secure, as compared to insecure, individuals form supportive, mutually satisfying relationships with others is seen as a further protective factor for mental health.

While the developmental pathways approach may appear relatively straightforward, risk-factor models are in reality very complex (Greenberg, 1999). Amongst the complexities to be acknowledged are that disorders are multiply determined; that risk factors may have different effects at different times, and depending on the presence or absence of other risks; and risk factors can operate at the level of the individual, family, community and society. In particular, Greenberg (1999) notes how combinations of risk factors, including parental mental illness, domestic violence and poverty, appear to predispose children to a variety of disorders.

Based on attachment theory, predictions have been made linking particular forms of insecurity to particular kinds of non-optimal developmental outcomes. Resistant attachment has been linked with outcomes of anxiety, low tolerance to frustration and depression arising from feelings of helplessness. Avoidant attachment has been linked with anger and aggression, lack of empathy and alienation associated with conduct problems, and depression arising from a sense of aloneness. Disorganised attachment has been linked to dissociation (see Weinfield et al, 1999). Research findings in relation to these predictions will be considered later in this chapter.

Attachment and psychopathology

There is much research underway that aims to uncover links between psychiatric disorders and prior attachment experiences. This focus is identified by Goldberg (2000) as 'one of the most rapidly growing areas of attachment research' (p. 214). Autonomous or secure attachment representations have been found to be very rare amongst adults and adolescents with psychiatric illness. The incidences of unresolved classifications are high.

In her review of the research to date, Goldberg notes the high frequency of disorganised attachment and unresolved and highly traumatic incidences of abuse and/or loss in samples of adolescents and adults with mental illness. In one of the few prospective studies to date, in which individuals have been followed from an early age through adolescence and/or adulthood, Carlson (1998) examined the consequences of attachment disorganisation/disorientation at age two years for later psychological functioning. She found a disorganised attachment classification in infancy was correlated with negative outcomes through to adolescence. These negative outcomes included behaviour problems at five years of age, internalising problems and dissociation symptoms ('confused, seems to be in a fog', 'strange behaviour', 'gets hurt a lot, accident prone', 'deliberately harms self or attempts suicide') during the high school years, and psychopathology at age 17 years.

This study is amongst the first to provide strong empirical support for the link between early attachment disorganisation (which, as we have already discussed, is linked to the occurrence of frightening and/or frightened behaviour by the caregiver) to later dissociative psychopathologies in the teenage years. Unfortunately, given the early childhood focus of this book, the precise implications of this research for the early childhood professional are unclear. This is because the paper does not detail the sorts of behaviour problems observed in preschool, with results reported only as a composite measure of scores on the Preschool Behaviour Questionnaire (Behar and Stringfield, 1974, as cited by Carlson, 1998) and the Behaviour Problem Scale (Erickson and Egeland, 1981, as cited by Carlson, 1998).

Disorders of attachment in childhood

Many of the symptoms of major psychiatric illness are not apparent until the adolescent years or beyond. It is therefore not surprising that there have been few studies of the links between childhood psychiatric disorders and attachment. However, 'Reactive attachment disorder of infancy or early childhood' has been identified, and is included in the American Psychiatric Association's *Diagnostic and Statistical Manual of Mental Disorders, Fourth Edition* (DSM IV-1994). The Manual describes the diagnostic features of the disorder as 'markedly disturbed and developmentally inappropriate social relatedness in most contexts that begins before age 5 years and is associated with grossly pathological care' (1994, p. 116). Pathological care is defined by three criteria. The first two relate to what might be called disturbances of attachment: 'persistent disregard of the child's basic emotional needs for comfort, stimulation, and affection' (criterion 1), and 'persistent disregard of the child's basic needs' (criterion 2). The third relates to attachment disruption: 'repeated changes of primary caregiver that prevent formation of stable attachments' (criterion 3). This criterion would include changes in foster-care placement.

Reactive attachment disorder is considered within the DSM IV description to take one of two forms. The first, termed 'inhibited', consists of the following presentation: 'persistent failure to initiate or respond in a developmentally appropriate fashion to most social interactions, as manifest by excessively inhibited, hypervigilant, or highly ambivalent and contradictory responses (e.g. the child may respond to caregivers with a mixture of approach, avoidance, and resistance to comforting, or may display frozen watchfulness)' (1994, p. 118). There are clear overlaps between this description of behaviour and criteria for disorganised attachment as discussed in earlier sections of this book.

The second form of reactive attachment disorder is termed 'disinhibited'. It consists of the following presentation: 'diffuse attachments as manifest by indiscriminate sociability with marked inability to exhibit appropriate selective attachments (e.g. excessive familiarity with relative strangers or lack of selectivity in choice of attachment figures)' (1994, p. 118).

The Manual reports that the occurrence of the disorder is very uncommon. It is generally agreed that the complete absence of attachment, or 'non-attachment' (Zeanah, 1996), is also rare, and restricted to situations, such as might apply in extreme cases of neglect, in which the child simply does not have sufficient contact with a caregiving figure to enable an attachment to form. Important understandings in this regard are emerging from studies of children reared during their early years in Romanian orphanages during the Ceauşescu regime, and subsequently adopted by North American families (e.g. Carlson and Earls, 1997; Chisholm, 1998).

The inclusion of reactive attachment disorder in the highly respected and influential DSM IV document has helped the clinical significance of attachment-related disorders to be mainstreamed. But there are those who have expressed some discomfort, especially with the narrow focus that has been taken (see Greenberg, 1999). For example, with all that is now known about the process of attachment formation and the subtle behavioural indicators of different attachment classifications, especially disorganisation, the Manual criteria appear over-simplified and inexact. The full outcomes of research do not appear to have been incorporated into the descriptions, definitions and diagnosis of the disorder.

Behaviour problems associated with an insecure attachment history

Attachment insecurity and attachment disorder are not the same, but clearly there is a continuum between the two. From a practical point of view, it seems the only way to distinguish between them is in terms of the severity of emotional and behavioural disturbance shown by the child, particularly around feelings of safety and personal distress (see Zeanah et al, 1993).

There have been attempts in recent years to gain better definitional precision. Empirical research and the clinical observations of those working with children who have experienced attachment-related trauma have been drawn together. For example, Lieberman and Zeanah (1995) have distinguished between non-attachment, disordered attachment and disrupted attachment, and have identified particular behaviours associated with each. As just one example, they differentiate several subtypes of disordered attachment. One involves the excessive inhibition referred to in the DSM IV criteria, another high-risk and reckless behaviour. Finally they describe role reversal, in which the child's behaviour takes on a highly 'parentified' style indicative of extreme relational distortion. The child's need for care and protection is subverted to meet the attachment 'needs' of the parent.

Those who have reviewed the literature on behaviour problems associated with different forms of insecurity—avoidant, resistant and disorganised (see Greenberg, 1999; Goldberg, 2000)—generally conclude that there is support for some, but not all, of the hypotheses linking different types of insecurity with aggression, anxiety or internalising problems. The hypothesis that avoidant and disorganised attachments put children at risk for aggressive, externalising problems and conduct disorders has been supported in a number of studies. Conduct problems include chronic non-compliance, intense and immature responses to limits and boundaries, strong tantruming, and frequent lying and/or stealing or other oppositions to family and societal rules (see Greenberg and Speltz, 1988). In contrast, there has been relatively little empirical support for the hypothesised link between resistant attachment and internalising problems, including anxiety and depression. This may reflect both the difficulty of identifying internalising problems in young children, and the relative infrequency of resistant attachment (Goldberg, 2000).

One recent study of resistant attachments over time used a detailed case-study approach. Hans et al (2000) report longitudinal data on two mother–child dyads from a sample of children studied during infancy, and at ages 3, 4, 5, 10 and 14 years. Detailed descriptions of mother–child interactions across the 14 years of the study are presented for two children, 'Kineta' and 'Gerome'. In line with other research (see chapter 4), the authors found that after infancy, the resistant child continues to use exaggerated emotional displays to gain the parent's attention. False affects emerge as early as the second year to control parental involvement by manipulating the adult's feelings towards discomfort. By age three years, alternating angry and helpless displays by the child were frequently observed, with coy, disarming behaviours used to minimise the risk of angry retaliations from the parent.

The authors found some evidence in their data for a link between resistance and pervasive anxiety in each child. For example, Kineta was reported to have 'a clear history of extreme levels of anxiety that had affected her functioning in school and other settings'

(p. 298), and both children were reported to experience a 'significant number of somatic signs that could be indicators of underlying anxiety' (p. 298). According to Hans et al, the pervasive anxiety experienced by the children most probably derived from their ongoing need to work hard at gaining attention and care from the mother. The displays of exaggerated affect, or acting in annoying, provocative ways, generally were successful in gaining the attention of the attachment figure, but the history of uncertainty about her continued availability meant that anxiety soon resurfaced. Hans et al (2000) note that anxieties of these kinds may become even more intense in situations where the child is required to be apart from the mother, such as in school. This is because the child can no longer actively monitor the mother, nor emotionally manipulate her to gain attention and control. The child may begin to apply the same strategies with the teacher and peers.

In discussing emotional development and adaptation in the preschool years, Sroufe (1995) notes a number of observations from his ongoing research (e.g. Sroufe, 1983, 1988, 1990) that indicate how previously established dyadic patterns between child and parent—secure and insecure—transfer to the child's style of engagement with people within the preschool setting. Typical teacher responses to these patterns were described in chapter 8.

Interventions

As we saw in the last chapter, Bowlby's view was that successful clinical interventions with adults ideally include therapeutic involvement, perhaps with a professional therapist but certainly with someone able to engender feelings of trust. The establishment of at least a fledgling sense of security, born of the therapist's ability to be 'reliable, attentive, and sympathetically responsive' and 'empathic' (1988, p. 140) was seen as essential to the process of overcoming a negative working model. The focus of therapy with the adult is to help him or her explore current, negative working models, then reconstruct them on the basis of the more positive interpersonal experiences with the therapist. When considering young children with unmet attachment needs, the primary focus of intervention is usually family based. The aim of interventions is generally to assist the child's parents or other carers within the family in ways that will facilitate their ability to provide sensitive, responsive care. The goal is to thereby move the child's experience of attachment relationships to greater security.

Family- and parent-focused interventions

Interventions may include support of various kinds aimed at reducing family stress, particularly in high-risk families where there may be a number of risk factors present, including poverty and/or domestic violence and/or substance abuse. Caregiver stress, it will be recalled, has long been identified by attachment theory as one of the main factors mitigating against high levels of caregiver sensitivity.

Other approaches include programs designed to enhance caregiver sensitive responsiveness through direct training and/or observation, with or without therapeutic interventions designed to alter the adult's attachment representations (e.g. Heinecke and Ponce, 1999). A recent example of this is the 'Circle of Security' (Marvin et al, 2002), a 20-week, group-based intervention combining parent education and psychotherapy and utilising attachment principles during all phases.

Alternative attachment figures

Another, sometimes complementary approach is to consider ways in which the child can be given opportunities to form secure attachments with other caregivers. The goal is to provide the child with caregiving experiences from which the experience of trust, perhaps for the first time, can emerge.

Research by Howes and Hamilton (1992) and Howes and Segal (1993) indicate that there is potential in this approach, since at least some of the children in these studies with a history of maltreatment did not generalise the maltreating model to new (foster) caregivers. While just over half the children in their sample who had been removed from parental care did form insecure attachments to new caregivers, the remainder (47 per cent) formed new secure attachments over a two-month period.

It can be a very challenging task to promote secure attachments in children with disturbed or disrupted attachment histories. This is because the insecure strategies they have developed in the past act to impede the process. For example, in children who have been placed in foster care due to prior maltreatment, it has been suggested that 'normal' levels of caregiver sensitivity may not be sufficient to promote secure attachments. Dozier et al (1999), for example, argue that the insecure attachment strategies infants develop in response to compromised caregiving in their families of origin may carry forward to new attachment figures and alienate them, describing the situation in the following way:

> For example, foster babies may behave in ways to suggest that foster parents are not needed [avoidant strategy] or are inadequate to soothe them [resistant strategy]. If foster parents respond reciprocally, these babies' expectations that others are unavailable or rejecting will be confirmed. To provide interactions that disconfirm babies' expectations, foster parents must see through the alienating strategies these children present (p. 195).

'Responding reciprocally' here means responding in a complementary way to the behaviour of the child. Using daily diary records over a number of months, foster parents were asked to record how the child responded in situations of distress, such as when accidentally hurt, scared or upset about separation (see case scenario, chapter 4). They also recorded how they responded to the child. Diary data revealed that when the infants responded to distress in a secure way (by seeking comfort) the foster parents responded sensitively. However, when the infants responded in an avoidant or resistant way, even autonomous caregivers reacted in kind—that is, they 'responded to avoidance or resistance in a complementary fashion, namely by acting as if they were not necessary to the child or were angry at being unable to help the child, respectively' (p. 208).

When a child's insecure strategies persist over time, even a highly sensitive and responsive adult may begin to behave in ways that undermine the child's security. It is very difficult, if not impossible, to avoid 'buying into' the insecure dynamic. In order to address this difficulty, Dozier et al (1999) developed an intervention designed to assist caregivers reinterpret the child's responses and thereby to respond to them in an ultimately more helpful fashion. The intervention consisted of three sessions, each conducted by a professional trainer. The first introduced the caregiver to attachment theory specifically in terms of the child's case history and current ways of responding. The second and third sessions focused on ways of reinterpreting the infant's behaviour and ways of responding in a therapeutic fashion, with 'booster' sessions provided on a six-monthly basis over the child's first three years.

This approach, along with other therapeutic interventions for foster and adopted children (e.g. Hughes, 1997) offers hope for those children who, unlike most (see Howes, 1999), have difficulty reorganising their insecure attachment representations. The principles applied in these programs may have useful applications for those who work in other settings, such as child-care centres, preschools and schools, and who attempt to form secure relationships with children who bring diverse attachment histories.

Certainly, within such an approach, the potential for professional caregivers to be such figures of security is considerable. In a recent review of the literature on multiple attachment relationships Howes (1999) notes:

> The bulk of the literature on attachment relationship formation with child care providers is based on typical children who have not necessarily had difficulties with prior relationships. A small literature examines relationship formation in atypical children whose prior relationship history is more problematic. These studies suggest that children with prior maladaptive relationships can form secure attachment relationships with new caregivers, and therefore that they construct each relationship based on interactions with a particular adult (pp. 677–8).

Approaches to preschool conduct problems that integrate an attachment perspective

A final approach to be considered concerns interventions with children who have conduct problems. Conduct difficulties often become most noticeable when the child moves to settings outside the home. But even before then, they are the cause of considerable parent–child conflict and distress and interfere with the child's effective functioning in a range of situations. Behaviour management or behaviour modification programs, based on principles of learning theory and operant conditioning, are the usual model of intervention. However, while these approaches yield fast, positive behaviour change, the outcomes are often not sustained, nor do they bring about progress in other relationships with teachers, peers and so on, or in other related areas of development (see Speltz, 1990).

In response to these problems, and based upon an understanding of the possible significance of attachment-related issues associated with conduct problems, some clinicians have developed new approaches in which operant learning and attachment perspectives are combined. One example, provided by Speltz (1990), involves parents and their children in a three-phase program. In the first phase, the focus is on the ways in which the child interacts with the parent during play, especially how the child gains and maintains parental attention and support. In the second phase, operant principles of behaviour management (reinforcement, punishment and extinction) are taught to achieve more successful adult limit-setting and child compliance. In the third phase, the program focuses on styles of parent–child communication, with the goal of achieving more harmonious mutual regulation. While it is not possible here to detail the program components further, Speltz (1990) presents an overview of the approach and a detailed case history which may be helpful to practitioners with an interest in this area.

Challenges for the future

In reviewing issues to do with attachment disorders and interventions informed by attachment theory, Rutter and O'Connor (1999) have warned of the difficulties and complexities in this area. They state that 'even when there is an undoubted attachment problem, it is by no means self-evident what form treatment should take' (p. 833). Amongst the questions they raise are the following:

What role should there be for cognitive restructuring? Should the focus be on present parent–child relationships, or on the origins of difficulties in past deficiencies in caregiving, or on both? . . . The most important constraints on the understanding of treatment, however, are (1) the uncertainty of what is needed for the children (as distinct from the parents) when their attachment problems derive from past, rather than present, experiences; and (2) the uncertainty regarding the benefits with respect to reduction in psychopathology that follow improvements in attachment security (1999, p. 833).

In Rutter and O'Connor's view, there is so far a paucity of research from which answers to these questions and concerns could come.

Implications and applications

CASE SCENARIO

In our final case scenario we return to Zamia, Eli's caregiver. Our focus this time is not Eli, however, but another child in Zamia's care, three-year-old Lachlan.

Lachlan has been attending child care at this centre for only three months and his behaviour has been challenging, to say the least. Zamia was aware from the beginning that Lachlan may have special needs. He is currently cared for in a foster placement, having been removed from his birth family at the age of 2¹/₂ years due to significant abuse and neglect.

Lachlan had initially been placed with another family, but the placement broke down. The current placement appears to be progressing well, although his foster parents have had major challenges. They describe Lachlan as 'very difficult to reach emotionally', he wets the bed most nights and occasionally soils his pants. He has been cruel to the foster carers' pet cat. At home and at child care he finds peer relationships difficult and is often aggressive. In fact, Zamia has become concerned about the infants when Lachlan is in the same room or play area outside. She observed Lachlan taking toys aggressively from Eli and on one occasion quite violently pushing one of the other toddlers. She has decided to seek the support of a resource specialist skilled in working with children who have special behavioural needs.

QUESTIONS FOR REFLECTION

- Which aspects of Lachlan's behaviour are consistent with a history of disturbed/disrupted attachment relationships?
- Which form of insecurity—avoidance or resistance—seems to underlie Lachlan's particular behavioural presentation?
- If you were the resource specialist consulted by Zamia, what insights might be provided by an attachment perspective?
- What interventions in the early childhood setting would be indicated by an attachment perspective?
- What other information about Lachlan would be helpful to Zamia in understanding Lachlan's needs?

DISCUSSION POINTS

Lachlan's pattern of responding is consistent with an insecure–avoidant attachment history, and the extent of prior neglect, abuse and attachment disruption suggests there may also be underlying disorganisation. We do not know from the brief history presented whether, and under what conditions, Lachlan has access with his birth family. This would be important for Zamia to know as a child's challenging behaviours may escalate in response to the complex emotions aroused during these reunions. It would also be helpful for Zamia to talk with Lachlan's foster carers regarding how they respond to Lachlan's behaviours at home and what they have found settles him.

The primary aim of any intervention with a young child who has unmet attachment needs is the nurturing of security. An early childhood curriculum based on attachment principles, with its regular, predictable routines and emphasis on sensitive, responsive and consistent caregiving, is ideally placed to do this. We have already seen in the case scenario presented in chapter 6 how attachment principles undergird Zamia's program. Accessing specialist resources and support professionals is also important for children like Lachlan who have suffered extensive attachment-related disruption, disturbance and distress.

Further readings

Greenberg, M.T. 1999 'Attachment and psychopathology in childhood' *Handbook of Attachment: Theory, research and clinical applications* eds J. Cassidy and P.R. Shaver, The Guilford Press, New York, pp. 469–96

Marvin, R., Cooper, G., Hoffman, K. and Powell, B. 2002 'The circle of security project: Attachment-based intervention with caregiver–pre-school child dyads' *Attachment and Human Development* vol. 4, pp. 107–24

Part V

Conclusion

14

Rethinking attachment in early childhood policy and practice

It is said that ideas are only as good as what you can do with them. If so, a theory dealing with development in early childhood might best be judged by its ability to generate productive research, and on the extent to which it—and the outcomes of the research—make a positive difference in the lives of people, particularly children and families. There is no doubt that attachment theory has achieved well on both these fronts. Attachment research is flourishing. As we have seen, major longitudinal and cross-sectional research programs inspired by attachment theory have begun to provide answers to important questions to do with children, their relationships and their development. Thousands of smaller scale studies, in combination, are also contributing new insights. Research considered in this book is fuelling exciting, provocative and ongoing debates and controversies. These in turn are generating more questions, more ideas, more research and, hopefully, more answers.

In the areas of child and family policy and practice, major changes in hospital procedures, and in the placement of children in need of protection, have occurred in response to an understanding of the attachment process, attachment needs and how separation affects children. Whenever possible, children in hospital now have the comfort and security of their attachment figures around them much of the time. Children removed from their family due to maltreatment are generally placed in family homes in the hope that they will have nurturing and loving care with the same caregivers over the period of time needed before successful reunification can be achieved. Child protection case plans reflect an appreciation of the negative effects of attachment disruption. Unfortunately, the reality for maltreated children is often far from the ideal—and many children experience multiple, short-term placements, moving from home to home before reunification or permanent placement. But attachment theory provides an ideal to be worked towards.

Early childhood policies and practices are the concern of this book. In chapter 1 you were challenged to 'rethink attachment'—to think again, and in new ways, about the significance and implications of attachment theory for your work with children and families in early childhood settings. In the chapters that followed, the theory and research flowing from it were presented to illuminate and emphasise what the theory has to say about child development in the context of early childhood services. Chapter-by-chapter case scenarios illustrated ways in which attachment theory can inform child-care provision, early childhood curricula, quality of care and teaching practices. In this final chapter, we draw together many of these implications. Conclusions are reached, based on an attachment perspective, about what needs to change, and what needs to be done much better, in order to nurture fully the wellbeing of our children and families.

Moving beyond the debate about whether child care is bad for children

After many years of debate and many hundreds, perhaps thousands, of studies, research has moved beyond the simple question of whether child care is bad for children. We now understand that child development, and the influences upon it, are far too complex for any one type of care arrangement to ever be—in and of itself—uniquely responsible for a child's developmental trajectory. The attachment perspective, embracing a developmental pathways approach, makes it clear that 'settings' of development are best construed in terms of interactions and relationships experienced within and between them. The quality of relationships establishes developmental 'potentials', and for any child there will be many significant relationships from which these potentials are built. It is the totality of each child's rearing experiences, interacting together, that ultimately will determine development. Attachment relationships with key caregiving figures—at home and in early childhood settings—are of special importance.

From an attachment perspective, early childhood settings are best understood through answers to the following questions:

- What sorts of interactions and relationships does the child—and the child's family—experience in this early childhood setting?
- How does the child's family feel about using the service?
- How well supported are the early childhood professionals themselves?
- How do policy and practice provisions in this setting impact on the ability of professionals to nurture the attachment needs of children?
- What attachment history do professionals bring to their work of caring for children?
- What attachment histories do the children bring?

How the setting impacts on the emotional wellbeing of parents, professionals and children will all impact on the child's development through the resultant quality of relationships experienced in the early childhood setting, and at home. It is this level of complexity in regards to child development that needs to be acknowledged if we are to understand better whether any setting of development is 'good' or 'bad' for children.

Connecting attachment theory and child-care policies

In 1999, Rutter and O'Connor presented a scholarly overview of the implications of attachment theory for child-care policies. In distinguishing attachment theory from other theories of development, they note that attachment theory emphasises:

- the need for the child's significant caregiving relationships to be characterised by sensitive responsiveness;
- the importance of attachment relationships that are sustained and continuous, rather than disrupted and disturbed;
- the feelings of fear, anxiety and distress that arise from the experience of separation from attachment figures, and in response to their inconsistency and/or rejection, and the negative impact of these feelings on psychological wellbeing; and
- the potential of caregiving relationships to be the source of the child's all-important sense of security in others and self, and thus the contribution of these relationships to promoting mental health and resilience, and protecting against psychological vulnerability, both currently and later in life.

We have considered all of these aspects of the theory, and research associated with them, in this book. The importance of sensitive responsiveness is discussed in chapters 3, 4, 6 and 7; the dangers of attachment disruption and disturbance in chapters 10 and 13; and the link between attachment and resilience in chapter 5.

In their analysis, Rutter and O'Connor (1999) also identify a number of contemporary policy concerns in relation to daily care of children away from their parents. These include:

- the effects of brief separation;
- the way(s) in which the child's development is influenced by different attachment figures, and in particular by attachment relationships differing in security (secure with one figure and insecure with others); and
- the significance of continuity of the caregiving figure in the child-care setting as against at home.

In relation to the first concern, they conclude that 'very young children are truly stressed by separation experiences, but they readily cope with brief separations during the day when these occur in the context of relationship continuity and good-quality caregiving' (p. 827). In relation to the second issue, they conclude that 'supplementary caregiver–child attachment relationships [relationships between early childhood professionals and children] may well be influential' (p. 828) but research has yet to establish whether one relationship is more influential than others and whether 'one secure relationship . . . [can] compensate for insecurities in others' (p. 835). In relation to the third issue, they conclude that the answer is not yet known.

Who can be an attachment figure? Do attachment relationships in early childhood settings matter?

Attachment theory's emphasis on the importance of relationships with all significant caregiving figures, not only parents, has been underlined in this book. Attachment figures, by definition, potentially include all persons from whom a child might reasonably expect care and protection from danger. As we have seen, Howes and her colleagues (see Howes, 1999) identify attachment figures as those who provide care, both physical and emotional, are continuous or consistent caregiving figures in a child's life, and who have an emotional investment in the child. Early childhood professionals potentially meet all these criteria. We can therefore conclude that:

- attachment relationships *are* built in early childhood settings;
- attachment relationships in early childhood settings can be secure *or* insecure;
- *secure* attachment relationships in early childhood settings *promote* the psychological wellbeing of the child; and
- *insecure* attachment relationships in early childhood settings will have a *negative impact* on the child's wellbeing.

As Honig (1998) states, regardless of the quality of attachments children have at home, professional caregivers are people to whom they can form secure or insecure attachments, with all the known impacts of these on their development. When the child's attachments to the parents are insecure, the special importance of secure attachments in child care are underlined.

If this aspect of attachment theory is somehow missed, overlooked or unacknowledged, it is all too easy for those who make decisions about early childhood policies to misunderstand the role of the early childhood professional, and the role of the early childhood setting in child development. If attachment theory is mistakenly represented as a theory about children and their parents primarily, then the professional caregiver's role risks being relegated to one of simply 'holding the fort' until mother and/or father return, at which time the real developmental influences of significance resume. This is not the case. And yet many policies and practices appear to be based on just such a view.

In this category of unacceptable practices and policies are included:

- child: staff ratios that are too high to allow the individualised, sensitive and responsive care from which secure attachments grow;
- staff rostering—particularly in baby and toddler rooms—that prevent children forming secure attachments because there are too many changes of staff, or inadequate attention to a primary care model of staffing; and
- transitions to child care that are too abrupt to allow the young child—and parents—time to build trust in the new caregivers before separation from the primary attachment figures occurs.

Despite Rutter and O'Connor's (1999) optimistic statement that: 'There is a general acceptance of the effects on psychological development of young children's early social experiences, of the need for individual caregiving, and of the importance of continuity in relationships' (p. 834), in practice there appear too many examples that this is not yet the case.

Reflecting on early childhood practices

Honig (e.g. 1998) has written at length about attachment and caregiving, and her work helps us to reflect on how attachment theory and research can impact on practices in early childhood settings. For example, in discussing the secure attachment relationship, Honig describes how the adult caregiver becomes for the infant a person who can be trusted 'to provide safety, comfort and reassurance' (p. 3). In particular the infant learns that:

- the caregiver can be relied on for comfort;
- the caregiver will help when emotions become overwhelming;
- the caregiver will not be intrusive in ways that 'stifle a baby's budding exploratory curiosity' (1998, p. 3); and
- 'he or she is . . . worthy of being supported, protected, and responded to in helpful and affectionate ways' (1998, p. 3).

Honig also underlines how each attachment relationship that the infant or young child forms is unique, and its quality (secure or insecure) reflects the 'innumerable small daily gestures of care' (1998, p. 7) experienced with that particular person. This aspect of relationships—the minute-by-minute, day-by-day way in which they form—has also been stressed in this book. Honig states that when a caregiver has one or a small number of infants assigned to him or her, it is possible for that caregiver to get to know each child well. This is essential if daily interactions are to nurture optimal security, autonomy and resilience.

In the case of children who come into the early childhood setting with a history of insecure attachments, the early childhood professional's role is most crucial in offering the child, perhaps for the first time, calm empathic responsiveness. In Honig's view, the same primary caregiver should remain with an infant, or small group of infants, until the age of three years.

The importance to the child of a positive, supportive relationship between the early childhood professional and the family has also been emphasised. Honig states that 'rapport and good will through specific attention to close positive communication' (p. 18) between staff and parents in early childhood settings is essential. It enhances the security of the attachment the child feels with the professional caregiver and with the parent since, as we have seen in chapter 11, levels of parental separation anxiety reduce as their confidence and trust in the professional grows.

Honig's suggestions reflect material presented throughout this book. She encourages prompt, consistent and appropriate responses to promote secure attachments. These should occur as routine characteristics of all the 'small daily gestures, reflections, and activities' (1998, p. 23) that take place during a normal day of caregiving. She also stresses respectful interactions, including use of the child's name, a calm tone of voice, and informing children, even infants, when and why you are about to leave the room and when you will return. She underlines the importance of touch, including caresses, baby massage and 'lap or snuggle time even for children who seem to avoid adult touches' (p. 24). Well-developed observation skills are necessary so that subtle attachment cues and signals are not missed. And finally, she acknowledges the importance of caregiver self-knowledge:

> We all have flash points for getting exasperated or feeling badly treated. Most of us can remember times when we had less than optimal family rearing conditions . . . Reflect on yourself and nurture your own life. Then you will have the inner resources to become the kind of nurturing teacher who will build a positive attachment between each child and yourself in the classroom (1998, p. 28).

Questions and answers about policy and practice implications

In chapter 1 (p. 6), readers were encouraged to reflect on a series of themes as they progressed through the text. Each theme is now revisited as a way of drawing out the practice and policy implications of attachment theory and research.

Theme 1: How does attachment theory translate into ways of interacting with children that nurture security, autonomy, feelings of competence and resilience?

In chapter 5, the links between secure attachment, feelings of competence and resilience were outlined. In chapters 6 and 7 we explored the two major tasks of the attachment relationship—to develop the child's sense of trust in others (security) and to develop trust in him or herself (autonomy). Ideally these feelings are established over the first three years or so of a child's life. In the normal course of events, trust in others is learnt first, during the infancy period when dependency is high. Autonomy and initiative develop as children become mobile and begin independent explorations of the world around them. The early childhood professional must be aware of, and sensitive to, these developmental stages, and know what interactions and activities promote optimal outcomes at each stage. We have considered ways of interacting that promote security, and ways of interacting that promote autonomy. These are described in detail in Rolfe (2002), and are summarised here.

Promoting security

Children develop trust and feel secure when their caregiver is *sensitive, responsive, warm and consistent*. What exactly do each of these mean?

- *Being sensitive* means being 'tuned in' to the child's feelings, and able to read their cues. This requires opportunities for relatively uninterrupted and sustained individual time with a child. This is when we can best get to know the young child, and the child can best get to know us. One-to-one interactions are the repository of attunement experiences, of joint attention and loving nurture. Being sensitive requires us to be relatively free from ongoing distractions when interacting with a child. It requires us to notice when children signal to us, even in a group setting. And it requires careful attention to how all children are feeling, even those who are less demanding of attention. The sensitive caregiver also understands that children of different ages signal their needs for comfort and attention in different ways.

- *Being responsive* means being psychologically available, and able to respond to children's cues appropriately. Responsiveness and sensitivity are inter-related, and most writings on attachment put them together in the one term: 'sensitive responsiveness'. You must know each child well, what comforts him or her, and provide whatever time is required to settle, soothe or reassure the child. This might mean giving your undivided attention to one child for an extended period and having colleagues who can support you when this is required. Children need caregivers who are patient, gentle, calm, reassuring, kind and clear, even in the face of strong negative feelings, such as the child's distress, frustration or anger. You need different strategies to try at these times, as some responses to a child's attachment needs are not effective every time. You need to work closely with the child's family to understand what works best to soothe and calm anxiety and distress.

- *Being warm* means responding to children with honest, positive affection. It means providing a child with feelings that you genuinely enjoy interacting with them. The early childhood setting must be an environment where appropriately intimate and loving relationships are both accepted and expected. Again, time is essential. Many young children need sustained physical closeness with their caregivers. Behaviour that is rushed or mechanistic is to be avoided.

- *Being consistent* means interacting with a child predictably, that is, to consistently present a predictable mood and way of responding. Children need to know that certain caregivers will be consistently available to them as well. This is particularly important for infants and toddlers. Children need age-appropriate limits and boundaries, applied fairly, calmly and predictably.

Promoting autonomy and competence

As we have discussed in other parts of this book, experiences that promote *autonomy, initiative, feelings of self-competence and high self-esteem* are important to promoting resilience. The importance of these feelings resides in their ability to promote children's views of themselves as agents with control over their lives and their destiny.

- Experiences that enhance feelings of *autonomy* assist the child develop their sense of being able to function independently and competently. Children need opportunities to make age-appropriate choices, to explore and try out skills independently while caregivers monitor their safety. They depend on caregivers to be available as a secure base when needed during their independent forays. Experiences within the early childhood setting that focus on the unique characteristics of each child and celebrate diversity will foster autonomy. So will respecting the rights of every child to decide whether or not to participate in a planned activity. Flexibility in the timing of routines, such as sleeping and meal times, allows children more control.

- Experiences that enhance feelings of *self-competence*, *efficacy* and *self-esteem* are those that help children feel good about themselves, their abilities and their relationships. Each child needs to feel valued unconditionally. Disapproval of inappropriate behaviour must not be a rejection of the child or an evaluation of her or him as less worthwhile. Constructive feedback is direct, accurate, specific and objective and is not derogatory, humiliating or demeaning.

- Children need to experience naturally occurring situations of manageable disappointment or failure so that they have opportunities to experience a range of emotions. Your role is to assist them to cope. Providing many opportunities for challenge at a level that can be mastered by the child with appropriate effort, persistence and support will help. So will modelling self-acceptance and respect for others.

Theme 2: What implications does attachment theory have for the way we set up early childhood environments, especially the interpersonal dimensions of the setting?

Attachment theory makes clear, unambiguous statements about the need for caregivers to have the necessary time, resources and emotional energy to provide that critical caregiving ingredient of sensitive responsiveness. The crucial cut-off in staff–child ratios may be debatable, but sensitive responsiveness as described here is unlikely to be achieved with caregiver:infant ratios greater than 1:3. Attachment theory also makes a clear and unambiguous statement about the importance of continuity of care, especially for infants and toddlers. If staff turnover is high, or the least experienced and less-trained staff are employed in infant and toddler rooms, continuity of care for the first three years may be difficult to achieve. But in a context of inadequate wages and conditions, staff turnover will remain high.

Finally, chapters 10 and 11 have made clear that separation experiences in the context of early childhood settings must be handled sensitively, or the security of children's attachments to parents and professional caregivers alike will be compromised. Too little attention has yet been paid to this aspect of the child–care experience. This is surprising given the emphasis on separation concerns in the child-care debate. Children's secure attachments are enhanced by a transition phase long enough for the child to develop confidence in the new caregiver before being left for extended times in the new setting. Attachment theory predicts that the child will be helped by experiencing first hand a positive relationship between their parents and the early childhood professional—that is, in understanding that the parent trusts the caregiver, the child is encouraged and affirmed to trust him or her too. Extended transitions may be challenging to achieve but attachment theory underlines their critical importance in the short and longer-term.

Adequate attention needs to be given to parents' separation feelings. Research described in chapter 11 makes it clear that some, if not all, parents experience feelings of sadness, anxiety and guilt about leaving their children, and this is usually more intense the younger the child. Policy and practice must be sensitive to these parental concerns and allow more opportunities for grief resolution.

Theme 3: How can I use attachment theory and research to understand better the behaviours of those in the early childhood community in which I work—the children, the parents, other professionals, myself?

There is much in this book about how children's behaviour and development reflects the security of their attachment history. There would be few, if any, chapters that do not touch on this topic in one way or another, and there is no need to reiterate the material again here. Attachment theory also has important things to say about adult attachment issues, and provides important insights into adult behaviour in the early childhood setting.

In relation to parents, the most important message from attachment theory is that the more parents are supported in the role, the more likely it is that their relationship with their child will be secure. Supporting parents and other significant people in a child's life maximise the child's opportunities for positive relationship experiences with them in the home.

To support parents, early childhood professionals need to develop partnerships with the family through which an understanding of the child and knowledge and respect for the culture of the family can grow. It is important to schedule time with parents that allows meaningful, uninterrupted dialogue about the child and any concerns the parents may have. Being willing and able to offer advice and support to parents if requested, particularly guidance and encouragement in relation to child development and child management issues, is important. So too is developing professional networks that enable parents or other family members to link with other community supports and resources if required. Being an active listener, vigilant for signs that a family is under stress or having problems coping, and having realistic expectations about the extent of parents' involvement in and contribution to the life of the early childhood setting helps.

A climate of supportive collegial relationships and shared curriculum goals within the early childhood setting will promote the ability of all to provide sensitive, responsive care. Chapters 3, 4 and 11 provide material relevant to understanding adult attachment needs, and are an important guide for self-reflection of the kind espoused by Honig (1998).

Theme 4: In what ways might I change/modify/develop my interactions with children, parents and colleagues to best nurture their wellbeing?

Hopefully there has been much in this book to guide processes of change. Developing new ways of relating may take considerable personal courage, dedication, perseverance and the encouragement and support of others.

Some words of caution

While this book has emphasised the significance of secure and insecure attachment patterns and explored how they are apparent in the developing social and emotional behaviours of the child, it is important to stress that the clinical identification and classification of these different patterns is a task requiring extensive, specialised training. Strange Situation coders must first attend a week-long training program and then score a large number of videotaped sessions to a high level of accuracy before they become certified. The same is true for the Adult Attachment Interview.

Observation is a highly subjective undertaking, and cues to quality of attachment are subtle and easily misunderstood and misinterpreted. There are many reasons why children may behave as they do, especially under diverse and changing conditions. It is the task of the early childhood professional to promote secure attachments. Classifying individual children and their relationships with significant others is a task best undertaken by those specifically trained to do so.

Final thoughts

When I teach my students about child development theories, I encourage them to take an eclectic approach, to sample from all that is available. I stress to them that the diversity of domains of psychological development, and its complexity, mean that it is unlikely any one theory could ever explain all that needs to be known.

For myself, attachment theory has provided many of the answers I have sought to questions about why people develop as they do. It makes sense, it rings true, and it is supported by a growing research literature that continues to raise interesting and provocative questions. It is a theoretical and empirical literature that does not shy away from difficult controversies and debates. Attachment theory is young. Those who have dedicated much of their professional life to testing its tenets are amongst the first to admit there are many issues yet to be resolved and many complexities yet to be explored.

This book has attempted to engage with the implications of attachment theory and research for early childhood professionals.

It has been about reflecting on and rethinking attachment and what it has to say about nurturing the psychological wellbeing of infants, children and adults in early childhood settings. There is much work still to be done.

Appendix

Helpful websites

International Attachment Network

Website: <www.attachmentnetwork.org>
The International Attachment Network (IAN) promotes the study of attachment and related topics amongst relevant professionals, including psychologists, teachers and social workers, and acts as a meeting place for the exchange of information and ideas. The IAN organises seminars, courses and workshops and publishes the journal *Attachment and Human Development* in conjunction with Taylor and Francis. The website advertises events, provides news and relevant articles and other information about attachment.

Attachment research at the State University of New York at Stony Brook

Website: <www.psychology.sunysb.edu/ewaters/>
This website is the link to the attachment research laboratory of Everett Waters and colleagues at the State University of New York at Stony Brook. It provides lists of relevant publications, information on attachment measures including the Attachment Q-Set, and other interesting information in relation to attachment theory.

Attachment research at the University of Western Ontario

Website: <www.ssc.uwo.ca/psychology/faculty/pedmor/pedermor.html>
This website is the link to the attachment research laboratory of
Greg Moran and David Pederson and colleagues at the University
of Western Ontario, Canada. It presents information on research
and measures of maternal sensitivity and attachment, recent
publications of the group, including masters and doctoral research
projects.

Focus Adolescent Services — Attachment and Attachment Disorders

Website: <www.focusas.com/Attachment.html>
This website presents much information relevant to attachment and
in particular to attachment disorders in children and adolescents.
There is a very extensive list of web-based links, book reviews and
information on upcoming conferences about attachment and
attachment-based interventions. Focus Adolescent Services is
described as an Internet clearinghouse of information and resources
to help and support families with troubled and at-risk teens: 'Our
mission is to provide information and resources to empower
individuals to help their teens and heal their families. Through
education, self-awareness, self-help, and personal responsibility,
families can rebuild their relationships and reconnect in positive
and loving ways. Professionals, journalists, youth workers, and students
also find valuable information at Focus Adolescent Services to help
them in their work and study' (from website).

World Association for Infant Mental Health (WAIMH)

Website: <www.msu.edu/user/waimh/main.html>
WAIMH is an interdisciplinary and international association that:

* Promotes education, research, and study of the effects of mental,
  emotional, and social development during infancy on later
  normal and psychopathological development.
* Promotes research and study of the mental health of the parents, families, and other caregivers of infants.

- Promotes the development of scientifically based programs of care, intervention, and prevention of mental impairment in infancy.
- Sponsors regional and biennial world congresses devoted to scientific, educational, and clinical work with infants and their caregivers.
- Encourages the realisation that infancy is a crucial period in the psychosocial development of individuals.
- Facilitates international cooperation among individuals concerned with promoting optimal development of infants and their families.
- Provides international networking via quarterly newsletters, computer-based information technology, and development of Affiliate Associations.
- Sponsors the *Infant Mental Health Journal* and provides members reduced rates for subscriptions (from website).

The website presents resources in the area of infant mental health including publications, videos and an extensive list of relevant web links, and information on the WAIMH World Congress.

National Child Protection Clearing House at the Australian Institute of Family Studies (AIFS)

Website: <www.aifs.gov.au/nch/nch_menu.html>
'The National Child Protection Clearinghouse is funded by the Commonwealth Department of Family and Community Services as part of the Commonwealth's response to the problem of child abuse. The National Child Protection Clearinghouse has operated from the Australian Institute of Family Studies since 1995 and provides an information/advisory service to workers in the field' (from website). It aims to inform policy, practice and research into child abuse prevention.

The website includes extensive information on resources, publications, crisis and counselling services in relation to child abuse and links to related websites.

References

Ainsworth, M.D.S. 1963 'The development of infant–mother interaction among the Ganda' *Determinants of Infant Behaviour* vol. 2, ed B.M. Foss, Wiley, New York, pp. 67–112

——1964 'Patterns of attachment behaviour shown by the infant in interaction with his mother' *Merrill-Palmer Quarterly* vol. 10, pp. 51–8

——1967 *Infancy in Uganda: Infant care and the growth of attachment* The Johns Hopkins Press, Baltimore

——1984 'Attachment' *Personality and the Behavioral Disorders* vol. 1, eds N.S. Endler and J. McV. Hunt, Wiley, New York, pp. 559–602

Ainsworth, M.D.S., Blehar, M.C., Waters, E. and Wall, S. 1978 *Patterns of Attachment: Assessed in the strange situation and at home* Erlbaum, Hillsdale, NJ

Ainsworth, M.D.S. and Wittig, B.A. 1969 'Attachment and exploratory behaviour in one-year-olds in a Strange Situation' *Determinants of Infant Behaviour* vol. 4, ed. B.M. Foss, Methuen, London, pp. 111–36

American Psychiatric Association 1994 *Diagnostic and Statistical Manual of Mental Disorders (4th edn)* APA, Washington, DC

Anthony, E.J. and Cohler, B.J. 1987 *The Invulnerable Child* The Guilford Press, New York

Australian Department of Family and Community Services 2002 *Warrki Jarrinjaku Jintangkamanu Purananjaku 'Working together everyone and listening': Aboriginal child rearing and associated research: A review of the literature* Commonwealth of Australia, Canberra

Belsky, J. 1986 'Infant day care: a cause for concern?' *Zero to Three* vol. 6, pp. 1–7

——1989 'Infant-parent attachment and day care: In defense of the Strange Situation' *Caring for Children: Challenge to America* eds J. Lande, S. Scarr and N. Gunzenhauser, Erlbaum, Hillsdale, NJ, pp. 83–5

——1999a 'Modern evolutionary theory and patterns of attachment' *Handbook of Attachment: Theory, research and clinical applications* eds J. Cassidy and P.R. Shaver, The Guilford Press, New York, pp. 141–61

——1999b 'Interactional and contextual determinants of attachment security' *Handbook of Attachment: Theory, research and clinical applications* eds J. Cassidy and P.R. Shaver, The Guilford Press, New York pp. 249–64

Belsky, J., Garduque, L. and Hrncir, E. 1984 'Assessing performance, competence, and executive capacity in infant play: Relations to home environment and security of attachment' *Developmental Psychology* vol. 20, pp. 406–17

Belsky, J., Rovine, M. and Taylor, D.G. 1984 'The Pennsylvania infant and family development project, III. The origins of individual differences in infant–mother attachment: Maternal and infant contributions' *Child Development* vol. 55, pp. 718–28

Belsky, J. and Steinberg, L. 1978 'The effects of day care: A critical review' *Child Development* vol. 49, pp. 929–49

Benoit, D. and Parker, K.C.H. 1994 'Stability and transmission of attachment across three generations' *Child Development* vol. 65, pp. 1444–56

Berk, L.E. 2000 *Child Development* 5th edn, Allyn & Bacon, Boston

Berlin, L.J. and Cassidy, J. 2001 'Enhancing early child–parent relationships: Implications of adult attachment research' *Infants and Young Children* vol. 14, pp. 64–76

Blehar, M.C. 1974 'Anxious attachment and defensive reactions associated with day care' *Child Development* vol. 45, pp. 683–92

Bowlby, J. 1958 'The nature of the child's tie to his mother' *International Journal of Psycho-Analysis* vol. 39, pp. 350–73

——1969/1982 *Attachment and Loss: Vol. 1. Attachment* 2nd edn, Basic Books, New York

——1973 *Attachment and Loss: Vol. 2. Separation, anxiety and anger* Basic Books, New York

——1980 *Attachment and Loss: Vol. 3. Loss, sadness and depression* The Hogarth Press, London

——1988 *A Secure Base: Clinical implications of attachment theory* Routledge, London

——1991 'Postscript' *Attachment Across the Life Cycle* eds C.M. Parkes, J. Stevenson-Hinde and P. Marris, Tavistock, London, pp. 293–7

Bretherton, I., Ridgeway, D. and Cassidy, J. 1990 'Assessing internal working models of the attachment relationship: An attachment story completion task for 3-year-olds' *Attachment in the Preschool Years: Theory, research and intervention* eds. M. Greenberg, D. Cicchetti and E.M. Cummings, The University of Chicago Press, Chicago, pp. 273–308

Bronfenbrenner, U. 1979 *The Ecology of Human Development* Harvard University Press, Cambridge, MA

Burhans, K.K. and Dweck, C.S. 1995 'Helplessness in early childhood: The role of contingent worth' *Child Development* vol. 66, pp. 1719–38

Bus, A.G. and van IJzendoorn, M.H. 1988 'Mother–child interactions, attachment, and emergent literacy: A cross-sectional study' *Child Development* vol. 59, pp. 1262–72

Cain, K. and Dweck, C.S. 1995 'The relation between motivational patterns and achievement cognitions through the elementary school years' *Merrill-Palmer Quarterly* vol. 41, pp. 25–52

Carlson, E.A. 1998 'A prospective longitudinal study of attachment disorganisation/disorientation' *Child Development* vol. 69, pp. 1107–28

Carlson, E.A. and Earls, F. 1997 'Psychological and neuroendocrinological sequelae of early social deprivation in institutionalised children in Romania' *Annals of the New York Academy of Sciences* vol. 807, pp. 419–28

Cassidy, J. 1994 'Emotion regulation: Influences of attachment relationships' *The Development of Emotion Regulation: Biological and behavioural considerations. Monographs of the Society for Research in Child Development* ed. N.A. Fox, vol. 59, pp. 121–34

Cassidy, J. and Shaver, P.R. eds 1999 *Handbook of Attachment: Theory, research and clinical applications* The Guilford Press, New York

Chisholm, K. 1998 'A three-year follow-up of attachment and indiscriminate friendliness in children adopted from Romanian orphanages' *Child Development* vol. 69, pp. 1090–104

Cicchetti, D., Cummings, E.M., Greenberg, M.T. and Marvin, R.S. 1990 'An organisational perspective on attachment beyond infancy' *Attachment in the Preschool Years: Theory, research, and intervention* eds M.T. Greenberg, D. Cicchetti and E.M. Cummings, The University of Chigaco Press, Chicago, pp. 3–49

Clarke, A. and Clarke, A. 2003 *Human Resilience: A fifty year quest* Jessica Kingsley, London

Clarke-Stewart, K.A. 1988 'The "effects" of infant day care reconsidered' Reconsidered: Roles for parents, children and researchers *Early Childhood Research Quarterly* vol. 3, pp. 293–318

Colin, V.L. 1996 *Human Attachment* McGraw-Hill, New York

Constantino, J. and Olesh, H. 1999 'Mental representations of attachment in day care providers' *Infant Mental Health Journal* vol. 20, pp. 138–47

Craik, K. 1943 *The Nature of Explanation* Cambridge University Press, Cambridge

Crittenden, P. 1981 'Abusing, neglecting, problematic, and adequate dyads: Differentiating by patterns of interaction' *Merrill-Palmer Quarterly* vol. 27, pp. 81–96

——1992 'Quality of attachment in the preschool years' *Development and Psychopathology* vol. 4, pp. 209–41

——1995 'Attachment and psychopathology' *Attachment Theory: Social, developmental and clinical perspectives* eds S. Goldberg, R. Muir and J. Kerr, The Analytic Press, Hillsdale, NJ, pp. 367–406

——2000a 'Introduction' *The Organisation of Attachment Relationships: Maturation, culture, and context* eds P.M. Crittenden and A.H. Claussen, Cambridge University Press, Cambridge, pp. 1–12

——2000b 'A dynamic-maturational exploration of the meaning of security and adaptation' *The Organisation of Attachment Relationships: Maturation, culture, and context* eds P.M. Crittenden and A.H. Claussen, Cambridge University Press, Cambridge, pp. 358–83

Crittenden, P.M. and Claussen, A.H. eds 2000 *The Organisation of Attachment Relationships: Maturation, culture, and context* Cambridge University Press, Cambridge

Crowell, J.A., Fraley, R.C. and Shaver, P.R. 1999 'Measurement of individual differences in adolescent and adult attachment' *Handbook of Attachment: Theory, research and clinical applications* eds J. Cassidy and P.R. Shaver, The Guilford Press, New York pp. 434–68

Davis, M. 1997 'Paternal separation anxiety' Unpublished Bachelor of Early Childhood Studies Honours Thesis presented to the Department of Learning and Educational Development, The University of Melbourne

Davison, L. 1994 'Maternal separation anxiety: An investigation of predictors and the effects of two intervention strategies' Unpublished report, Royal Melbourne Institute of Technology

DeMeis, D.K., Hock, E. and McBride, S.L. 1986 'The balance of employment and motherhood: Longitudinal study of mothers' feelings about separation from their first-born infants' *Developmental Psychology* vol. 22, pp. 627–32

DeWolff, M. and van IJzendoorn, M. 1997 'Sensitivity and attachment: A meta-analysis on parental antecedents of infant attachment' *Child Development* vol. 68, pp. 571–91

Dowlby, R. 2003 'On being emotionally available' *Reflections: National Gowrie RAP Publication* Issue 12, pp. 4–6

Dowlby, R. and Swan, B. 2003 'Strengthening relationships between early childhood staff, high needs children and their families in the preschool setting' *Developing Practice: The child, youth and family work journal* vol. 6, pp, 18–23

Dowlby, R., Warren, E. and Mares, S. 2001 'A new collaboration between psychiatry and child care: The establishment of a mentor group' Paper presented at the Australian Early Childhood Association Biennial Conference, Sydney

Dozier, M., Stovall, K.C. and Albus, K.E. 1999 'A Transactional intervention for foster infants' caregivers' *Rochester Symposium on Developmental Psychopathology, vol. 9: Developmental approaches to prevention and intervention* eds. D. Cicchetti and S.L. Toth, University of Rochester Press, New York, pp. 195–219

Dozier, M., Stovall, K.C., Albus, K.E. and Bates, B. 2001 'Attachment for infants in foster care: The role of caregiver state of mind' *Child Development* vol. 55, pp. 1467–78

Dunn, J. 1993 *Young Children's Close Relationships: Beyond attachment* Sage, London

Easterbrooks, M.A. and Goldberg, W.A. 1990 'Security of toddler–parent attachment: Relation to children's sociopersonality functioning during kindergarten' *Attachment in the Preschool Years: Theory, research, and intervention* eds. M.T. Greenberg, D. Cicchetti and E.M. Cummings, The University of Chicago Press, Chicago, pp. 221–44

Edwards, C. and Raikes, H. 2002 'Extending the dance: Relationship-based approaches to infant-toddler care and education' *Young Children* vol. 57, pp. 10–17

Egeland, B. and Farber, E.A. 1984 'Infant–mother attachment: Factors related to its development and changes over time' *Child Development* vol. 55, pp. 753–71

Emde, R.N. 1980 'Emotional availability: A reciprocal reward system for infants and parents with implications for prevention of psychosocial disorders' *Parent–infant Relationships* ed. P.M. Taylor, Grune & Stratton, Orlando, Florida, pp. 87–115

Erikson, E. 1963 *Childhood and Society* 2nd edn, Norton, New York

——1968 *Identity, Youth and Crisis* Norton, New York

Fahlberg, V.I. 1994 *A Child's Journey Through Placement* UK edn, BAAF, London

Fein, G.G. 1995 'Infants in group care: Patterns of despair and detachment' *Early Childhood Research Quarterly* vol. 10, pp. 261–75

Flavell, J.H. 1986 'The development of children's knowledge about the appearance–reality distinction' *American Psychologist* vol. 41, pp. 418–24

Fonagy, P. 1999 'Psychoanalytic theory from the viewpoint of attachment theory and research' *Handbook of Attachment: Theory, research and clinical applications* eds. J. Cassidy and P.R. Shaver, The Guilford Press, New York, pp. 595–624

Fonagy, P., Steele, H. and Steele, M. 1991 'Maternal representations of attachment during pregnancy predict the organisation of infant–mother attachment at one year of age' *Child Development* vol. 62, pp. 891–905

Fonagy, P., Steele, M., Steele, H., Higgitt, A. and Target, M. 1994 'The Emmanual Miller Memorial Lecture 1992. The theory and practice of resilience' *Journal of Child Psychology and Psychiatry* vol. 35, pp. 231–58

Fox, N.A. and Fein, G. 1990 *Infant Day Care: The current debate* Ablex, Norwood, NJ

Freud, A. 1965 *The Writings of Anna Freud: Vol. 6. Normality and pathology in childhood: Assessments of development* International Universities Press, New York

Fury, G., Carlson, E.A. and Sroufe, L.A. 1997 'Children's representations of attachment relationships in family drawings' *Child Development* vol. 68, pp 1154–64

George, C. and Solomon, J. 1999 'Attachment and caregiving: The caregiving behavioural system' *Handbook of Attachment: Theory, research and clinical applications* eds J. Cassidy and P.R. Shaver, The Guilford Press, New York, pp. 649–70

Glantz, M.D. and Johnson, J.L. eds 1999 *Resilience and Development: Positive life adaptations* Plenum, New York

Goldberg, S. 2000 *Attachment and Development* Arnold, London

Goossens, F. and Melhuish, E.C. 1996 'On the ecological validity of measuring the sensitivity of professional caregivers: The laboratory versus the nursery' *European Journal of Psychology of Education* vol. 11, pp. 169–76

Goossens, F. and van IJzendoorn, M. 1990 'Quality of infants' attachments to professional caregivers: Relation to infant–parent attachment and day-care characteristics' *Child Development* vol. 61, pp. 832–7

Greenberg, M.T. 1999 'Attachment and psychopathology in childhood' *Handbook of Attachment: Theory, research and clinical applications* eds J. Cassidy and P.R. Shaver, The Guilford Press, New York, pp. 469–96

Greenberg, M.T., Cicchetti, D. and Cummings, E.M. eds 1990 *Attachment in the Preschool Years: Theory, research, and intervention* The University of Chigaco Press, Chicago

Greenberg, M.T. and Speltz, M.T. 1988 'Attachment and the ontogeny of conduct problems' *Clinical Implications of Attachment* eds J. Belsky and T. Nezworski, Erlbaum, Hillsdale, NJ, pp. 177–218

Greenberg, M.T., Speltz, M.L. and DeKlyen, M. 1993 'The role of attachment in the early development of disruptive behaviour problems' *Development and Psychopathology* vol. 5, pp. 191–213

Grossmann, K.E. 1995 'The evolution and history of attachment research and theory' *Attachment Theory: Social, developmental and clinical perspectives* eds S. Goldberg, R. Muir and J. Kerr, The Analytic Press, Hillsdale, NJ, pp. 85–122

Grossmann, K., Fremmer-Bombik, E., Rudolph, J. and Grossmann, K.E. 1988 'Maternal attachment representations as related to patterns of infant–mother attachment and maternal care during the first year' *Relationships Within Families: Mutual influences* eds. R. A. Hinde and J. Stevenson-Hinde, Oxford University Press, Oxford, pp. 241–69

Grossmann, K.E. and Grossmann, K. 1991 'Attachment quality as an organizer of emotional and behavioral responses in a longitudinal perspective' *Attachment*

Across the Life Cycle eds C.M. Parkes, J. Stevenson-Hinde and P. Marris, Tavistock/Routledge, London, pp. 93–114

Grossmann, K., Grossmann, K.E., Spangler, G., Suess, G. and Unzner, L. 1985 'Maternal sensitivity and newborns' orientation responses as related to quality of attachment in northern Germany' *Growing Points of Attachment Theory and Research. Monographs of the Society for Research in Child Development* eds I. Bretherton and E. Waters, vol. 50 (1–2, Serial No. 209), pp. 233–57

Hans, S.L., Bernstein, V.J. and Sims, B.E. 2000 'Change and continuity in ambivalent attachment relationships from infancy through adolescence' *The Organisation of Attachment Relationships: Maturation, culture, and context* eds P.M. Crittenden and A.H. Claussen, Cambridge University Press, Cambridge, pp. 277–99

Harrison, L. 2003 'Attachment: Building secure relationships in early childhood' *Research in Practice Series*, Early Childhood Australia, Canberra

Harrison, L. and Ungerer, J. 1997 'Child care predictors of infant–mother attachment security at age 12 months' *Early Child Development and Care* vol. 137, pp. 31–46

——2002 'Maternal employment and infant–mother attachment security at 12 months postpartum' *Developmental Psychology* vol. 38, pp. 758–73

Harwood, R.L., Miller, J.G. and Irizarry, N.L. 1995 *Culture and Attachment: Perceptions of the child in context* The Guilford Press, New York

Hazan, C. and Shaver, P.R. 1987 'Romantic love conceptualised as an attachment process' *Journal of Personality and Social Psychology* vol. 52, pp. 511–24

Heinicke, C. 1956 'Some effects of separating two-year-old children from their parents: A comparative study' *Human Relations* vol. 9, pp. 105–76

Heinicke, C.M. and Ponce, V.A. 1999 'Relation-based early family intervention' *Rochester Symposium on Developmental Psychopathology, vol 9: Developmental approaches to prevention and intervention* eds D. Cicchetti and S.L. Toth, University of Rochester Press, New York

Heinicke, C. and Westheimer, I. 1966 *Brief Separations* Longmans, London

Hock, E. 1984 'The transition to daycare: Effects of maternal separation anxiety on infant adjustment' *The Child and the Day Care Setting: Qualitative variations and development* ed. R.C. Ainslie, Praeger, New York, pp. 183–205

Hock, E., DeMeis, D.K. and McBride, S.L. 1988 'Maternal separation anxiety: Its role in the balance of employment and motherhood in mothers of infants' *Maternal Employment and Children's Development: Longitudinal research* eds A.E. Gottfried and A.W. Gottfried, Plenum, New York, pp. 191–230

Hock, E., McBride, S. L. and Gnezda, M. T. 1989 'Maternal separation anxiety: Mother–infant separation from the maternal perspective' *Child Development* vol. 60, pp. 793–802

Hock, E. and Schirtzinger, M.B. 1992 'Maternal separation anxiety: Its developmental course and relation to maternal mental health' *Child Development* vol. 63, pp. 93–102

Hoffman, M. 1985 'Affect, cognition, and motivation' *Handbook of Motivation and Cognition* eds R. Sorrento and E.T. Higgins, Guilford, New York, pp. 244–80

Holmes, J. 1993 *John Bowlby and Attachment Theory* Routledge, London

Honig, A.S. 1998 'Attachment and relationships: Beyond parenting' Paper presented at the Head Start Quality Network Research Satellite Conference (East Lansing MI, 20 August, 1998) (ED 423043)

Howard, S., Dryden, J. and Johnson, B. 1999 'Childhood resilience: Review and critique of literature' *Oxford Review of Education* vol. 25(3), pp. 307–23

Howe, D. 1995 *Attachment Theory for Social Work Practice* Macmillan, London

Howe, D., Brandon, M., Hinings, D. and Schofield, G. 1999 *Attachment Theory, Child Maltreatment and Family Support: A practice and assessment model* Erlbaum, Mahwah, NJ

Howes, C. 1997 'Teacher sensitivity, children's attachment and play with peers' *Early Education and Development* vol. 8, pp. 41–9

——1999 Attachment relationships in the context of multiple caregivers' *Handbook of Attachment: Theory, research and clinical applications* eds J. Cassidy and P.R. Shaver, The Guilford Press, New York, pp. 671–87

Howes, C., Galinsky, E. and Kontos, S. 1998 'Child care caregiver sensitivity and attachment' *Social Development* vol. 7, pp. 25–36

Howes, C. and Hamilton, C.E. 1992 'Children's relationships with child care teachers: Stability and concordance with maternal attachment' *Child Development* vol. 53, pp. 879–92

Howes, C., Phillips, D.A. and Whitebook, M. 1992 'Threshold of quality: Implications for the social development of children in child care' *Child Development* vol. 63, pp. 449–60

Howes, C. and Ritchie, S. 1998 'Changes in child–teacher relationships in a therapeutic preschool program' *Early Education and Development* vol. 4, pp. 411–22

Howes, C., Rodning, C., Galluzzo, D.C. and Myers, L. 1988 'Attachment and child care: relationships with mother and caregiver' *Early-Childhood Research Quarterly* vol. 3, pp. 403–16

Howes, C. and Segal, J. 1993 'Children's relationships with alternative caregivers: The special case of maltreated children removed from their homes' *Journal of Applied Developmental Psychology* vol. 14, pp. 71–81

Howes, C. and Smith, E.W. 1995 'Relations among child care quality, teacher behavior, children's play activities, emotional security, and cognitive activity in child care' *Early Childhood Research Quarterly* vol. 10, pp. 381–404

Hughes, D.A. 1997 *Facilitating Developmental Attachment: The road to emotional recovery and behavioural change in foster and adopted children* Jason Aronson Inc, Northvale, NJ

Joseph, R. 1999 'Environmental influences on neural plasticity, the limbic system, emotional development and attachment: A review' *Child Psychiatry and Human Development* vol. 29, pp. 189–208

Kagan, J., Kearlsey, R.B. and Zelazo, P.R. 1978 *Infancy: Its place in development* Harvard University Press, Cambridge, MA

Karen, R. 1994 *Becoming Attached: Unfolding the mystery of the infant–mother bond and its impact on later life* Warner Books, New York

Kellman, P.J. and Arterberry, M.E. 1998 *The Cradle of Knowledge: Development of perception in infancy* MIT Press, Cambridge, MA

Kobak, R. 1999 'The emotional dynamics of disruptions in attachment relationships: Implications for theory, research, and clinical intervention' *Handbook of Attachment: Theory, research and clinical applications* eds J. Cassidy and P.R. Shaver, The Guilford Press, New York, pp. 21–43

Lamb, M.E., Bornstein, M.H. and Teti, D.M. 2002 *Development in Infancy: An introduction* Erlbaum, Mahwah, NJ

Lamb, M.E. and Sternberg, K. 1990 'Do we really know how day care affects children?' *Journal of Applied Developmental Psychology* vol. 11, pp. 351–79

Lieberman, A.F. and Zeanah, C.H. 1995 'Disorders of attachment in infancy' *Child and Adolescent Psychiatric Clinics of North America* vol. 4, pp. 571–687

Luthar, S.S., Cicchetti, D. and Becker, B. 2000 'The construct of resilience: A critical evaluation and guidelines for future work' *Child Development* vol. 71, pp. 543–62

Lyons–Ruth, K. and Jacobvitz, D. 1999 'Attachment disorganisation: Unresolved loss, relational violence, and lapses in behavioural and attentional strategies' *Handbook of Attachment: Theory, research and clinical applications* eds J. Cassidy and P.R. Shaver, The Guilford Press, New York, pp. 520–54

Mahler, M.S., Pine, F. and Bergman, A. 1975 *The Psychological Birth of the Human Infant* Basic Books, New York

Main, M. 1991 'Metacognitive knowledge, metacognitive monitoring, and singular (coherent) vs multiple (incoherent) models of attachment: findings and directions for future work' *Attachment Across the Life Cycle* eds C.M. Parkes., J. Stevenson-Hinde and P. Marris, Routledge, London, pp. 127–59

——1995 'Recent studies in attachment: Overview with selected implication for clinical work' *Attachment Theory: Social, developmental, and clinical perspectives* eds S. Goldberg, R. Muir and J. Kerr, Analytic Press, Hillsdale, NJ, pp. 407–74

Main, M. and Goldwyn, R. 1984 'Predicting rejection of her infant from mother's representations of her own experience: implications for the abused-abusing intergenerational cycle' *Child Abuse and Neglect* vol. 8, pp. 203–17

Main, M. and Hesse, E. 1990 'Parents' unresolved traumatic experiences are related to infant disorganized attachment status: Is frightened and/or frightening parent behavior the linking mechanism', eds M.T. Greenberg, D. Cicchetti and E.M. Cummings *Attachment in the Preschool Years: Theory, research, and intervention* The University of Chigaco Press, Chicago, pp. 161–82

Main, M., Kaplan, N. and Cassidy, J. 1985 'Security in infancy, childhood, and adulthood: A move to the level of representation' *Growing Points of Attachment Theory and Research. Monographs of the Society for Research in Child Development* eds I. Bretherton and E. Waters, vol. 50 (1–2, Serial No. 209), pp. 66–106

Main, M. and Solomon, J. 1986 'Discovery of a new, insecure–disorganised/disoriented attachment pattern' *Affective Development in Infancy* eds T.B. Brazelton and M.W. Yogman, Ablex, Norwood, NJ, pp. 95–124

——1990 'Procedures for identifying infants as disorganised/disoriented during the Ainsworth Strange Situation' *Attachment in the Preschool Years: Theory, research and intervention* eds M. Greenberg, D. Cicchetti and M. Cummings, University of Chicago Press, Chicago, pp. 121–60

Marfo, K. 1992 'Correlates of maternal directiveness with children who are developmentally delayed' *American Journal of Orthopsychiatry* vol. 62, pp. 219–33

Marris, P. 1991 'The social construction of uncertainty' *Attachment Across the Life Cycle* eds C.M. Parkes, J. Stevenson-Hinde and P. Marris, Tavistock/Routledge, London, pp. 77–90

Marvin, R., Cooper, G., Hoffman, K. and Powell, B. 2002 'The circle of security project: Attachment-based intervention with caregiver–pre-school child dyads' *Attachment and Human Development* vol. 4, pp. 107–24

Maslin-Cole, C. and Spieker, S.J. 1990 'Attachment as a basis for independent motivation: A view from risk and nonrisk samples' *Attachment in the Preschool Years: Theory, research and intervention* eds M.T. Greenberg, D. Cicchetti and E.M. Cummings, University of Chicago Press, Chicago, pp. 245–72

Masten, A.S. 1999 'Resilience comes of age: Reflections on the past and outlook for the next generation of research' *Resilience and Development: Positive life adaptations* eds M.D. Glantz and J.L. Johnson, Plenum, New York, pp. 281–96

——2001 'Ordinary magic: Resilience processes in development' *American Psychologist* vol. 56(3), pp. 227–38

Matas, L., Arend, R. and Stroufe, L.A. 1978 'Continuity of adaptation in the second year: The relationship between quality of attachment and later competence' *Child Development* vol. 49, pp. 547–56

McCartney, K., Scarr, S., Rocheleau, A., Phillips, D., Abbott-Shim, M., Eisenberg, M., Keefe, N., Rosenthal, S. and Ruh, J. 1997 'Teacher–child interaction and child care auspices as predictors of social outcomes in infants, toddlers, and preschoolers' *Merrill-Palmer Quarterly* vol. 43, pp. 426–50

Moore, T.W. 1969 'Effects on the children' *Working Mothers and their Children* 2nd edn, eds S.Yudkin and A. Holme, Sphere Books, London, pp. 112–34

Muir, D. and Slater, A. 2000 *Infant Development: The essential readings* Blackwell, Malden, MA

NICHD Early Child Care Research Network 1997 'The effects of infant child care on infant–mother attachment security: Results of the NICHD study of early child care' *Child Development* vol. 68, pp. 860–79

Oppenheim, D. 1997 'The attachment doll-play interview for preschoolers' *International Journal of Behavioral Development* vol. 20, pp. 681–97

Oppenheim, D., Sagi, A. and Lamb, M.E. 1988 'Infant–adult attachments on the kibbutz and their relation to socioemotional development 4 years later' *Developmental Psychology* vol. 24, pp. 427–33

Oppenheim, D. and Waters, H. 1995 'Narrative processes and attachment representations: Issues of development and assessment' *Caregiving, Cultural, and Cognitive Perspectives on Secure-base Behaviour and Working Models: New growing points of attachment theory and research. Monographs of the Society for Research in Child Development* eds E. Waters, B. Vaughn, G. Posada and K. Kondo-Ikemura, vol. 60 (2–3, Serial No. 244), pp. 197–215

Osofsky, J.D. and Eberhart-Wright, A. 1992 'Risk and protective factors for parents and infants' *Future Directions in Infant Development Research* eds G.J. Suci and S.S. Robertson, Springer-Verlag, New York, pp. 25–42

Pearson, J., Cohn, D., Cowan, P. and Cowan, C. 1994 'Earned and continuous security in adult attachment: Relation to depressive symptomatology and parenting style' *Development and Psychopathology* vol. 6, pp. 359–73

Pederson, D.R., Gleason, K.E., Moran, G. and Bento, S. 1998 'Maternal attachment representations, maternal sensitivity, and the infant–mother attachment relationship' *Developmental Psychology* vol. 34, pp. 925–33

Perry, B.D., Pollard, R.A., Blakley, T.L., Baker, W.L. and Vigilante, D. 1995 'Childhood trauma, the neurobiology of adaptation, and "use dependent" development of the brain.' How "states" become "traits"' *Infant Mental Health Journal* vol. 16, pp. 271–89

Phelps, J.L., Belsky, J. and Crnic, K. 1998 'Earned security, daily stress, and parenting: A comparison of five alternative models' *Development and Psychopathology* vol. 10, pp. 21–38

Piaget, J. 1926/1930 *The Child's Conception of the World* Harcourt, Brace & World, New York

Posada, G., Gao, Y., Wu, F., Posada, R., Tascon, M., Schöelmerich, A., Sagi, A., Kondo-Ikemura, K., Haaland, W. and Synnevaag, B. 1995 'The secure-base phenomenon across cultures: Children's behavior, mothers' preferences, and experts' concept' *Caregiving, Cultural, and Cognitive Perspectives on Secure-base Behaviour and Working Models: New growing points of attachment theory and research. Monographs of the Society for Research in Child Development* eds E. Waters., B.E. Vaughn., G. Posada and K. Kondo-Ikemura vol. 60, nos. 2–3 (Serial No. 244), pp. 27–48

Radke-Yarrow, M. 1991 'Attachment patterns in children of depressed mothers' *Attachment Across the Life Cycle* eds C.M. Parkes, J. Stevenson-Hinde and P. Marris, Tavistock/Routledge, London, pp. 115–26

Raikes, H. 1996 'A secure base for babies: Applying attachment concepts to the infant care setting' *Young Children* vol. 51(5), pp. 59–67

Randolph, E.M. 2000 *Children who Shock and Surprise: A guide to attachment disorders* 3rd edn, RFR Publications, Sacramento, CA

Rauh, H., Ziegenhain, U., Muller, B. and Wijnroks, L. 2000 'Stability and change in infant–mother attachment in the second year of life: Relations to parenting quality and varying degrees of day-care experience' *The Organisation of Attachment Relationships: Maturation, culture and context* eds P.M. Crittenden and A.H. Claussen, Cambridge University Press, Cambridge, pp. 251–76

Robertson, J. 1953 'Some responses of young children to loss of maternal care' *Nursing Times* vol. 49, pp. 382–6

Robertson, J. ed. 1962 *Hospitals and Children: A parent's-eye view* Gollancz, London

Robertson, J. and Robertson, J. 1971 'Young children in brief separation: A fresh look' *Psychoanalytic Study of the Child* vol. 26, pp. 264–315

Rolfe, S.A. 1997 'Families settling into high quality child care: From sadness, anxiety and guilt to relief, comfort and support' Paper presented to the New Zealand Early Childhood Development Unit, Auckland

——2000 'The brain research phenomenon' *Every Child* vol. 6, pp. 8–9

——2002 'Promoting resilience in children' *Research in Practice Series* Early Childhood Australia, Canberra

Rolfe, S.A., Lloyd-Smith, J. and Richards, L. 1991 'Understanding the effects of infant day care: The case for qualitative study of mothers' experiences' *Australian Journal of Early Childhood* vol. 16(2), pp. 24–32

Rolfe, S.A., Nyland, B. and Morda, R. 2002 'Quality in infant care: Observations on joint attention' *Australian Research in Early Childhood Education* vol. 9(1), pp. 86–96

Rolfe, S.A. and Richards, L. 1993 'Australian mothers "construct" infant day care: Implicit theories and perceptions of reality' *Australian Journal of Early Childhood* vol. 18(2), pp. 10–22

——1994 'Families developing in the context of quality care: The experience of Australian mothers' Paper presented as part of the symposium 'Quality of Day

Care and Quality of Family Life', XIIIth Biennial Meetings of the International Society for the Study of Behavioural Development, Amsterdam

Rutter, M. and O'Connor, T.G. 1999 'Implications of attachment theory for child care policies' *Handbook of Attachment: Theory, research and clinical applications* eds J. Cassidy and P.R. Shaver, The Guilford Press, New York, pp. 823–44

Sander, L. 1975 'Infant and caretaking environment' *Explorations in Child Psychiatry* ed. E.J. Anthony, Plenum, NY, pp. 129–65

Schaffer, H.R. and Emerson, P.E. 1964 'The development of social attachments in infancy' *Monographs of the Society for Research in Child Development* vol. 29(3), pp. 1–77

Seifer, R., Schiller, M., Sameroff, A.J., Resnick, S. and Riordan, K. 1996 'Attachment, maternal sensitivity and temperament during the first year of life' *Developmental Psychology* vol. 32, pp. 12–25

Sims, M. and Hutchins, T. 1999 'Positive transitions' *Australian Journal of Early Childhood* vol. 24, pp. 12–16

Smith, A. 1996 'Educare for infants and toddlers in New Zealand childcare centres: Is it a reality and how important is joint attention?' Paper presented at the Conference of the International Society for the Study of Behavioural Development, Quebec City

——1999 'Quality child care and joint attention' *International Journal of Early Years Education* vol. 7, pp. 85–98

Solomon, J. and George, C. 1999 'The place of disorganisation in attachment theory: Linking classic observations with contemporary findings' *Attachment Disorganisation* eds J. Solomon and G. George, The Guilford Press, New York, pp. 3–32

Speltz, M.L. 1990 'The treatment of preschool conduct problems: An integration of behavioural and attachment concepts' *Attachment in the Preschool Years: Theory, research, and intervention* eds M.T. Greenberg., D. Cicchetti and E.M. Cummings, The University of Chigaco Press, Chicago, pp. 399–426

Sroufe, L.A. 1983 'Infant–caregiver attachment and patterns of adaptation and competence in the preschool' *Minnesota Symposia in Child Psychology* ed. M. Perlmutter, vol. 16, Erlbaum, Hillsdale, NJ, pp. 41–83

——1985 'Attachment classification from the perspective of infant–caregiver relationships and infant temperament' *Child Development* vol. 56, pp. 1–14

——1988 'The role of infant–caregiver attachment in development' *Clinical Implications of Attachment* eds J. Belsky and T. Nezworski, Hillsdale, Erlbaum, NJ, pp. 18–38

——1990 'An organisational perspective on the self' *Transitions from Infancy to Childhood: The self* eds D. Cicchetti and M. Beeghly, University of Chicago Press, Chicago, pp. 281–307

——1995 *Emotional Development: The organisation of emotional life in the early years* Cambridge University Press, Cambridge

Sroufe, L.A. and Waters, E. 1977a 'Heart rate as a convergent measure in clinical and developmental research' *Merrill-Palmer Quarterly* vol. 23, pp. 3–27

——1977b 'Attachment as an organisational construct' *Child Development* vol. 48, pp. 1184–99

Steele, H. and Steele, M. 1994 'Intergenerational patterns of attachment' *Attachment Processes in Adulthood, Vol. 5: Advances in personal relationships* eds. K. Bartholomew and D. Perlman, Jessica Kingsley, London, pp. 93–120

Stern, D.N. 1985 *The Interpersonal World of the Infant* Basic Books, New York

Stifter, C., Coulehean, C. and Fish, M. 1993 'Linking employment to attachment: The mediating effects of maternal separation anxiety and interactive behavior' *Child Development* vol. 64, pp. 1451–60

Stovall, C. and Dozier, M. 2000 'The development of attachment in new relationships: Single subject analyses for ten foster infants' *Development and Psychopathology* vol. 12, pp. 133–56

Teti, D.M. 2000 'Maternal depression and child–mother attachment in the first three years' *The Organization of Attachment Relationships: Maturation, culture, and context* eds P.M. Crittenden and A.H. Claussen, Cambridge University Press, Cambridge, pp. 190–213

Thompson, R.A. 1999 'Early attachment and later development' *Handbook of Attachment: Theory, research and clinical applications* eds J. Cassidy and P.R. Shaver, The Guilford Press, New York, pp. 265–386

Tizard, B. 1977 *Adoption: A second chance* Open Books, London

Tulving, E. 1972 'Episodic and semantic memory' *Organisation of Memory* eds E. Tulving and W. Donaldson, Academic Press, New York, pp. 381–403

Urban, J., Carlson, E., Egeland, B. and Sroufe, L.A. 1992 'Patterns of individual adaptation across childhood' *Development and Psychopathology* vol. 3, pp. 446–60

van IJzendoorn, M.H. 1995 'Adult attachment representations, parental responsiveness, and infant attachment: A meta-analysis on the predictive validity of the Adult Attachment Interview' *Psychological Bulletin* vol. 117, pp. 387–403

van IJzendoorn, M.H. and DeWolff, M.S. 1997 'In search of the absent father: Meta-analyses of infant–father attachment: A rejoinder to our discussants' *Child Development* vol. 68, pp. 609–14

van IJzendoorn, M.H. and Sagi, A. 1999 'Cross-cultural patterns of attachment: Universal and contextual dimensions' *Handbook of Attachment: Theory, research and clinical applications* eds J. Cassidy and P.R. Shaver, The Guilford Press, New York, pp. 713–34 van IJzendoorn, M.H., Schuengel, C. and Bakermans-Kranenberg, M.J. 1999 'Disorganised attachment in early childhood: Meta-analysis of precursors, comcomitants, and sequelae' *Development and Psychopathology* vol. 11, pp. 225–49

Waters, E. and Valenzuela, M. 1999 'Explaining disorganised attachment: Clues from research on mild-to-moderately undernourished children in Chile' *Attachment Disorganization* eds J. Solomon and C. George, The Guilford Press, New York, pp. 265–87

Waters, E., Vaughn, B.E., Posada, G. and Kondo-Ikemura, K. 1995 eds 'Caregiving, cultural, and cognitive perspectives on secure-base behavior and working models: New growing points of attachment theory and research' *Monographs of the Society for Research in Child Development* vol. 60, nos. 2–3 (Serial No. 244)

Watson, J. and Kowalski, H. 1999 'Toddler–caregiver interaction: the effect of temperament' *Early Child Development and Care* vol. 159, pp. 53–73

Weinfield, N.S., Sroufe, A.L., Egeland, B. and Carlson, E.A. 1999 'The nature of individual differences in infant–caregiver attachment' *Handbook of Attachment: Theory, research and clinical applications* eds J. Cassidy and P.R. Shaver, The Guilford Press, New York, pp. 68–88

Werner, E. 1989 'Children of the garden island' *Scientific American* vol. 260, pp. 2–6

Werner, E. and Smith, R.S. 1992 *Overcoming the Odds: High risk children from birth to adulthood* Cornell University Press, New York

Winnicott, D.W. 1965 *The Maturational Processes and the Facilitating Environment* International University Press, New York

Young, J. Z. 1964 *A Model of the Brain* Oxford University Press, London

Zeanah, C.H. 1996 'Beyond insecurity: A reconceptualisation of attachment disorders in infancy' *Journal of Consulting and Clinical Psychology* vol. 64, pp. 42–52

Zeanah, C.H., Mammen, O. and Lieberman, A. 1993 'Disorders of attachment' *Handbook of Infant Mental Health* ed. C.H. Zeanah, The Guilford Press, New York, pp. 322–49

Index